Roy and Brenda

Isaiah

Tim Scott

BREATHE

For my Brenda

[illegible]

4:10

BREATHE

Overcoming Anxiety, Depression and Negative Emotions

By Timothy R. Scott, Ph.D.

XULON PRESS ELITE

Xulon Press Elite
2301 Lucien Way #415
Maitland, FL 32751
407.339.4217
www.xulonpress.com

Printed in the United States of America.

Paperback ISBN-13: 978-1-6628-1510-2
eBook ISBN-13: 978-1-6628-1511-9

To my wife, Kimberly Scott, you found me,
and your love saved me.

You have taught me the journey of joy.

Thank you for telling me to go to God's Word
to find answers for life's fears.

Table of Contents

Preface

More than Insomnia:

It's 2:00 a.m. and my mind starts racing as I wake from a sound sleep. I'm flooded with thoughts, negative thoughts of stress about work, fear of failure and incompetence. My body temperature rises and the covers seem like they're on fire. I'm hot and my mind is on high alert as if there is some great danger. I can't go back to sleep because my mind won't shut down. I pray, "Lord, please give me sleep." But my mind won't stop. It is as if every thought is being forced into my mind by an outside source. I haven't opened my eyes yet but I'm hoping it is close enough to morning that I can just get up and get on with my day. I look and see that it is 2:00 a.m. Here I am again, another night of sleepless anxiety.

I try to distract my mind by praying for everyone I know and yet my mind resists the distraction and I'm back to obsessing about the latest stressor to hit my plate. No, it is not always a big deal, but I always make it huge and insurmountable. In the middle of the night, I'm beginning to think I'm going crazy. I focus on the stressor so much I have become convinced the solution is that I need a life change, you know, I need to run.

I finally have had enough and I get out of bed and move to the living room. I turn on the TV for a distraction and find myself drifting in and out of sleep the rest of the night. In and out of anxiety and hopelessness of this never going away. I don't live in fear of monsters under my bed like in my childhood. Now I have these "grownup" fears, the fear of my own emotions that are out of control. The strange thing is that the fear is more about the fear than an actual problem I'm facing. Yes, that's right, I'm afraid of fear. The fear is like an unending battle with my emotions that seems to destroy my love for life. I'm at a loss to know what to do.

I'm writing this book as a tool for the countless number of people who have a similar problem with anxiety. This is not a book about insomnia but something much deeper; it is about anxiety and negative emotions, the kind of emotions that terrorize your mind. The kind of emotions that, if not checked and changed, will result in despair and depression. Many of us feel there is no hope for us, no place to turn. We feel alone and helpless. I personally felt alone, and as a Christian leader, I felt shame over these uncontrollable emotions because I thought I should have more faith and more strength.

My wife has said to me many times, "Tim, you will always have problems and stresses in your life, so you better figure out how to resolve your reaction to them. You are your greatest enemy." It sounded like this when she said it, "Man up, you loser, stop being a baby!" Those were not her words, but I was sure I knew what she meant…insecure much?

I see myself as a fixer and this was going to be my next fix. I was going to fix once and for all my emotional instability. I loved God and I loved serving God, so I needed to get over this disabling emotional immaturity and "Man up!" Yes, my words to me. What I found was that I had been teaching the principles for years. I just had never assimilated them into life principles. I was about to enter a whole new freedom. If you are broken, tired and emotionally drained, this book is for you. The "breathe" concept hit me like a train when I realized my emotions were my responsibility. Hang on and take this journey with me, a journey into a whole new way of thinking and feeling. God's gift of joy is about to rise up in your soul.

Chapter 1 – Learning to Breathe

THE CAUSE OF NEGATIVE EMOTIONS

"Set your mind on the things above, not on the things that are on earth." (Colossians 3:2)

After a difficult night of sleep, you wake up with a sense that something is wrong and that there is impending doom, sometimes called a "foreboding." You think something bad is going to happen. Your evidence for this foreboding is weak and maybe non-existent, but nevertheless you have a sense that things are bad. You take your shower and get ready, the whole time thinking life is monotonous and maybe even meaningless. Your children are awake now and you must get them off to school. You push through because you must, you're a mom and moms push through. People ask you when you arrive at work, after having dropped off the kids, "How are you?" You respond, "Fine!" But, if only you could respond the way you are really feeling, you would unload about the misery of life.

"Why does this happen to me?" you think, and then you see him, the guy who is overwhelmingly happy. You wonder, "How is it that he is always happy?" But you have known him for ten years and even when life for him has been difficult, you see his response of a quick resilient return to joy. You are even upset that someone is so resilient and you are so fragile. You want off this cycle of misery.

You have concluded that your thoughts and emotions are passive, they happen to you, they just come into your mind, you have no control. People have told you to think positive thoughts. You would, but you can't. You have prayed that God would help you to be filled with joy, filled with resilience. You can't even dream of being resilient, you just want to get through the day with this knot in your stomach. Emotions seem to run your life. You hate being in your own head.

You have anxiety. In fact, you don't just have it, it identifies you. It rules your life.

Breathing is fundamental to life and health. We all know this. What we may not know is that we can control much of our breathing and impact our health. We need to learn to breathe well. This seems ridiculous to say because we have been breathing all our lives. We are experts at breathing, right? The same is true about thinking. We have been thinking our whole lives, but many are under the delusion that we can't control our thinking. We need to learn to breathe and to think for our health. By breathing and thinking well, we can make significant changes in our lives.

Linda's Story

As a young child, Linda was a lively, funny, and intelligent girl. She would fill a room with joy with her personality and energy. However, Linda's life changed into a life of woundedness, loneliness and eventually self-destructive behavior. What happened was not a moment of trauma but a slow contamination of her heart with toxic words that created fear, anger, and negative emotions.

Carbon monoxide is a colorless, odorless, and tasteless gas, very hard to detect. Linda's heart was being filled with toxic gas, and she didn't know it. She was living in a world of manipulation, shame, and guilt. The real problem was that this was coming from the person she should have been able to trust the most, her mother. Linda's mother was not malicious, but ignorant of how to love well. She centered most of her influence and child rearing on herself, not her children's needs. (Many parents struggle with the notion that raising children is about them, not the child.) This created a world that was toxic for Linda. It was insidious, because just like carbon monoxide it was undetectable. It wasn't like she was in pain from being beaten or molested, which would make sense. But she was in her own home, seemingly safe, and yet day-by-day slowly moving into the darkness of a wounded heart. She was betrayed by selfish parenting. By the time she was thirteen, Linda was set for a life of lonely retreat and emotional struggle that would define every day of her life.

Linda's story is tragic and led to a life of destruction and pain for her and the ones who loved her. I will trace her life throughout this book. I don't do this to disparage her, but to show how beauty can be wounded and destroyed. Counselors struggled to help her because she was resistant to giving up her strongly held beliefs. Linda could have made meaningful change in her life if she had learned to think well. This book is for those who desire to change their thinking and thereby their emotions and live in the freedom of real joy.

The two dimensions of breathing

We all know how to breathe, right? It is a simple process we don't even need to think about. Actually, if we think too much about our breathing, we may start to hyperventilate. In my first Breathe 90 class (Breathe 90 is a ninety-day program I wrote to overcome negative emotions), I had everyone take a deep breath, focusing on their breathing as intensely as possible. I said, "Go ahead, take a deep breath, inhale and count to four, then slowly exhale counting to six. There, doesn't that feel great? Do that five times and you will relax a bit." We did this as a class for a few minutes, and I saw a woman who looked as if she was about to pass out. I told her she needed to stop breathing for a moment. She laughed and so did the rest of the class. I of course didn't mean to say, "stop breathing," I should have said, "change your breathing patterns." If you stopped breathing, you would have a serious problem. The fact that she started laughing stopped her hyperventilation and she felt better. For her, too much focus caused her to take shallow breaths that resulted in hyperventilation and a loss of blood to her brain. Breathing is essential to life and breathing properly is essential to optimum physical and emotional health. I taught them how to breathe diaphragmatically and to stop breathing thoracically. This is a major issue in emotional freedom from stress and anxiety.

As I walk my journey out of anxiety, negative emotions, depression, and anger, I'm learning a lot about breathing and the importance of this simple act. However, breathing has become more to me than just a relaxation method; it has become a metaphor for the whole matter of emotional control and anxiety. Let me explain: if you were to describe breathing to a young child, you would speak of two aspects of breathing, inhale and exhale. This is so clear and intuitive to all of us because we all breathe. But to me, breathing became more than a physical exercise; it became a metaphor for emotional healing.

If we allow this concept of breathing to be a metaphor for our life's experiences, we might conclude that life is two-dimensional, i.e., inhale and exhale. Inhaling represents our environment, those things that influence us. The influences in our lives, such as family, friends, boss, spouse, finances, the national economy and so forth, that impact the way we feel and even the way we act. We simply cannot ignore the power of influence. Exhaling then represents our actions. We exhale out behavior.

We should understand there is a strong connection between inhaling and exhaling, influence and behavior. We are hopeless to stop bad behavior if we have negative influence we can't change. This concept of behavior's connection to influence has permeated our culture; it is even used in the court of law to excuse bad and even illegal activity. What is the answer? How can we change?

Attempts at making the change

If life is two-dimensional, inhale and exhale, influence and behavior, how can we change? One method is to modify. When the influence is negative, we simply modify our environment, if possible, to bring about a positive change in the way we think and feel. To some degree this is not only effective but also essential. However, in many cases this doesn't get to the source of the problem and change in feelings doesn't come with environment modification. Divorce, emancipation, bankruptcy, or separations from failed friendships may not be the real answer. A lot of time is spent in counseling to locate and eradicate negative inhale/environment. The regression into earlier influences is a part of many approaches in dealing with negative emotion. Of course, I'm not saying this is not helpful. I'm suggesting there is a simpler, more effective way.

Exhale/behavior, the other side of the two dimensions is equally difficult. We conclude our behavior is bad and know we need a change, but change doesn't come easily. We work hard at modifying our behavior, only to find we have replaced one bad behavior for another. What is wrong with us? To make matters worse, our emotions seem to be subject to our inhale/environment, and we know we can't change many aspects of these influences in our lives. We are stuck in a bad environment, which fuels bad behavior and even worse negative emotions. What's the answer?

A friend of mine, who identifies himself as an alcoholic and has patterns of thinking sometimes referred to as "cognitive distortions," made a significant change in his life. He stopped drinking. He had a problem, however; he replaced his drinking with an addiction to sex, including porn and prostitutes. To him, this was an acceptable replacement of addictions. He could live with sexual addiction but not alcohol addiction.

There must be a better way than behavior modification. Cognitive distortions are ways of thinking that include generalizations, exaggerating, and catastrophizing, among many other distorted thoughts. The better way is found in what I call "The third dimension of breathing." People who struggle with emotional negativity must get a strong understanding of this third dimension.

The third dimension of breathing

Back to our description of breathing, inhale and exhale and that's all there is, right? No, we are missing the most important part of breathing and the key to understanding the control of our behavior and our emotions. The crucial step between inhale and exhale is the "**exchange**." God has designed the lungs to exchange oxygen for carbon dioxide. Without this step, there is no reason to inhale and exhale, and even more importantly, we would die. Oxygen is essential to life. The exchange metaphorically is the process of exchanging thought for thought, truth for lie. For those of us who tend toward negative emotions, thinking is our only path to recovery.

Therapy that doesn't direct the change of your thinking, that is, the exchange of truths for lies, will keep you stuck in dependency on the support of your counselor. These well-meaning counselors unknowingly have created a dependency and not a transformation of the heart. All that has been done in this form of therapy is an addition of support in your "inhale/environment." As you will see in this book, our Creator has given us a way to overcome negative emotions such as anxiety, anger, defensiveness, and depression through this exchange; transformed thinking.

Thinking is the great exchange in life. I have studied happy people over the last few decades. You know, those people who are consistently happy and joyful. I have found the common denominator: healthy thinking. People with all kinds of negative influences have learned to exchange the lies of life for truth that makes them emotionally stable and happy. What is it about positive, happy people that make them that way? They have no more ability to keep changing their environment than the people who are miserable. They, in most cases, have as many negative influences in their lives as miserable people. What is it then? The answer is clear: they know how to exchange the negative with positive. This may even be intuitive to them. In my case, I needed to learn a new way of thinking. I had to change the lies I believed about myself and about life and come to a better exchange. I am intuitively analytical and creative, a deadly combination. My thinking gets me going with all kinds of different possibilities and my creativity causes me to exaggerate those possible scenarios into catastrophic events. Here is how it works:

Catastrophizing: The unhealthy third dimensions

As you go through each day, a constant conversation goes on in your mind. You are thinking, reacting, feeling, and responding to stimulus all day. Have you ever stopped to think about the things you say to and about yourself? You may say things like: "I'm not as good as her." "I deserve better than this." "I'm an idiot." "I'm a failure." This conversation going on in your head is the exchange in the third dimension of breathing. In scripture, God repeatedly directs us to control our thinking. These directives should be taken seriously and understood as the key to living a life free from negative emotions.

My problem, and the problem of millions also, is the tendency to catastrophize the situations in life. Negativity in life is fixated on and then blown out of proportion. People who catastrophize are people who are both analytical and creative. It seems the combination of analysis and creativity cause a number of us to take a situation and drive it to a conclusion that is catastrophic.

The way it works psychologically is this: because of the analytical tendencies of your mind, you look at every detail of life and try to figure it all out. But the other part of your mind, the creative side, likes to imagine, so you take your clear analytical thinking and create scenarios that are fantastic and even catastrophic. You have taken a small manageable thing and turned it into an unmanageable catastrophe.

One day, I was sitting in a restaurant with some friends. We were being loud and maybe even obnoxious. There was a lady across the restaurant who seemed to be repeatedly looking at us. I noticed her looking, but didn't think much about it. After some time, this woman approached our table and confronted us about laughing at her. We were shocked and told her that we were sorry, but assured her we were not laughing at her. The fact of the matter was, we barely even noticed her. She clearly had an inner conversation going on in her head, coming from a place of insecurity and maybe even self-centeredness, that caused her to assume the laughter was about her. It was logical to her that we were discussing something about her and were disrespecting her in some way. Her inner conversation was one of unhealthy exchange in the third dimension of breathing.

If you're not sure if you're a catastrophizer here is a checklist for you:

- ☐ I have irrational thoughts that cause me to make events far worse than they actually are.
- ☐ I project things into the future with the worst-case scenario, and yet I rarely have a solution.
- ☐ I avoid some opportunities in life because I think they will go wrong.
- ☐ Negativity seems to affect my entire outlook on life.
- ☐ I feel sorry for myself because my life seems to be worse than other's.
- ☐ I tend to miss solutions because all I can think about is the negative scenarios.
- ☐ I seem to see things more negatively than other people.

Did you check any of these indicators? If so, the healthy ways to deal with these unhealthy thoughts at the end of this chapter will be helpful to you. I have always lived with the motto, "Expect the worst and hope for the best." This mindset crippled my life, because while I was expecting the worst, I couldn't even see the best. Catastrophizers tend to miss the joys of life, and they make themselves and people they love miserable. If you are a catastrophizer, your misery is not because of negative circumstances, it is because you create your own misery. Please listen to me: I'm a recovering catastrophizer. The catastrophizer is one who is stuck in negativity and fear. Let me show you something from my research about negative thinking:

Triggered Negative Thoughts (TNTs): Stuck in negative emotions

Years ago, a friend of mine who worked with explosives admitted to me how scared he was of the materials he was handling. He was afraid at any time they could blow unexpectedly. I realized his fears were deep and were really having a negative impact on his marriage and life. This threat was real, the possibility was actually there. I encouraged him to leave that line of work, which he did. As he got into a safer line of work, the threat was gone and he was more relaxed. But what about people who feel a threat when one doesn't exist? Most people who struggle with negative emotions are concerned about two things:

1. How life could go wrong
2. The unending fears that plague their minds

There are triggers that set our minds on a course of emotional turmoil. They are to us like TNT, a powerful explosive. I use TNT to mean Triggered Negative Thoughts. It is an explosive and can destroy our emotional stability, robbing us of our joy and happiness. Life becomes miserable. My friend who worked with explosives found relief just getting away from the danger. You too can get away from the explosives in your mind by learning the principles of healthy breathing, where the exchange is a healthy truth-for-lies transaction. This is a life where your environment is not the enemy and your behavior is in line with your values and not subject to erratic extremes.

Dr. Daniel Amen, in his book, ***Healing Anxiety and Depression***[1], developed a concept he called "ANTs," Automatic Negative Thoughts. I have learned much from his work but have decided to focus, not on the automatic aspects of negative thinking, but rather on the triggers for these negative thoughts. These triggers may go back to childhood or your spouse saying negative things about your appearance; it may be your boss constantly rejecting your work, or you fill in the scenario. If we look carefully at the triggers, we can understand the exchange failure of the third dimension of breathing, which is why we think the way we do and how to correct it. If we obsess about the triggers, we may blame our environment for our emotional turmoil. However, if we fail to understand these triggers, we will fail to address our responses to them. So, the key is to become aware of the triggers that set our emotions upside down and address our responses with truth.

Getting a grip on our emotions is simply understanding the thoughts that drive those emotions and then correcting this thinking with diligent focus on truth. Here is the hard truth about negative emotions: It is your fault! Yes, that's right. You are the cause of your negative thoughts. You have the power to change your thinking but have not developed the tools to think differently. Anger, shame, and fear are emotions that can be controlled and corrected with a focus on truth. Focus is important, but reinforcement of positive truths is crucial. (More about reinforced thinking in Chapter 3.) When I say it is your fault, I'm not saying you are morally or ethically responsible, but that your thinking has not been changed. The Bible says things like, "take every thought captive," (2 Cor. 10:5) and "set your minds on things above," (Col. 3:2) and "think on these things," (Phil. 4:8). If God tells us to, we must

1 Healing Anxiety and Depression, Daniel G. Amen M.D., G.P. Putnam's Sons, New York, New York, 2003, pages 186-190

be able to change our thinking. We must learn to find the triggers for negativity and apply specific truths to combat them and reinforce them in continually focused thinking.

Here is how negative thoughts work: We develop patterns of negative thinking by thinking in absolutes. We might say, "I'm only valuable when I have a certain amount of money," or "If my children turn out well, I will be a good person," or "I will be valuable when I experience a certain level of success." We cannot accept value short of reaching goals, often-unobtainable goals. Or we develop patterns of negative thinking in the generalizing of events. We might say, "This is the worst day ever," or "My life has never been so bad." We suffer from a sense of low self-worth and continue to generalize our failure to reach our goals. We look to blame someone, anyone outside ourselves, so we can find emotional relief. This produces only anger and not resolution. We are afraid we will never "become" or "arrive," so we experience despair. We are trapped in negative emotions. These are just two of many possible scenarios of emotional negativity.

Negative Triggers

With sensitive hearts, we are subject to triggers that drive us into negativity. It could be a missed deadline at work, a friend's passing negative comment about your appearance, or even remembering a shame-inducing event in your past. These triggers seem to control our thinking and our emotions. The key again is to learn how to think. The purpose of this book is to give the tools and principles of emotional stability in a world of triggers. Don't blame the inhale/environment for your emotions; take control through proper thinking.

Julie and TNTs:

When I met Julie, she was a married mother of two children. She was smart and she and her husband were obviously financially set. Her kids were perfectly dressed every time I saw them in church. Julie didn't allow her kids to go to the kid's programming. I asked why they didn't go and she said, "We want them to worship with us in the service." I couldn't argue with the fact that the kids were well-behaved in service. To be honest, they seemed a little too well-behaved from my experience. (I will never forget the day my brother and I were playing marbles on the pew of the last row of our large church auditorium, Yes, my dad was preaching and one of the marbles hit the floor and started rolling down the slanted wood auditorium floor, only stopping every once in a while, when it hit a leg of one of the pews; then it would start rolling again until it reached the front, in what seemed like forever. The whole time, my father waited in silence for it to stop and said, "I will talk to you boys when we get home." This was Bill Scott code for a good spanking. Believe me, my dad and mom saw to it that we were in children's programming always after that.) *Well, back to Julie; she seemed to have everything under control, that is, under* her *control. The word "control" is the key word. She was always so worried about her kids turning out well, she put a lot of pressure on them to perform and be good. Later I would learn from counseling her and her husband that she did this in every aspect of her life and marriage, including their sex life.*

The years passed and her little kids became adults and essentially walked away from their parents, the church and the moral values given by Julie. Julie and her husband came to me for counsel about how to get their kids back. As I began to explore with Julie and her husband their adult children's attitudes, I began to see two clear problems. Julie was a negative thinker and Julie was a catastrophizer.

Their marriage was on the rocks and her view of God was negative and distant. Julie had very little joy in her life and she had made herself, her husband and their children miserable. She also had not one friend she could go to in a crisis. Julie was alone and couldn't get anyone to agree with her controlling ways. Julie was unwilling to see that she and her thinking were the problem. It was her husband and her kids and even the church and God. Pretty lonely place to be, wouldn't you say?

For a period of time, Julie lived alone, and to my knowledge had almost no contact with her children and her ex-husband, who had remarried. But worst of all, she was shut off from God. She didn't pray or fellowship with others.

In recent years, Julie has started a process of finding the triggers in her life. She realized that as a child her mother was also a controller and her dad was unfortunately an absent but nurturing father. Her mother created fear scenarios in Julie's life about kidnappers, rapists, boys who only wanted sex, and a myriad of negative thoughts about life. Even God, in her mother's view, was angry and unapproachable. Every time Julie would hear a positive complement, she would dismiss it and reject the notion that things could be positive. Julie has begun to realize her fear and negativity and is beginning to explore the truth about God's love for and protection of her. Julie is on the road to recovery and is making progress toward joy.

Thinking is a decision:

Most people perceive thoughts as passive. That is, people think they have no control over their thoughts or their emotions. In all your pursuit of recovering from negative emotions, you need to understand our Creator, who knows our minds better than anyone, has warned us about careless thinking. We have become disciplined in so many areas of our lives, but somehow, we conclude our thinking is not within our control. God would not ask us to be "careful how we think" if there was no way to be in control our thoughts. **Proverbs 4:23, "*Be careful of how you think; your life is shaped by your thoughts.*"**

We literally have the capacity to control our thinking. Look what the scriptures say about this control:

> ***"1 Therefore if you have been raised up with Christ, keep seeking the things above, where Christ is, seated at the right hand of God. 2 Set your mind on the things above, not on the things that are on earth. 3 For you have died and your life is hidden with Christ in God."* (Colossians 3:1-4)**

Notice that we have the capability to "*set our minds on things above.*" The word for mind from the original language of the book of Colossians is "*phren,*" which has more to do with the emotions than the intellect. Some translations state this as "setting your affections." This is not exactly right either. The word is used in this way: a person focuses attention on something based on a belief. For example, if you believe your house is only a temporary dwelling for you and your family, you will be less likely to maintain it as if you owned the property. You lack what is called "pride of ownership." What if you truly believed "you have died in Christ and you are hidden in Christ"? Would that make a difference? The discipline here is not to focus your emotions on things above, but rather to focus on the fact that your life is not about this world and your life now is about Christ and your destiny with Him in eternity. Truly believing this would change the way you think about the things that disturb you today. You would be free emotionally from the entanglements of this life because your life today is only a temporary experience waiting for the real fulfillment of life in Heaven.

Chapter 1 Life Skills:

Realize your thoughts are real; they form your beliefs. Cognitive distortions such as generalizing, catastrophizing, and exaggerating must be understood as the problem, not your environment or even your behavior.

Realize your emotions can't be controlled by other emotions but by thoughts. Emotions have no intelligence; they react or respond to stimulus. Negative thinking is a bad habit that can and must be changed.

Don't attack the negative thoughts; replace them with truth. The spiral of negativity happens when we try to attack the negative thoughts with more negativity. The best way is to fill your mind with positive truths.

Write down your TNTs and then write a rational response to these thoughts.

Ask these questions about your negative beliefs:

> Is there any evidence for these beliefs?
>
> What is the evidence against these beliefs?
>
> What is the worst that can happen if you give up these beliefs?
>
> And what is the best that can happen if you give up these beliefs?

Here are some helpful ways to minimize catastrophizing:

Acknowledge that you are a catastrophizer.

Take the thoughts to their conclusion and ask, "Is this really possible?" And if so, "Is it something you can handle with God's grace?"

Replace these thoughts with reasonable and positive scenarios.

Repeat these scenarios until the negative becomes unreasonable to you. This will take time but is well worth it.

Begin today to keep on your computer or in a notebook a thanksgiving journal. Write down everything you are thankful for, such as a beautiful day, the smile of a child, a moment with your favorite pet, your health, today's food, etc. Think on those journal entrees throughout the day. If you keep this journal faithfully and focus on those positive things, you will see a tremendous change in your mood and disposition.

Chapter 2 – Emotional Defiance

Emotions That Take Control of the Mind

"Examine me, O LORD, and try me; test my emotions and my heart." (Psalm 26:2)

The alarm goes off and you say, "Today is going to be different, I'm not going to worry, I'm not going to let anxiety rule me, I'm not going to allow my anger to be seen by that jerk at work who always pushes my buttons, I'm not going to let the finances be a source of fear for me." Then things start to go sideways for you emotionally.

Your thoughts go to projects that are incomplete at work, the fear that the car is not going to make it long enough to pay for a new one. Your mind goes to the last fight you had with your spouse that wasn't really ever resolved. You feel regret, anger, and fear of not having the marriage you always wanted. You start to think about your college roommate who has it all, a loving spouse and enough money to live without worry. How are you going to make it? How are you going to get through the day? Why does life have to be so hard? Why do other people have it so much better than you?

You don't want to, but you can't stop your mind from comparing your life to others' lives. You see people seemingly so happy compared to you. You see that life can be peaceful, but you don't have that peace. You're getting angry thinking about it. Your attention goes to God. "Why is He not helping me and bringing ease into my life and bringing peace to my mind?"

You are now in Emotional Defiance. The place of the loss of control. Your emotions are ruling your life.

Just like a defiant child, your emotions can fight against you. You can have a revolt going on in your soul. This is painful and destructive, but most of all it is unnecessary. In this chapter, I want to discuss how we arrive at emotional defiance and how to overcome this defiance.

Linda's Story

Linda was a cute thirteen-year-old girl who was smart and had a bubbly personality. She was friendly and was liked by most people in her school. Linda, at thirteen years old, the summer before eighth grade, hit puberty and saw a radical change in her body during the three months of her summer break from school. In her words, she was a "FAT" little girl until puberty. Her favorite place to go as a young girl was to her grandparents' ranch where horses and other animals were her great joy. She loved living close enough to go there often. Linda's grandmother and grandfather loved her with very few expectations. She felt totally accepted, even as a little girl. At home, things were a little different; the expectations were a bit of a hurdle for her. She felt like she could never totally please her mother. She always felt she was not thin enough or pretty enough for her. Her mother unknowingly had created an emotional distance from Linda by constantly trying to get her to improve her appearance. She was frustrated by the rejection and her inability to please her mother.

Over the next year, her body changed dramatically and she became thin and, in her words, "prettier." That next year she entered high school, taller and thinner and stunningly beautiful. Her previously chubby cheeks had thinned and now revealed a beautiful face with almost perfect bone structure. Linda's hair was long and healthy; her body was shapely and trim. Her face was stunning and there was a new confidence in her walk for the first time in her life. She didn't know exactly why, but knew she was getting positive input from her mother for her new beauty. Years later she would look at childhood pictures and say, "I remember back when I was fat and happy."

Yes, things changed that fall for Linda. Her friends also changed their opinion of her. Linda walked on the campus of her school and for the first time in her life got favorable looks from everyone. It seemed the whole world had changed, as she was now more popular, especially with the boys. That fall in ninth grade, Linda found the tragic reality of living in a fallen world: ***Beautiful people, especially girls, get more positive attention.*** *She loved her newfound attention and thrived socially. It was everywhere: her school, her neighborhood and even at her church. That's right, life had changed for Linda, but not necessarily for the good.*

That moment of realizing what pleased the world would change Linda forever. It would ultimately end her life in a tragic death. Linda started down a dark path of life in the shadows and experienced the loneliness God never intended for His children. This path was a life of lies. This path is the one chosen by many of us and is so pervasive in humanity that it has become totally acceptable, yet deadly.

(Throughout this book we will trace Linda's life and see how she unknowingly learned the tragedy of living without joy and happiness, a life in the shadows, a life without intimacy with God and others.)

Living with a deficit worldview:
This world functions in a deficit reality. That is, a reality of the never-ending pursuit of fulfillment, how to get what you want that you don't have. It impacts your relationships with others, with God and even with ourselves. The fallen world runs on three principles that govern this deficit reality:

1. Pursue things that make you feel good.
2. Pursue things that are pleasing to your eyes.

3. Pursue things that you believe will make this life about you.

Here is how the scriptures state the three principles:

> "*15 Do not love the world or the things in the world; if anyone loves the world, the love of the Father is not in him. 16 For all that is in the world, the* ***lust of the flesh*** *and the* ***lust of the eyes*** *and the* ***boastful pride of life****, is not from the Father, but is from the world. 17 The world is passing away, and also its lusts; but the one who does the will of God lives forever.*" (1 John 2:15-17)

In verse 17, we are given the truth about these principles: They are temporary and won't satisfy permanently. Only living for God will produce permanent fulfillment. All other pursuits are futile in bringing about emotional security. We pursue these things thinking they will magically turn into permanent satisfiers. To put the principles simply:

1. The lust of the eyes: ***If you see it, get it!***
2. The lust of the flesh: ***If you want it, get it!***
3. The pride of life: ***If you believe it will enhance your life, get it!***

Linda couldn't see the eternal for the temporary, and this led to a tragic misconception that led to living life with a wrong worldview and terrorized her entire life. Without knowing it, Linda slipped into a life of deficit emotions. From that point on, she needed the approval of every man and woman in her world, and for them to think of her as beautiful, to maintain happiness. If that approval were lost her happiness would be lost. This change was subtle at first and yet became pervasive in her life over time. The joy of life diminished in light of the need to be accepted as beautiful. She was outwardly humble when people gave her compliments for her beauty, but inside was craving the acceptance. Linda was not a malicious girl but lived so entrenched in the shadows, she couldn't see the love of her Heavenly Father who wanted her beauty to radiate from the inside out.

Living with emotional defiance:
Millions of us have accepted something that is a lie, and we believe it with our whole hearts. The lie is that life is only about the moments we live on this planet during our lifetime. I call this, "life in time." We don't realize that "life in eternity" begins in this lifetime and we need to live for our destiny, not just live for this lifetime. We intuitively race to the temporary, life in time, to produce love, acceptance, and security. This sets us up for what we will refer to in this book as "Emotional Defiance." We truly believe if we can get people to esteem us higher, we will be better people. Instead of having to grow up, we try to manipulate the people in our world to love and accept us. This is always a flawed strategy and will never lead to peace and joy. God said, in Colossians 3:2, "*set our affection on Heaven not on things of this earth.*"

Emotional defiance is when your emotions take over control of your mind. It is life out of balance. When life becomes dominated by emotions, the behavior will be without purpose and meaning.

The emotions work as "passive responders" or "reactors" to your thoughts and beliefs. Your emotions are not intelligent. When the emotions take control of your life, as in anxiety or panic attacks, the life in your soul is in emotional defiance. Your emotions become the ruling force of life. This is understandable in a four-year-old, but totally unacceptable in the life of an adult. We rightly expect adults to act maturely. Maturity, among other things, is the balance of emotions with proper beliefs. Emotional defiance in contrast to maturity is the cause of the emotional chaos of panic attacks, anxiety, depression, rage, and other forms of negative emotions.

If someone you love, a parent, sibling or friend, tells you that you are ugly, you may accept that and store it in your heart (i.e., your frame of reference). The immediate feelings of rejection and pain are soon gone, but the heart stores these thoughts as a frame of reference for the future. Now when someone looks at you, you may pull up that reference belief, "I'm ugly." Seeing a flaw in the mirror may trigger this, and your frame of reference is again, "I'm ugly." You probably will unconsciously say this throughout the day to yourself, which reinforces the lie. Now you are set up to be trapped in emotional defiance. Because beauty is relative, you are probably missing the truth about your actual appearance.

The real problem is not your appearance, but your belief that your appearance sums up your value. Your value is not what others think about you, but about how God values you. Life is about loving God and living your life with purpose. Beauty fades, but loving God is forever (1 Jn 2:17). This is only one example of emotional defiance. Emotional defiance can be illustrated whenever "the lie" is accepted in your beliefs.

The relationship between kidneys and emotions:

In ancient times, the Jewish people didn't have a word for emotions. The Hebrew word for emotions used in Old Testament scriptures is the word *Kilyah,* meaning, kidneys. The word *Kilyah* referred not only to the kidneys but also to the adjacent adrenal gland. The kidneys and adrenal glands are held in a sack on either side of the body. The word is used many times in the Old Testament; here are a couple of examples:

Here is an example of how it is used literally: "*You shall take all the fat that covers the entrails and the lobe of the liver, and the two kidneys (Kilyah) and the fat that is on them, and offer them up in smoke on the altar.*" (Exodus 29:13)

Kilyah here are not just the kidney but the "fat that is on them." This is a reference to the sack and fat deposits that held both kidneys and adrenal gland.

Here is an example of how it is used figuratively as emotions: "*Examine me, O LORD, and try me; test my emotions (Kilyah) and my heart.*" (Psalm 26:2)

Why would God want man's emotions tested? This is how God loves man, who is subject to emotional defiance. God wants us to grow and mature, and we will only grow in the context of testing. He allows the testing of our emotions for the purpose of emotional maturity. If God just took care of every problem without any investment on your part, you would never grow into the mature adult you need to be.

A simple overview of the purpose of the kidneys reveals three functions:

1. Filtration
2. Selective reabsorption
3. Excretion

Every day, a person's kidneys process about 200 quarts of blood to sift out about two quarts of waste products and extra water. The wastes and extra water become urine, which flows to the bladder and is excreted. This sophisticated system is one of the physical designs by God to give man the best opportunity for a toxin-free body. Why would the scriptures use the kidneys as a metaphor for emotions? Well, simply, the emotions are meant to be filters for life. That is when you see beauty in life, such as a mother with her child, your emotions filter this and give you joy. However, if you were to see an abusive mother, your emotions filter this and reject it.

As previously said, the term kidney refers to the adrenal gland as well. Why would scripture use this as a metaphor? The adrenal glands work interactively with the hypothalamus and pituitary gland in the following way: the hypothalamus produces hormones, which stimulate the pituitary gland. The pituitary gland, in turn, produces hormones, which stimulate the adrenal glands. When there is a perceived threat, the body goes into reaction. This in the Hebrew was the best way to describe emotional defiance.

The adrenal glands prepare the body for fight or flight: The heart beats faster, the blood is prepared for coagulation, the eyes dilate and the blood flows to the extremities to prepare for strong resistance or flight. This is the body's self-defense system against threat. On an emotional level, the mind perceives something as a threat and the emotions react in such a way as to protect. Because the emotions have no intelligence, they will continue to react until there is a change in belief about the threat. We will run or fight.

Here is where things get difficult: oftentimes there is no real threat, only a perceived threat, and yet your adrenal gland flushes the body with these hormones due to stimulants like coffee or even our own thoughts that scare us. This may result in a panic attack and strange irrational thoughts (more on this in Chapter 8).

Nurturing Response: King David's healthy emotions
When the emotions are functioning in a healthy way, we would refer to this as a "Nurturing Response" (kidneys)

> *"7 I will bless the LORD who has counseled me; Indeed, my mind (Kilyah) instructs me in the night. 8 I have set the LORD continually before me; Because He is at my right hand, I will not be shaken. 9 Therefore my heart is glad and my glory rejoices; my flesh also will dwell securely."* (Psalm 16:7-9)

Notice that David is being instructed/nurtured in his emotions/kidneys during the night. This took place because his belief system was focused on the Lord (verse 8) This put him in a position of emotional stability, "I will not be shaken." But further, the sensitive heart of David was filled with gladness, rejoicing, and security. This is the emotion working to benefit David because his belief was that God was "at my right hand."

I have had many nights where I know my emotions were working properly and filtering the beauty of life. Nights that were sleepless turned out to be a blessing of truth filtering through my heart and emotions, loving the life God has given me, embracing with joy the children and family God has put in my life, loving the sense of accomplishment when a job was completed well. The emotions can be of great blessing when they are in a positive filtering form. They actually "instruct" us by showing us the beauty of life; this is done while we muse at night over the blessing of life. This can even be done to filter out the things that don't matter, such as the rejection of a hostile enemy or an unlovely encounter. When functioning properly, emotions will sort through the blessing and dismiss the unimportant in our lives.

Alarm Reaction: Asaph's unhealthy emotions

Emotions in defiance is an "Alarm Reactor" (adrenal gland.) Asaph was a man of emotional struggle, as recorded in Psalm 73. He found himself struggling with the control of his emotions. In Psalm 73, we find his journey from emotional defiance to balanced living. Notice the psalmist Asaph in his conflicted life and the three options he tried to correct his misery:

Option 1: Environment (Inhale) modification:

> "*1 1 Surely God is good to Israel, to those who are pure in heart! 2 But as for me, my feet came close to stumbling, my steps had almost slipped. 3 For I was envious of the arrogant as I saw the prosperity of the wicked.*" (Psalm 73:1-3)

> "*13 Surely in vain I have kept my heart pure and washed my hands in innocence; 14 For I have been stricken all day long and chastened every morning. 15 If I had said, "I will speak thus," Behold, I would have betrayed the generation of Your children. 16 When I pondered to understand this, it was troublesome in my sight 17 Until I came into the sanctuary of God; Then I perceived their end. 18 Surely You set them in slippery places; You cast them down to destruction. 19 How they are destroyed in a moment! They are utterly swept away by sudden terrors! 20 Like*

> *a dream when one awakes, O Lord, when aroused,*
> *You will despise their form."* (Psalm 73:13-20)

Asaph had become fixated on the injustice of life and longed for things to be set right. He took this even farther in his assessment of life and personalized it. He admits in verse 2 that even though God is good, he was nevertheless living with emotional instability and was to the point of a breakdown, "I almost slipped." He rightly concluded the source of his emotionally precarious condition was that he had made life about himself and compared his life to the life of people he believed deserved less than him.

He now was in a predicament. How would he be able to reconcile that God is good (v. 1) with the fact that his life was filled with misery and the wicked were prospering? This is the dilemma of many of us, and unless we reconcile the issues, we will conclude like Asaph the only way to live is to run to the sanctuary and hope for the destruction of the wicked. If he could experience the change in his environment (the inhale of life), then he could live with peace of mind.

This didn't work for him, and this will not work for you. Simply getting a divorce or getting away from an unkind boss, or whatever seems to be the source of your misery, will not bring peace of mind. You need to have another option.

Option 2: Behavior (Exhale) modification:

> *"13 Surely in vain I have kept my heart pure, and washed my hands in innocence, 14 For I have been stricken all day long and chastened every morning."* (Psalm 73:13-14)

Asaph tried a second option, and so do most of us. We seek to modify our behavior. If I could simply be more controlled in my actions, my life will come to a point of fulfillment. I have often modified my behavior and found that even though the change was good, it didn't produce the peace of mind and joy I desired.

Asaph had "cleansed his hands," that is, changed his behavior in verse 13, only to find that life was still filled with misery. I do think it is good to make significant changes in your behavior when you are living with destructive actions. My point is that you will need to make a more fundamental change in your life to be balanced. Asaph saw the third option, the one that would change his life, and if we truly understand and apply this option, we will experience huge change to real balance.

Option 3: Thinking (Exchange) modification

> *"21 When my heart was embittered And I was pierced within, 22 Then I was senseless and ignorant; I was like a beast before You. 23 Nevertheless I am continually with You; You have taken hold of my right hand. 24 With Your counsel You will guide me, And afterward receive me to glory. 25 Whom have I in heaven but You? And besides You, I desire nothing on earth. 26 My flesh and my heart may fail, But God is the strength of my heart and my portion forever. 27 For, behold, those who are far from You will perish; You have destroyed all those who are unfaithful to You. 28 But as for me, the nearness of God is my good; I have made the Lord GOD my refuge, That I may tell of all Your works."* (Psalm 73:21-28)

Asaph describes the condition of his emotional defiance in verses 21-22: Asaph was out of balance **mentally**: "bitter" and "senseless." He was out of balance **emotionally**: "pierced within (Kilyah – emotions)" He was out of balance **spiritually:** "I was like a beast before you [God]." Asaph was out of balance and only came into emotional control when he had a change in his beliefs in verses 24-28.

Asaph concluded the truth about his relationship to God in eight ways:

1. I'm always with God (v. 23).
2. God protects me (v. 23)
3. God guides me in this life (v. 24).
4. At the end of this life I will be in Heaven (v. 24).
5. All I need in heaven is God (v. 25).
6. All I want in this life is God (v. 25).
7. The nearness of God is my good and my strength (v. 28).
8. My purpose in life is to tell of God's greatness (v. 28).

When you begin down the road of the proper "exchange," that is, you let truth permeate your beliefs, you will experience power, joy and peace. You should be very careful to approach the emotional challenges of life, taking the correct option above.

These are important options in changing your life. However, from the journey of Asaph, the most important thing you can do is to change your thinking and beliefs. If truth permeates your thinking, you will have the courage to change your environment when necessary, the wisdom to know when an environmental change is not necessary, and the personal power and resolve to change your behavior once and for all.

My journey into anxiety started at an early age:
It was my seventh birthday and I was having four friends over for my party. That morning my mom asked me, "Timmy, what do you want for breakfast for your special day?" I loved her sweet care of my heart. My mom and dad were stable, loving, and godly parents. Their love for me was obvious, but somehow, I felt lost in a family of six kids vying for attention. My friends arrived and my brother Dan, the older and more charismatic brother, was entertaining them while my younger brother, one of the kindest people alive, was winning my friends' hearts. I can remember feeling left out, insignificant even though these boys were there for me and all the presents were mine. I started down an emotional reaction to the party by believing I was less important on a day where I had high expectations of attention. I retreated to my bedroom for a good sulk and self-pity. I probably was hoping for the rescue of my mother.

My mother did come into the bedroom, and with wisdom told me I was not seeing things as they truly were. I was allowing a fun day, she said, to be ruined by my emotions, and she even said it was time to grow up in the face of my persistent selfish pity party. The growing up would not take place for over forty years. I was in emotional defiance, something that would be a pattern my whole life. As I got older, I would learn, for the most part, socially acceptable ways to sulk and feel sorry for myself. Life was about my gratification and no one seemed to agree to make life about Timmy. I was angry and on a dangerous and emotionally deadly course of life.

My emotions were playing out the "breathe" concept in ways that would be tough to break. I focused on my "inhale" environment and justified my bad behavior "exhale." Years later I learned the principle to live with the proper "exchange" and started to recover to emotional health. The process would be the most difficult task of my life, and yet the most rewarding. I was feeling the same despair of a world upside down like Asaph, but I only knew of two options, which would be my undoing. I spent most of my life trying to change my environment or my behavior without ever really getting to the problem: my thinking, and beliefs, that is, the exchange.

Once I realized I was responsible for my thinking, I was able to make real meaningful change in my life. I realized I needed to stop saying, "I'm just emotional," or "This is just the way I am." I needed to change my mind and thereby change my direction.

Emotional defiance leads to a hardened heart

There was another consideration that I needed to take into account. A life of emotional defiance practiced over time would result in hardening of the heart. This means that to change, there needed to be a change of sensitivity to divine truth. To make matters worse, emotional defiance has a cumulative impact on our hearts. We are warned about this in Ephesians 4:

> *"17 So this I say, and affirm together with the Lord, that you walk no longer just as the Gentiles also walk, in the futility of their mind, 18 being darkened in their understanding, excluded from the life of God because of the ignorance that is in them, because of the hardness of their heart; 19 and they, having become callous, have given themselves over to sensuality for the practice of every kind of impurity with greediness."* (Ephesians 4:17-19)

Notice the connection between behavior and thinking in verse 17. What you do is directly connected to what you believe. If your belief system is the "futility of the mind," you will eventually live out a reckless lifestyle. In verses 18 and 19, the point is made that a few things occur when ignorance rules the mind:

Step 1: Behave in the futility of the mind.
Step 2: Your thinking will become confused.
Step 3: You become alienated from the life of your Creator.
Step 4: Your heart begins to harden to the point that you become insensitive to truth.
Step 5: You lose your moral compass and your behavior becomes reckless.

The word "greediness," translated from the original Greek in verse 19, comes from the root meaning "to hold on too much or repeatedly," that is, habitually. The implications of this are staggering. You are being warned that if you walk away from divine truth, it will result in your eventual **habitual** moral failure. When people try to modify their environment or their behavior without changing their belief system, they will fail. Permanent and meaningful change comes by the transformation first of the mind and then the emotions as well as behavior become in check.

John's struggle with emotional defiance:
John was a man who struggled profoundly with pornography. By the time he and his wife came to me, this had become an unbearable problem in their marriage, with years of sexual rejection of his wife, in preference of porn. John truly loved his wife but believed many lies about sex and intimacy. He had replaced the value of intimacy with eroticism. Eroticism became such a part of his life it took up much of his undisciplined moments.

To explain the pornography, John started by telling me it was his wife's fault because she lacked a desire for sexual experimentation.

He said, "I'm just more sexual than her." My heart sank as I watched the painful expression on her face. She responded by saying, "The truth is, he is more committed to porn than to me." John's wife was very interested in intimacy with John, even after all the lies and rejection. Of course, the reality was that his addiction to porn preceded his desire for sexual experimentation in bed. His wife was rightly unwilling to explore some of John's more extreme sexual fantasies, which had come about through reading and viewing pornography.

John had slowly gotten addicted to pornography at work on his computer. As time went on, this problem came home, with many nights viewing pornography in the late hours. This left his wife feeling abandoned and rejected. John wanted a protocol that would change his addiction. My approach was different from what he expected. I helped him develop a strategy that included the transformation of his mind. John didn't need a moral reason to stop. He was already feeling guilt and shame. He came to me because his wife was demanding counseling or she was ending the marriage. John needed to believe he could truly change and be safe with that change.

John and I together developed a strategy. Once we established John's true desire for change, we developed among other things the following:

1. **Memorization and meditation**: Memorization of scriptural truths that related to the principles of sex and marriage. These truths would be meditated on at least six times a day in a biblical protocol for meditation. (More on this in Chapters 3 and 8)
2. **Analyzing triggers**: John needed to know the triggers for lustful thoughts to develop strategies to avoid these triggers. In a few weeks of analysis, John and I were able to

locate what caused the temptations. His strategy for dealing with these triggers included the removal of unneeded computers from his life and an accountability partner for his computer use.

3. **Thanksgiving journaling**: Journaling thankfulness for his wife would be critical to focus back on her, in terms of intimacy and fulfillment. We can only see the replacement of the bad with the good when we embrace God's provision for us with thanksgiving. For example, if you long for a bigger and better house, the discontent comes from a lack of gratitude for what God has provided. Thanksgiving began to permeate John's mind as these statements of thanks were repeated over and over.
4. **Weekly Reviews**: We weekly reviewed the journals and started seeing significant progress. John still struggles with his fantasies and yet is porn-free. He is seeing a profound change in his love and appreciation for his wife, and their marriage is strengthening. With strong prayer, John's wife is beginning to trust John, especially because John is beginning to trust himself.

Note: Through many hours of counsel, John became convinced that he needed to take responsibility for his addiction. He was not sick, he was not a victim, he was not a passive recipient of his own bad behavior, and he was solely to blame. Once he took responsibility for his actions and his thinking, he was in a position to make significant and meaningful change in his life. Stated simply, John grew up in this area of his life.

There must be an exchange of lies for truth in the mind. The concept of "Breathe" is to commit to a new way of thinking. Behavior modification without a change of beliefs will lead to other forms of reckless behavior. This is the warning we shared earlier in Ephesians 4:17-19. We must listen to this warning and learn to live the life filled with joy and freedom.

Chapter 2 Life Skills:

The intuitive worldview for man is to seek gratification, which puts us in a deficit situation where the world needs to cooperate with our desires.

Emotional defiance is when your emotions take control of your mind. This is a dangerous but avoidable reality. To overcome this defiance, you must write down specific truths that apply to your real value before God and focus on these.

As you see from the Hebrew word for emotions, "kilyah," our emotions are often reactionary. They need a good input of truth to respond well. The goal is to have our minds flooded with truth so truth will stimulate a proper response in our emotions.

Here is an approach that may be helpful to you:

Write down what you believe about yourself.

> Write down scripture that speaks to who you are in Christ (See Appendix 1).
>
> Once you have compiled a list of truths, repeat them over several times a day to yourself.

Spend maximum time with a friend who speaks "right things," the power of truth:

> *"And my inmost being (Kilyah) will rejoice, when your lips speak what is right."* (Proverbs 23:16)

Start writing a Thanksgiving journal every day.

Write down daily all the things you are thankful for. Do not include any negatives. Keep this thanksgiving journal as a discipline of life. Try to write as early in the day as possible.

Memorize: "*Do not fear for I am with you; Do not anxiously look about you, for I am your God. I will strengthen you, surely I will help you, Surely I will uphold you with My righteous right hand.*" **(Isaiah 41:10)**

Chapter 3–Reinforced Strategic Thinking:

Giving Voice to A Truth-based Inner Conversation

"Be anxious for nothing, but in everything by prayer and supplication With thanksgiving let your requests be made known to God." (Philippians 4:6)

You just missed the final off-ramp on your way to work and this is going to put you about five minutes late to the office. You are frustrated, but instead of just accepting the situation and rerouting to your office, you begin to berate yourself. You say to yourself, "You stupid, idiot," "How could you be so stupid?" "Why don't you think?" "Your boss is going to fire you." You continue on to work and arrive a couple of minutes late and get to work. While sitting at your desk, working away, your boss comes by and says, "Hey, I noticed your report from yesterday, good job." Okay, it turned out fine, right? No, it didn't turn out fine. You just caused a little bit of death to come to your soul, by thinking negatively and reinforcing that through repeated self-deprecation.

Each time you do this, you are stockpiling negativity in your soul. This adds up over time. You are doing grave damage to your well-being. But this is so common.

I was in the locker room of my gym one day, getting ready after a shower. I heard a man on the other side of the lockers, on the phone in a heated conversation. This man was using some pretty foul language and berating a guy named Walter. "Walter, you screwed up," he said. "You are a loser." It was loud and it was rude. I assumed he had a Bluetooth in and just didn't realize how loud he was.

I was getting ready to leave and it so happened that this man was leaving at the same time, I noticed he didn't have a Bluetooth in his ear, and I noticed his name on his work shirt said, **Walter**. Wow, was this guy vocalizing his inner conversation? It could have been some guy named Walter he was talking to, but I'm pretty sure he was talking to himself.

We may wonder about his sanity. However, before you criticize too much, you should be aware that we all talk to ourselves all day long. We carry on a conversation in our own minds that determines the quality of our life. Some are healthy and some are destructive. Destructive self-talk is a major reason for negative emotions. This conversation can be changed and, in many cases, must be changed to deal with negative emotions. Oh, and by the way, it is probably wise to avoid talking out loud to yourself, or others will wonder about your sanity as well.

Linda's Story

Linda became convinced from her experience that beauty was the way to acceptance and the acceptance of others was what life was about. She truly believed people would love her the most when she was thin and beautiful. But most tragic of all, she believed her worth was attached to the opinions of others. This is the problem of mankind in this world we live in.

As Linda went through the fall semester of her freshman year, she noticed an ever-so-slight "decline back into being fat," in her words. According to Linda, she had read in history about the Romans and their use of vomiting to be able to purge what they had eaten so they could go on eating even more. She thought if this was possible, maybe she could control her weight with this method. She tried that first time, thinking this would be a temporary solution to gaining weight. It worked. She was successful in getting rid of what she had just eaten. She thought, "I can do this when I overeat." However, it turned out to be a lifetime struggle, which at its peak would take place between ten and twelve times every day. She took the first steps toward a secret world of "binging and purging," long before she heard the term "Bulimia Nervosa."

This behavior proved to be a deadly trap, reinforcing her belief that she was only valuable when thin and beautiful. She had found a way to cheat the biological system. This lie about her value being attached to her beauty was reinforced at church, school, and most tragically, at home.

When any bad behavior begins, it seems to be a manageable action, but as time reinforces the behavior, addiction to that behavior increases. Linda was careful during the day what she would eat. But at night she would binge on as much food as she could, only to purge it a short period of time later. She thought this behavior would only last during her high school years and then be set aside for adulthood. She had no idea this would be a lifestyle dominating her life for forty years.

Because Linda's experience reinforced the idea that beauty was equal to love, it became her belief, her worldview. When anything becomes our belief, true or false, we begin to think and act according to that belief. She was in a difficult situation because her behavior made her feel worthless and yet the social acceptance from friends and family reinforced the lie. Linda lived with a lot of fear of being exposed for her bulimia, and so withdrew to a degree in those early years to controllable social interaction. There was no guile in Linda's heart and certainly no desire to hurt anyone; she was just trying to make it in a world of distorted values.

Most profound, for Linda, was the inner conversation about herself and life. She regularly would say how worthless she was, and compare herself to others. Her grandmother Lillian was someone she loved dearly. Her grandmother was, in Linda's view, happy and enjoyed life, but she also was "old and fat," Linda's words. She would many times say, "When I'm old I can be fat and happy, but for now I have to maintain beauty and youth to be accepted." Her belief now had gone from just beauty to include youth. Those two things were Linda's primary values for acceptance the rest of her life. She said this to herself over and over again until it was so reinforced in her beliefs that almost nothing, including years of counsel, could dislodge these false beliefs from her heart.

Linda fantasized about those days of not worrying about looks or how thin she was. Her inner conversation was dark and self-defeating. She would slam her cell door, putting herself in her own mental prison. Daily she lived in the darkness of this cell, while pretending to be happy. She was tragically trapped in her world of self-deprecation and destructive inner conversation. Her fantasies about being old and happy were a break from the darkness. Daily Linda was speaking the lies of a fallen world, to the point that her belief system was framed by this need to be accepted by a skewed standard of youth and beauty.

The inner conversation:

The term "self-talk" has always bugged me because it sounded shallow and trite. Remember the crazy skit from SNL of Stuart Smalley looking into the mirror and saying, "*Because I'm good enough, I'm smart enough, and doggonit, people like me.*" If this is an example of self-talk, I'm out. However, the truth of the matter is that we all are talking to ourselves throughout the day. That's right, all day long you have an inner conversation going on, when preparing for a difficult meeting, a confrontation, or maybe just musing about life. This conversation often is harmless, but sometimes it has devastating impact on our emotions. If we are intentional about this conversation going on in our minds, we can change the course of our lives.

Linda's life became complex as she spoke into her own life dark and devastating words such as, "I'm worthless" or "I'm too fat today." She developed patterns of bad thinking. She developed a habit of telling herself lies. Of course, this was unwitting. She was heading down a dark road of hopelessness and despair. Linda's biggest enemy was herself. Others admired and even coveted her beauty and kindness while she rejected herself and lived in self-loathing and self-rejection. Years later, she went to a therapist who spent hours trying to find the source and the blame for her problems. This turned out to be unhelpful, because what Linda needed was a new set of beliefs about true value and her relationship with her Creator. She also needed tools to be able to reinforce these truths into her thinking so she could move out of the darkness into the light.

Reinforced Strategic Thinking, RSTs

As I researched the cause of my own anxiety, fears and anger, the Lord laid on my heart a concept that revolutionized the way I thought and lived. I realized the "Breathe" concept was profound to me: that is, living a healthy life is not about the inhale/environment or the exhale/behavior, but in the exchange/thinking. Thinking is where life is really lived. I saw concepts in scripture like meditation, thanksgiving, prayer, worship, forgiveness and many other disciplines were done in the mind through intentional thinking. This should have been intuitive, but for me it took great pain to drive me to the concept of intentional thinking and its power to change my life. I developed and practiced for the first time what I call *Reinforced Strategic Thinking* (RST) and found measurable change in my mood and disposition.

Reinforced Strategic Thinking refers to three very specific disciplines.

1. **Thinking:** Thinking is foundational for emotional healing. Scripture says repeatedly, "Think on these things." It is clear from this directive that we have the compacity to change/redirect our thinking. We are not subject to passive thoughts ruling our minds unless we allow it. People who are happier and more filled with joy tend to think about the positive outcomes, whereas the people who struggle with misery tend to think on negative outcomes.

   Throughout each day, we stockpile messages to our brain with seemingly harmless statements like, "*I'm not going to make it*" or "*I'm not good enough.*" However, these messages are destroying our sense of self and our drive to live with purpose and courage. We need to stop these thoughts and focus our thoughts on what is positive and truth-based, like, "*God is with me*" and "*I can make it today,*" or "*God has uniquely gifted me and what I offer to the world is significant.*"

2. **Strategic**: When we focus our thinking, it must have direction. The direction is toward the point of weakness in your soul. For example, if you tend toward fear, you should focus on this truth: "*For God gave us a spirit not of fear but of power and love and sound mind.*" (1 Tim. 1:7) Memorizing this verse, targeting the fear in your soul, will give great relief to the anxiety controlling your thoughts, mood, and even your actions. Over time, this focused "strategic" truth will transform your mind.

3. **Reinforced**: Truth must be reinforced through the discipline of repeated focus. This discipline in the RST approach is crucial for success. In fact, this is where most people fail to have the transformation. You can't just say once, "*...God gave me a sound mind*." It must be repeated, reinforced over and over throughout the day and every day for weeks, until the truth takes dominance of your mind and soul.

We have heard it said, every thirty-five days your skin replaces itself and your body makes these new skin cells from the food you eat. What you eat impacts the quality of this replacement. Most of us realize the food we eat impacts the quality of our physical health. The old saying, "You are what you eat," is true. We have enough evidence from nutritionists that one of the best things we can do for our physical health is to eat the right foods, healthy foods. When we eat garbage, inevitably we will have physical problems with inflammation, disease and weakness. I have never had a Cinnabon roll and thought, "This is going to make my body healthy." In fact, I know it has no real value to my health at all. But I eat it anyway, hoping the moment of eating pleasure will outweigh the damage.

Thinking is like eating. Over time, what you think will impact how you feel and eventually will create healthy or unhealthy souls. Your soul metabolizes those thoughts just like food is absorbed in your body. It is absolutely vital that you change your thinking strategically and reinforce healthy thoughts. We need to discipline our thoughts and understand a new way of thinking.

Reinforced Strategic Thoughts in Scripture:

RST is a process of repeatedly focusing truths on your weakness, and then your mind will inevitably change. Your soul will move from complaining to joy, from fear to confidence, from negative to positive, from defeated to success. You have the power to change your mind and your life. Your misery will fade and your joy will spring forward into a new life. When all the dust of personal improvement and self-help settles, I believe RST is the *only way to have permanent meaningful change* in your life.

RST is the key to overcoming a life that has been surrendered to lies and self-deception. One of the most profound passages on RST is Philippians 4.

> *"Rejoice in the Lord always; again, I will say, rejoice! 5 Let your gentle spirit be known to all men. The Lord is near. 6 Be anxious for nothing, but in everything by prayer and supplication with thanksgiving let your requests be made known to God. 7 And the peace of God, which surpasses all comprehension, will guard your hearts and your minds in Christ Jesus. 8 Finally, brethren, whatever is true, whatever is honorable, whatever is right, whatever is pure, whatever is lovely, whatever is of good repute, if there is any excellence and if anything, worthy of praise, dwell on these things. 9 The things you have learned and received and heard and seen in me, practice these things, and the God of peace will be with you."*
> (Philippians 4:4-9)

It will be helpful for us to dig into this well-known passage in scripture, because in it the Lord gives us the keys to a transformed emotional life. What if you could move from fear and hopelessness to a life of joy and peace? Philippians 4 gives us this insight. Let's take a look at this insight:

In the original Greek language of the New Testament, it is very clear that *rejoice* is in the form of a command, but notice also it is restated for emphasis, "*and again I say rejoice.*" If God gives us a command, He must know that we have the capacity to carry out that command. Rejoice is the opposite of worry and anxiety. But just being directed to rejoice doesn't give us the capacity to rejoice. What is so practical about this passage is that the command is followed by details of how to fulfill it. These details, if understood correctly and applied intentionally, will change your life.

First, joy produces a gentle spirit. Philippians 4:5 gives the secondary directive to let your "moderation" or "gentle spirit" be known or seen by men. We are being instructed to let gentle responses to be what people see. The word translated here as moderation means "to yield upon," that is, to not react. By the way, as a recovering reactor, this is easier said than done. How do you respond to the attacks and threats in your life? Do you react and are you defensive? The number one tool for overcoming defensiveness is to understand and believe "*the Lord is near.*" This statement is for the reader to get a picture of the presence of a God who provides, not a God who rejects you but is present in the midst of turmoil. The next verse says, "*Let your request be made known to God.*" You see, the Lord wants us to know He is the ever-present God who provides and mitigates the reaction to an anxiety-producing threat. If we could truly believe this truth, we would see a marked change in our defensiveness. (More on defensiveness in Chapter 12.)

Second, joy will include freedom from anxiety. The key to removing anxiety and living with joy is through prayer. Not just any prayer but a specific kind of prayer. This is prayer that is coupled with thanksgiving. I have seen so many people approach

God in prayer, asking for help, only to feel worse than before they prayed. They come out frustrated and even impatient or angry with God. We demand results from God, telling Him to cooperate with our request, and then we are angry with Him when He doesn't comply. Prayer becomes a negative exercise of request in futility. We ask why God doesn't do what we want Him to. Remember this! The point of prayer is not to get God to do what you want but rather to express to Him what you want with the heart of thanksgiving for what you already have. God knows what you need.

We miss the point of prayer when we enter into, "Demand Praying," the idea of entitled requests. Demand Praying ignores the directive of Philippians 4:6. Look at it carefully. The prayer is coupled with thanksgiving. When we say thanks, we are saying, "What I have is enough." I'm grateful for whatever it is I'm facing, including a threat. The context of anxiety is clear that whether real or perceived, we are in a situation where we feel threatened. Our request puts the need on the shoulders of God and the thanksgiving diminishes the strength of the anxiety, the threat.

A real powerful consequence is that thanksgiving centers us in the moment, which is where life is meant to be lived. When we are in the moment, God gives us grace to handle what is, not what may come. What may come is in God's hands and we simply are able to enjoy the moment. When the moment is difficult, God enters in our hearts with comfort, so we can handle it.

Third, joy involves the presence of God's peace that will protect your mind. Philippians 4:7 gives a promise, "*The peace of God will guard your mind*." This promise of protection is based on our following the directives, requesting with thanksgiving. The peace God gives exceeds the "*comprehension*" or reason of man.

This is a supernatural intervention of God in the life of an obedient follower who seeks the Lord over self-preservation.

Fourth, the passage takes a turn to another and very important aspect of mental peace and joy. In Philippians 4:8, we are told to dwell on the positive aspects of life. He lists: Things that are true, honorable, lovely, good report are to be focused on. Thinking correctly will result in a foundation for change in behavior. In Philippians 4:9, the reader is encouraged to behave in the truth. Thinking right is crucial but it must be followed by change in behavior. We must act upon truth and then "the God of peace will be with us."

The key word in this passage is the word "dwell" in verse 8. The word "dwell" is translated from the word "*logizomai*" in the original New Testament language of Greek. This word in English is "logistics." The meaning is profound in the Greek and should be considered in the context of the directive to overcome anxiety, learn to rejoice and to live in peace. "*Logizomai*" in the accounting context is the calculation of the needs of income and expense. In the military context it is the calculation of required supplies for a military operation to be successful. As "dwell" is used here in Philippians 4, it is speaking to the need for the one who is anxious to intentionally and with strategic calculation focus on the positive aspects of life to find release from a life burdened with anxiety. This is the source of my teaching on RSTs. If we are going to experience real peace, we must follow the directive of giving voice in our minds to the positives of life, for example, truth, good report and pure things. We give voice through RSTs. Reinforced Strategic Thinking works as a spiritual principle to release the power of God as is clearly seen in Philippians 4:8-9.

I have noticed people who live in a state of consistent misery do so by focusing on the negative. I have also noticed that those who live life with joy and peace naturally focus on the positive. The simple truth is that the way you think impacts your emotions. For those of us who intuitively think negative, we need to intentionally change our thinking. RSTs are the only sure way I know that we can change the natural bent we have toward negativity.

Mark's story and the USA:

I got a call from a man who was concerned about a friend of his named Mark. Mark had fallen into deep depression and couldn't snap out of it. He was at the point of suicide. The darkness was overwhelming in his life. His mind had so attached to all things negative that it was ripping at his confidence and self-worth. And tragically, Mark had lost hope of ever changing and this hopelessness was pervasive in his soul. Mark needed to change this thinking.

Mark was a Navy SEAL. As a SEAL, his world was a performance-oriented value system. When I first started dealing with Mark, it was over the phone and we communicated through email. I had never seen him and asked him to describe himself to me: What did he look like? What were his strengths and weaknesses? What was the most important thing? And who was the most important person in his life?

Mark lived a distance from me, so it was some time before we counseled in person. We finally set up a time for our first face-to-face meeting. Mark walked up to my office and I was shocked to see what he looked like. He was tall, strikingly handsome, and obviously fit. Mark was a man of high intelligence, a physical man and a fifth-degree black belt. He had achieved much in this life. I was so shocked at Mark's appearance because he had described himself as "overweight and hideous." He was ripped and handsome, so this didn't square with his statement of himself. I needed to probe to find out if he truly believed he was hideous or was this contrived.

*In time I found out that Mark's wife had left him for another man. Mark, who clearly was given to TNTs and rejection from a woman was a huge trigger for him. This trigger left him emotionally devastated and filled with negativity. He began to speak lies to himself. He began to develop a habit of speaking to himself in very self-deprecating terms. If you had been able to hear his inner conversation you would have wanted to slap him and yell, "**Snap** out of it! I patiently listened to the heart of a man who was wounded not so much by the betrayal of his wife but by the self-betrayal of his mind. He had turned this into a life-threatening situation. Every day the conversation went something like this: "The one who knew you best has rejected you. You are worthless and hideous. Women will never find you attractive and you are not worth a woman's love." His conversation in darkness increased over time, developing fear, anxiety, anger and depression. His depression developed so deeply that suicide became the most reasonable course of action.*

One thing to keep in mind, Mark was admired and respected as a Navy SEAL and as a man. Mark was kind and wouldn't hurt others. If Mark heard anyone talking about themselves as he spoke about himself, he would run to their rescue and encourage them with truth and compassion.

Going back to Mark's state of mind; he was suicidal. Mark would fantasize about taking his pistol and putting it in his mouth and ending it. Mark told me that he would put his gun beside his bed to have it ready to kill himself when he got the courage to do it. Mark was serious about suicide, but was scared to death. Mark was a follower of Jesus. He believed God had given him eternal life through the sacrifice of Christ. His love for God was real and yet it seemed God wasn't going to take away his pain. Others had tried to help him by saying, "Mark, you need to pray harder and read your Bible more." Mark was a Navy SEAL, so if you gave him a discipline to do, he was on it. He dutifully prayed with great intensity and spent a good amount of time reading the Bible. It didn't help. He was at the point where there was no hope.

One night, with his pistol to his head and about to pull the trigger, he decided to give me a call. His mind was racing with fear and hopelessness. We arranged to get together. The stakes were high and the threat of suicide was real. One day he would have enough despair to overcome the fear of death, and he would pull the trigger.

Here is what Mark and I did in counseling. We talked about a method of approaching the Triggered Negative Thoughts (TNTs) I call USA. I asked Mark the question: Who do you work for? He responded by saying the Navy. I said, "Well, who actually pays your salary?" He said, "The United States." I said, "Mark, let's use the USA to be able to remember how to approach your problem."

USA stands for: **1. Understand the source of your emotions, 2. Strategic thinking, and 3. Action**. I told Mark these three things were crucial to overcome his depression and other negative thoughts.

> **U — Understand the source of your emotions**:
> We spent some time talking about how he was blaming his wife and the whole world for his troubles. I told him something I don't think many would normally want to say to someone who was suicidal. I said: "Your negative emotions are your fault and nobody is making you afraid, nobody is making you angry and

nobody is making you depressed. You are doing this on your own." I told him he had to intentionally stop blaming the "triggers" for his depression.

S — Strategic thinking:
Mark needed to get a grip on the lies plaguing his mind. As I mentioned, Mark was a black belt in Karate. I had him stand to his feet in my office and said, "What would you do if I threw a punch at you? Would you throw a punch at me?" He said, "No, I would deflect your punch." I said, "Let's try it." So, I threw a punch at his head, and before I knew it I was on the couch he had been sitting on. He had taken my momentum and my strength to use it against me. I told Mark, "What you are trying to do is face negative emotions by attacking the emotions. What you need to do is deflect them with truth. You take the negativity and its force and use it to your benefit. One way is to take the negative scenario to its logical conclusion and then ask yourself, 'Can I live with this?'" We did this in a couple of areas and found his belief was that God would give him the grace and strength to handle each one of these conclusions.

Another way of defeating these negative emotions is to have strategic truths that replace the negative thoughts. These RSTs must be strategic and applied directly to the negative area.

A — Action:
In Philippians 4, we discussed five points of the passage and left off the sixth. Here it is: take action. Philippians 4:9, "*The things you have learned and received and heard and seen in me, practice these things, and the God of peace will be with you.*" The point Paul is making is crucial in emotional recovery. It is not enough to understand the source of your emotional problems

and the need to apply strategic thinking. We have to move to the third part of USA: Action based on these truths. As we act, the truths become reinforced in a life of new thinking and living. As days and weeks of reinforced thinking and living are experienced, the habits change.

This is the point of the breathe concept we need to accept; the areas of inhale/environment that cannot be changed and understanding the importance of the exchange/thinking. But we must also exhale/behave truth to be completely balanced and whole and have permanent change.

Mark is living to a great degree a transformed life as he recovers from the habit of negative thinking. He is no longer fixated on suicide and is moving toward wholeness and balance.

Here are some of the RSTs that Mark and I came up with for his strategic need:

Negative thought: "I'm a failure."
RST response: "Today is enough; I can accomplish my next step today."

Negative thought: "I'm going to live in fear all of my life."
RST response: "God has not given me the spirit of fear but of a sound mind."

Negative thought: "I'm ugly and hideous."
RST response: "My looks are not the sum of who I am."

Negative thought: "My life has no future and I should just kill myself."

RST response: "God has given me this day as what He has made. I will rejoice and be glad in it," and "My life is a gift of God to me and others with whom I have contact."

(See Appendix 2 for RSTs to use in your recovery from negative thinking.)

The Pollyanna Syndrome:
Pollyanna was a novel written in 1913 about an orphan who endures difficulties and yet consistently seeks the positive in the midst of a world of negative. Pollyanna plays what she calls "The Glad Game," in which she imagines the best in every situation. She is resilient and pushes back at difficult with the vitality of a positive heart. She is so positive she irritates many. My wife Kimberly is the Pollyanna in my world. I have said many times, "If she lost a leg in an accident, she would spend a moment lamenting its loss and then she would say, 'Well, this is great, because now I only need to buy one shoe.'"

The Pollyanna syndrome has come to mean a person who unrealistically and illogically imagines life with extreme optimism. While we should avoid the extreme and irrational, it would be helpful to pursue the positive. I think there are people who dwell on the negative and justify it by saying, "I'm a realist," or "I look at things as they are." In their declaration of realism, they have altered reality to be about negative interpretation of life. I know this was my life for most of my adult years, and remains my default without an intentional refocus. We need a balance of realism with a clear understanding of what is true.

The Law of Inevitability

The problem with many of us is what I will call the Law of Inevitability. This law states that you cannot change who you are. You can make some modifications in your inhale/influences and even in your exhale/behavior, but you cannot significantly be transformed. For example, you may hear that a man who hit his wife will always be a "wife beater." This idea is found in many articles and books. Please understand, I have great concern for a man who ever raises a hand to his wife, but to lock someone into a lifelong sentence of "wife beater" is dangerous. I recently was talking to a Christian friend who works with accused sex offenders. Even though she is very disgusted by sexual aggression and bad sexual behavior, she thinks a lot of damage has been done through the overreaction of the legal system. Men and woman are being labeled "sex offender" for life, and according to my friend, some didn't always commit an act worthy of that title. Once labeled, you are stuck legally and socially. The stigma is damning and sometimes unwarranted. Society wants to err on the side of safety. I get this, but we must be careful. In one case a sixteen-year-old boy had sex with a thirteen-year-old girlfriend. Should he be labeled a sex offender? He was until he turned twenty-one, and still feels the stigma today.

The real problem psychologically is when we self-label. We take on a label based on behaviors and then we wrap our identity around that label; e.g., alcoholic, hoarder, OCD or sex addict. These labels and our views of ourselves can be self-imposed life sentences. Whenever you wrap your identity around a behavior, you lock yourself into a certain lifestyle of compliance with that label or spend the rest of your life fighting the very thing you see as your identity. Most people say if you drink excessively to the point where alcohol becomes your identity, you will either be a "practicing alcoholic" or you will be a "sober alcoholic," but in either case you are an "alcoholic." This labeling is a lie that is perpetuated in most Christian recovery programs. This is unfortunate and deadly.

The Law of Inevitability promotes the notion that even though one would like to change, the reality is, "I can only modify my behavior and my environment." We might say:

"I was born this way; there is nothing I can do about it."
"This is the way I think."
"I have always been moody and negative."
"I have a disease that can't be cured."
"I'm just crazy and there is no way out."

I have heard these and more. In fact, I have said some of them myself. What I have realized about the Law of Inevitability is that it ignores the Law of Redemption. God has given Jesus Christ to die for my redemption, to buy me back from slavery.

Let's take a look at the Law of Redemption: There are three Greek words translated "redeem" in the New Testament:

Agorazo–To buy in the marketplace
Exagorazo–To buy and take out of the marketplace
Lutroo–To purchase and set free a slave

These words are used in a specific context in the New Testament. God reveals man is a slave to sin, the Law of God and to sinful behavior. Through redemption, God through Christ has purchased man back from sin, the condemnation of the law of God and also from bondage to sinful behavior. We become new creatures in Christ Jesus.

Here is the context of how redemption is used in the New Testament: In the first century, there were slaves who would be bought in the marketplace. The price would be set, the slave would be sold, and the new owner would have the power over that slave. The New Testament was written with this backdrop. In some cases, a slave would be purchased and taken out of the marketplace and then set free. This is the picture the New Testament gives of the one who believes in Jesus Christ.

Christ has paid the price for our freedom through His death on the cross and His resurrection from the dead. When we believe in Him, that death is applied to our lives and we are purchased, removed from the marketplace and then set free. This new freedom extends to our behavior. We are free to live lives that are free from bad behavior. This is not automatic but is available to all who will tap into the redemptive power through Christ.

For those who are calling themselves names like "Alcoholics," "Sex addicts," "Drug addicts," "Hoarders," or whatever habit, they are living under the Law of Inevitability, not under the Law of Redemption. The lie of inevitability is destroying many who desperately need to get ahold of the truth of redemption. The resurrection of Christ gives us new life with new capacity with new power. Identifying behavior as a disease will keep us stuck in that Law of Inevitability. The Law of Redemption calls us to take responsibility for our behavior with God's resurrection power. We can overcome, we can change, and we can have transformed thinking and living. Behavior is not inevitable.

You may say: Well, Tim, that sounds great but how does it work? I don't have the power to change. I have prayed for God to deliver me and I'm still stuck. How can I change?

Here is how it works:

The Filling of the Holy Spirit and RSTs:
The filling of the Spirit is the means by which God allows for the transformation of the mind and life of the believer. It is the way for biblical truth to move from academic understanding to practical life-transforming living. The Holy Spirit takes the truth our minds are exposed to, and as we submit to Him, He implants truth into our lives, changing the way we believe, think and live. This is crucial in the development of emotional stability. **(See Appendix 4 for a further discussion on how the Filling of the Holy Spirit works.)**

Chapter 3 Life Skills:

The inner conversation: There is a constant inner conversation going on in your mind. What happens in your thinking is what will determine your emotional health and stability. Your beliefs will determine your emotions and even your actions. If you can change your beliefs, you can overcome emotional excess and bad behavior.

RSTs and the transformed mind: It is time to change: It is not outside of you. It is not in your past. It is not in your future. It is in this very moment where the exchange must take place. You can live free by changing the inner conversation to a truth-based conversation. I believe one positive RST is worth twenty statements of praise from another person.

Prayer is the Key to joy:
We will experience peace and joy when prayer takes the focus off our need and places it on God, who is faithful. This produces a heart of joy and peace because we are relieved of anxiety.

USA:
Step 1: Understand the source of your emotions
Step 2: Strategic thinking is essential
Step 3: Actions will strengthen your beliefs

Your way of thinking is a learned and reinforced habit and is subject to choice. You have the power to change your thoughts. You must first acknowledge the source, then you can "rethink." Once you acknowledge and understand that it is within your power, you must gain strategic thinking skills (See Appendix 2). Now you can put these new thoughts into action, which will reinforce and strengthen your new beliefs.

Law of Inevitability verses the Law of Redemption:
In Christ, God has provided redemption as the way to be free from any habit in your life. You can be set free through the Law of Redemption. Every time you think of your identity in terms of your behaviors, consciously reject this notion and speak out loud if you can, or at least in your mind, the truth: "I am a new creature in Christ."

The Filling of the Holy Spirit:
In all your pursuit of freedom from emotional extremes, do not leave out the power of the Holy Spirit to change your emotional stability. Remember to read the Bible daily and pray that God will implant it into your life.

Try this:
It may be helpful to keep a "thought journal" with reasonable responses. What are my thoughts? Scale your thoughts as negative or positive 1 to10, with 10 being most positive and 1 being most negative. What promoted these thoughts? What is really troubling me? Or what is really making me happy? (**See a sample "Thought Journal" in Appendix 5)**

Write down from the Appendix 2 the RSTs that apply to your area of need and repeat them at least twenty times a day this week.

Chapter 4–Fear and Worry

The Emotional Matrix

"I sought the Lord, and He answered me, and delivered me from all my fears." (Psalm 34:4)

Tommy was a young boy struggling through life. His brothers teased him incessantly, he was bullied at school and his parents didn't seem to care, at least in Tommy's mind. He was constantly getting in trouble in school for outbursts of anger. His parents were told that if he didn't stop with these outbursts, he would be suspended.

His parents were worried about his education and even his mental health, so they sent him to a child psychologist. The psychologist listened to Tommy's description of his outbursts and the complaints about his behavior. When Tommy was all done telling his story, the psychologist looked at him for an awkward moment and said, "What are you afraid of?" Tommy was dumbfounded and said, "What do you mean, I get in trouble for getting angry all the time" He said, "Let's not worry about your anger right now, just think for a minute and tell me what makes you afraid." So, Tommy began to think.

For the next several weeks, Tommy and his counselor talked about Tommy's deepest fears. Those fears, it was discovered, had to do with the teasing and the bullying. Tommy was afraid of being different, being seen as unlikeable, and most of all being rejected. Those real fears were driving the anger. The psychologist helped the parents to see that the teasing at home was devastating to Tommy's emotional health, and to see the importance of setting rules with their children to combat the culture of teasing and bullying at home. There would be no way for the parents to control the bullying at school, Tommy was going to have to learn to overcome. Tommy having a safe place at home for acceptance and love began from his brothers. Of course, this took time and was not easy, but the family began to have a cultural change.

The counselor also helped Tommy to learn to speak powerful words of life to his own heart, by writing down his greatest strengths and to repeatedly speak these to himself. As Tommy's siblings became more supportive of Tommy and as he began to speak words of life into his own soul, he started to have a new confidence in himself. His confidence impacted the way he was seen at school by other kids. Tommy and his family began to see a dramatic decline in his outbursts of anger, the fear was subsiding, and the anger was disappearing.

The above vignette is oversimplified, but shows the connection between fear and negative emotions. As you will see in this chapter, I am convinced that at the core of all negative emotions there exists the root emotion, fear. Fear is the enemy of the human experience. As you read this chapter, keep your mind open to the possible fears in your life fueling the other negative emotions.

Emotional Literacy:

People typically don't know their real emotions. When they are asked what they are feeling, they might say, "I'm angry," when they are actually afraid or they are feeling disrespected. The average person is an emotional illiterate. They don't know what they are feeling, but they do know that they are uncomfortable and want it to stop.

Unless we really get to the core of our emotions, we will not be able to change them. I hope the teaching you receive in the next four chapters will assist you in becoming more aware of your real emotions.

I met Linda in college:
It was our freshman year and the newness of college with academics and dorm life was spinning our heads around. For me, basketball practice and studies were the main things on my mind, until I saw Linda. She was radiant, filled with life and beautiful. She had just been voted head cheerleader by the student body. Yes, this new student was so bubbly and friendly and attractive, she was voted head cheerleader two months into her first year in college.

Behind the personality, most people had no idea that she was filled with pain and fear because she had mastered her disguise. She would say in the years to come, "I know how to dance in the light for moments of time and then I retreat to my private dark world." She had become so good at performing in front of others that no one noticed the pain beneath the surface. She made sure nobody got close and nobody entered in. She had a wall a mile high protecting her from the world that would reject her if they only knew. At least, that was how she saw things. In her words, she was fat and ugly and a complete loser, she hated herself for not being good enough. The reality, of course, was that she was fit and attractive and people wanted to be around her.

As a teenager, I only saw her as beautiful, happy, and kind. I pursued her for dating, I wanted to get to know her. Without knowing it, I really wanted her beauty, thinking it would make me a better person, more acceptable. I didn't consciously think this, but in my immature thinking, I didn't know what was important and what mattered.

Her looks and her friendly but sometimes distant demeanor intimidated the other guys in the dorm. But not me, I overcame my fear and approached her and asked her to go on a date. We began to date and explore a relationship. She trusted me and liked my humor and felt no threat because she didn't take our relationship seriously. In fact, she told me early on, "Tim, you are not a guy I would want to marry, but I love our friendship." For some reason, even though that went to a deep place within me, I ignored it and pursued her anyway. Within a short period of time, we were dating exclusively and she was feeling protected by having a boyfriend to keep away other boys in the school. Little did I know that the nature of our relationship was a friendship and an unspoken and unacknowledged arrangement of non-intimacy.

Within a year and a half, we were married. We were kids without a real understanding of marriage and yet a strong moral sense of commitment from our Christian upbringing. We were going to be together for life, no matter what. Linda found me to be a good protector and eventually a stable provider. I saw Linda as my ticket to acceptance and felt it was my duty and privilege to take care of her. In a sense, I was like a big brother, not a husband. As the years went on (twenty-eight years, to be exact) I grew to love her in a very paternal way. She was weak and vulnerable and my role, as I saw it, was to conceal her eating disorder, depression and fears. I perceived this as noble and loving and even my biblical responsibility. Of course, the truth was that it served my fears as well. I didn't know how to reach her heart. The best I could do was to get counseling for her and for us. Counseling never seemed to work for us. We spent many hours talking through our issues and even praying about them, but no real change came for either of us; we were afraid and the fear was destroying our lives.

I lived in fear of our relationship being exposed to our world. Our world revolved around family and church. I had become a pastor in my early twenties and loved to preach, but was a fear-based leader. We thought we had concealed our failed marriage, but people, of course, saw through this. I was always afraid of our marriage being exposed and Linda was afraid her secret bulimia would become known. We protected our failures from every attempt of people to enter in. We had a few casual friends but no intimate ones.

Fear can produce some "crazy" behavior. Linda and I lived a secret and separate life. We were friends and yet we knew we were supposed to be lovers. We loved each other from a distance and we were for the most part kind to each other. We rarely spoke about our real feelings; it was as if we had conspired to be silent. We lived a lie and ignored our pain.

Linda's fear drove her to withdraw from situations where she would be out of control or exposed. She lived in fear of her addiction being seen, but she also lived in fear of the darkness of her low self-esteem. Linda wanted intimacy and acceptance and feared it would never be realized in her life. She hoped one day a miracle would happen and she would be free from her self-destructive behavior.

I lived in fear of our marriage being seen as a failure, and more profoundly I lived in fear of never experiencing intimacy in marriage. Not that I would know what to do with real intimacy. I wanted what my parents appeared to have had; a strong loving partnership where, although imperfect, they truly had intimacy. I was afraid to embrace Linda with all my heart because I was afraid of going into the darkness of her depression. I was also afraid of rejection and selfish. She was afraid I would never accept her and love her unconditionally. I hate to admit it, but her fears of rejection were probably well founded in those early years.

Fear was our everyday companion. It impacted our communication, our parenting, our finances, our friendship, our sex life and even our walk with God. We were crippled together by fear. We lived in a glass house with blankets over our heads, thinking no one could see. We went to extremes to find happiness and nothing worked. Fear had become our master and there was seemingly no way to extract ourselves from fear's control and dominance.

The parable of the boy and the tigers:
A young boy heard there were tigers coming into small villages in India around where he lived. He had never personally seen the tigers, nor had he known anyone who had been attacked by a tiger. In fact, the tigers were known to stay away from people for the most part. Tigers would only attack people when there was no other prey available, even though humans were an easy prey for them.

As the young boy grew, he never saw a tiger, but many nights he was sure he heard the roar of tigers surrounding his house. This boy became so afraid of the tiger that it affected his life. He wouldn't leave his village to find a good job; he never married because he was afraid he couldn't protect a wife and family. The boy grew to become a man without much of a life. He was lonely and lived in fear. The tiger never came to his village; the tiger never really posed a threat to him or anyone else he knew. The boy grew to an old age, and on his deathbed, he asked his nurse, "Can you make sure there are no tigers coming?"

I have never been afraid of tigers. I have never been insecure about my safety because of tigers, and I imagine I never will be afraid of them. If I lived in India and tigers were surrounding my village, it would give me something else to fear.

You may be thinking how ridiculous this boy in the parable was. However, stop and think of your anxiety and your fears. Can you trace them to a real threat? What tigers do you fear? What I mean is, what is crippling you even though there is no real threat? Much of our fear is concerning threats that are not real. But fear doesn't need reality to impact your life. In fact, you may be surprised to know that most of our fears and anxieties have nothing to do with real threats.

Fear, the first negative human emotion:
In the Garden of Eden there was a beautiful experience of communication with God and man. Marriage was perfect and Adam and Eve enjoyed life on a level that we will not experience again this side of Heaven. What happened? I suspect you have heard of the "spiritual fall of man." God said, "Don't eat of the tree of the knowledge of good and evil or you will die." (Gen. 2:17) They did, and they died spiritually that day and began to die physically as their bodies would now age. Along with the spiritual fall of man, there were many consequences; most obvious was their psychological fall. What does that look like?

> *Then the eyes of both of them [Adam and Eve] were opened, and they knew that they were naked; and they sewed fig leaves together and made themselves loin coverings. 8 They heard the sound of the Lord God walking in the garden in the cool of the day, and the man and his wife hid themselves from the presence of the Lord God among the trees of the garden. 9 Then the Lord God called to the man, and said to him, "Where are you?" 10 He said, "I heard the sound of You in the garden, and I was afraid because I was naked; so, I hid myself." 11 And He said, "Who told you that you were naked? Have you eaten from the tree of which I commanded you not to eat?" 12*

> *The man said, "The woman whom You gave to be with me, she gave me from the tree, and I ate." 13 Then the LORD God said to the woman, "What is this you have done?" And the woman said, "The serpent deceived me, and I ate."* (Genesis 3:7-13)

Note the first function of man after sin was not an action but a thought. They "knew they were naked." Remember, they had been naked their whole existence and were certainly stimulated sexually by the appearance of each other because God had directed them to be together sexually and have children. So, what is this awareness of nakedness? Let's look back at Genesis 2:24-25, just a few verses earlier:

> *For this reason, a man shall leave his father and his mother, and be joined to his wife; and they shall become one flesh. 25 And the man and his wife were both naked and were not ashamed.* (Genesis 2:24-25)

The knowledge of their nakedness in Genesis chapter 3 was not about sex but about their shame. Genesis 2:25 makes it clear that before their sin there was a nakedness without shame. This seemingly unnecessary statement in 2:25 becomes crucial to understanding what they "knew" in Genesis 3:7. Whereas before their sin they were aware of their nakedness and sexually attracted to each other, as evidenced in the directive to become one flesh, they now had become distorted in their perspective of their sexuality and their relationship. They would never be the same; they had fundamentally changed from innocent to a fallen human state.

What emotion did this shame produce? Immediately they covered their "loins," showing fear of being seen in shame. We at this point can only surmise this; however, in Genesis 3:10, Adam expressly states fear is behind the coverup and the hiding. Fear was the matrix for the other emotions and dysfunctional action Adam and Eve would take to cover their guilt and shame. Note, there is always a connection between fear and shame. Here are their actions immediately following their sin:

1. Covered their nakedness out of shame, Genesis 3:7
2. Hid from God out of fear, Genesis 3:8-10
3. Blamed others to remove personal responsibility, Genesis 3:12- 13

If you study the emotional pathologies of man, you would be able to trace each problem back to just a few things we see in the garden: shame, fear, hiding in our relationships with others and hiding in our relationship with God and failure to take personal responsibility for our actions. There is the core problem of the fallen man. It was an immediate reality for man because he died just as God had warned him in Genesis 2:17. Unfortunately, this fall is passed from Adam and Eve to all mankind.

It should be noted that God's plan included purchasing back man from this death, called "redemption," and a reconnection with God, called "reconciliation." Also, God, out of love, would send His own Son, Jesus Christ, to die for the sins of man to make man righteous again, called "justification." We blew it, but God fixed it in Christ. (For a simple study on this look at: Romans 3:23, Romans 6:23 and Romans 8:1-4. These verses in light of our understanding of what happened in the Garden are an eye-opener to the need of man and the love of God.)

So, fear was the first emotion of man after he sinned. This was man's first negative emotion and is the matrix of all other negative emotions.

Fear is the matrix of negative emotions:

Most people go through life without ever analyzing their emotions. It is helpful to understand what God has to say about our emotions and what we learn from observation of man. Ask yourself these questions:

> Why do I get so angry?
> Why am I so controlling?
> Why am I so critical of others?
> Why am I so hard on myself?
> Why am I so defensive?

Fear is the source of all negative emotions in the soul. Anger is seen typically as a primary emotion. However, I have become convinced in my research and observation that anger is a secondary emotion that is sourced in fear (More on this in Chapter 5.) The following three statements put fear in the proper perspective:

> "Find the fear, fix the problem."
> "Find the fear, resolve the anger."
> "Fear will be resolved when lies are completely replaced with truth."

The man outside my bedroom window:

It was probably about 2:00 AM and I was startled and awake. I had just had a dream that was so vivid, I was sure it was real. At least in my eight-year-old mind. One of those dreams that might sound silly in the morning but was terror-filled in the middle of the night.

There was no conciliation that my three brothers were sharing the same room with me and they were peacefully sleeping.

I lay there for probably less than two minutes and then jumped out of bed. (I say jumped because of course there were monsters under my bed, ready to get a bite of my skinny little leg. Can you say fearful child?) I ran into my dad and mom's room, and while running I calculated the need to be a dad-size problem. Mom wouldn't do in this situation. The dream was that a man was looking at me outside my bedroom window and had the scariest eyes I had ever seen. In my dream, I woke up my brother and asked him to come with me to see how this man could see into our bedroom, which was too high for someone to see in. We went to the door in the living room and looked out. We could see the man standing on a ladder, looking in our window. Before we could pull our heads back in the door, the man looked at my brother with his piercing eyes and shot death rays into him and my brother dropped dead at my feet. That was when I woke up. So, you can see this was a dad-size issue and the death ray man would kill my sweet mom.

So, I woke up my dad. He was not glad to be awakened out of sleep for another of my fear episodes. But he got up anyway and tried to encourage me to see there was no threat and prayed with me. I wasn't having it, even though my brother was in his bed, peacefully asleep. So, after my dad prayed with me and tried to comfort me, I told my dad it was real. So, my dad said, "Come here and look out the window and see that everything is okay." He pulled back the drapes and said, "Look." To our surprise, we looked out the window and saw a ladder standing at my window. My dad had to admit this was a problem in proving the dream was not real. I got to sleep in my dad's bed that night.

It took about a week before I could sleep in my own room. This was only after one of my older brothers informed us that he had put the ladder there to get in through our window the day before my dream. Not until that truth was revealed was I able to dismiss it as only a nightmare.

Fear for me was a lifetime problem as a child. It was childlike fears at first, but as I grew they became adult fears; e.g., fear of failure, fear of rejections. We all have fear, but some live a lifestyle of fear. Unfortunately, my fears took a dominant role in my life. Fear drove me to accomplish in one situation, and drove me to avoid trying in another situation. Fear is not a friend to the human heart.

King David's fear-based behavior:
David wrote Psalm 34 to communicate the right and wrong way to handle fear. He writes in the superscription to Psalm 34, "*A Psalm of David when he feigned madness before Abimelech, who drove him away and he departed.*" David self-protected by pretending to be insane. This was clearly not David's best moment. There is some debate about what this false insanity was about, but the most important thing in reading this psalm is that you see the bondage David was experiencing was not so much about the external threat, but his internal struggle with fear. In Psalm 34:4 it says, "*I sought the LORD, and He answered me, and delivered me from all my fears.*" In Psalm 34, David used two Hebrew words for fear:

1. "*Megorah*" means terror or panic.
2. "*Yare*" means a fear or respect due to understanding the nature of the person or thing feared.

For example, if you are afraid of a non-poisonous snake to the point you think it might kill you, it would be the "megorah" fear, the fear that is not necessarily appropriate to the threat of a snake that cannot kill a human. If you are afraid of a murderer holding a gun to your head, the word "yare" would be the right word to use because the threat is really based on fact. When David speaks about the threat of Abimelech, he uses "*megorah*" to describe his fear. He was afraid of the threat and became terrorized internally by that threat, even though God had promised protection. This fear didn't create rational response. But when he speaks of the fear of the Lord, he uses the word "*yare*," meaning he respects the nature of God and this fear causes him to see the power of God's presence, which makes him want to be a better man. What a difference. Fear can be good or it can be bad. We are encouraged to have the fear "*yare*" of the Lord, but not to fear man.

After David's failure to trust God in light of the threat from Abimelech, he wrote Psalm 34 to explain how we can overcome fear and live in the peace that comes from God.

> "*4 I sought the Lord, and He answered me, and delivered me from all my fears. 5 They looked to Him and were radiant, and their faces will never be ashamed. 6 This poor man cried, and the Lord heard him and saved him out of all his troubles. 7 The angel of the Lord encamps around those who fear Him, and rescues them. 8 O taste and see that the Lord is good; how blessed is the man who takes refuge in Him! 9 O fear the Lord, you His saints; for to those who fear Him there is no want. 10 The young lions do lack and suffer hunger; but they who seek the Lord shall not be in want of any good thing.*" (Psalm 34:4-10)

David gives his process in overcoming fear:

1. It is God who removes the fear, verse 4.
2. Those who come to Him will never be ashamed or rejected, verse 5.
3. When the poor (afflicted) call on Him, He saves them, encamps around them and rescues them, verses 6-7.
4. When we taste and see the Lord (terms describing intimacy), take refuge in Him and fear Him, we will never be left to want, verses 8, 10.

What does this "fear of the Lord" mean? As we already mentioned, the term fear is "yare," a respect for the nature of the person or thing feared. To understand the fear of the Lord, we must know a few things:

1. The fear of the Lord is a respect for God's nature.
2. The fear of the Lord involves seeing His presence with us.
3. The fear of the Lord is a lifestyle of appropriate behavior, as it says in Psalm 34:11-18.

Like David, we do things out of fear to avoid pain. This is what Linda and I did, we avoided dealing with pain out of fear, not knowing that when we as followers of Christ turn our fears over to the Lord, He takes care of us. We were more afraid of the fear of man and his rejection than the fear of the Lord. If we had by faith in the Lord broken through our fears, we would have been given the grace to change and become mature in our emotions and actions. We relegated our lives to fear, failure, and the lack of intimacy with others.

The real tragedy is that we really wanted to serve God and follow Him but worked together to support each other's fears. We were trapped like the boy/man who feared tigers. We were afraid of something that was not a threat. We had the Lord who was willing to protect us, and yet couldn't live what David said in Psalm 56:4, "*In God, whose word I praise, In God I have put my trust; I shall not be afraid. What can mere man do to me?*" Just like the fear of unseen tigers, we gave man the power and lived crippled with emotions dominating our minds and lives. Living this way is a tragedy, to be sure. How are you doing with your fears? Do you give the power to man to determine your worth and acceptance?

Defining our terms:

Fear: Fear is apprehension from small to great. When fear dominates the mind, it controls the life. Fear is a distressing emotion aroused by a perceived threat. It is a basic survival mechanism occurring in response to a specific stimulus. Fear perceives danger and flees from it or fights it. Fear is related to the specific behaviors of escape and avoidance, whereas anxiety is the result of threats, which are perceived to be uncontrollable or unavoidable.

Worry: Worry is concern over possible events. Worry is both negative thinking and imagery, which are used to avoid potential threats. Excessive worry is the main component of Generalized Anxiety Disorder (GAD.) As I have mentioned previously, worriers are usually intelligent and creative people. Someone who is analytical tends to overanalyze situations, including threats. If that analytical person is also creative, the scenarios will become creatively exaggerated. When this happens, there is a departure from the real threat to a new problem, that is, our own anxiety.

Anxiety: Anxiety is a feeling of apprehension or fear brought on by worry. When worry focuses away from reality to imaginations, it turns to anxiety. When anxiety becomes habitual, one's life will be dominated by fear. Anxiety is fear gone rogue.

There are two primary directions of fear:
After it is all said and done, there are really only two directions of fear. Understanding these two directions will help us to know what causes us to be crippled:

1. Fear of things happening to us (examples: dying, getting sick, getting old, being left alone, being ignored, being disrespected, being attacked verbally or physically, running out of resources.)
2. Fear of things we have to do (examples: making a public speech, learning to drive, leading a business, raising kids, making decisions, sticking up for ourselves, confronting people.)

Think about how crippling life is when fear causes us to be immobilized so we avoid circumstances and people and we are unable to perform certain tasks we wish we could do. If we could overcome our fear, we could do and experience wonderful things. Fear is at the core of our emotional struggle and our dysfunctional behavior.

Fear that makes sense is easier to combat. When fear is not easily seen, it can become overwhelming and unmanageable. For example, if you are afraid of speaking to your boss about something, you may be able to build up the courage, prepare your attitude and information, and go talk to him. However, if you're afraid of being insignificant or afraid of being rejected, you will develop strategies to overcome that fear, which are usually unhealthy and ineffective in removing fear.

For example: I have been a father for over forty years and am now a father of seven children. I have learned a lot about kids and more about myself. Here is just one thing I know about my fear and myself: I'm afraid of failure and this drives me to seek to control my world. On our son Malachi's sixteenth birthday, he invited his friends to stay the night. My wife's tendency is to let the kids come over and let them hang out. I have a different approach; I want rules clarified, what food can be eaten, what is the pick-up time. My need to control just looks like a dad trying to make things go smoothly, a manager if you will. But behind my need to control is fear: fear of not being respected, fear of my kids doing things that will shame the family, fear of being inconvenienced, and most of all fear of failure. These fears drove my need to control the party. I took some of the joy out of the party for Malachi and for his friends. The kids had a relatively good time, but it could have been a good time for me as well if I could have just relaxed. Controlling your world is a tough job. I don't recommend it.

Three steps to overcoming fear:

<u>Step 1: You must identify the fear</u>: Most fear is based on unknowns, so you can take the power away from fear by analyzing it through what you know to be real.

A low sense of self-worth creates an emotional void. When this void is filled with fear, it increases the intensity of the low self-esteem. The lower our self-esteem, the greater the likelihood we will have fear rule our lives. (Note: The opposite of low self-esteem is confidence, not high self-esteem. High self-esteem is usually nothing more than narcissistic arrogance.)

In counseling I will ask people to do the following exercise:

List five of your fears:

List five things that define you (Don't include what you have, but who you are.):

What happens when this exercise is completed is they develop a foundational picture of how they view the world and its impact on them and how they view their value in this world. Fear is connected to the threats we see around us in combination with our opinion of our selves. If you can truly look at who you are and what real threats there are in this world, you can get a picture of your fear. It may take several times to get an honest list. In counseling we work at this, and so should you. Go ahead and make the list on a sheet of paper without taking too much time to think about it. Then after some time, come back to the lists you made and ask yourself, "Is this really honest and how I truly feel?"

Once this has been honestly dealt with, you will be ready to go to the next step:

Step 2: You must take fear to its logical conclusion (i.e., worst-case scenario). Take your fears to their logical conclusion, then create solutions and ask if this is manageable. The way that most people fight fear is to constantly ruminate over the possible scenarios and then try to push back emotionally against the fear, only to have fear increase with obsession over the scenarios. This doesn't resolve the fear. The problem with this method is that it goes nowhere, at least nowhere positive. Again, what we must do is confront our fears by taking them to their logical conclusion and then ask ourselves if we could truly live with the end result. We should objectively analyze the seriousness of the threat.

Follow this exercise and see how it works:

Write down the worst thing that can happen with your fears from step 1:

Now ask a question of each fear:

1. How serious is the threat?
   No threat (1...2…3…4…5) Great threat

2. What is the worst-case scenario?

3. What is the likelihood of the worst case happening?
   Very likely (1...2…3…4…5) Very unlikely

4. What can I do to minimize this threat?

5. Can this threat change how I define myself?
   Very likely (1...2…3…4…5) Very unlikely

Step 3: You must replace the lies with truth: To reverse the negative power of fear, we must think in an intentional and reinforced process of replacing lies with truth. This is what we called *Reinforced Strategic Thinking* in Chapter 3. What we are doing with RSTs is applying truth to our lives. Once this truth forms our new belief system, we will have truth dominating our minds and hearts. No significant and lasting change will take place until the truth permeates the mind, the heart, and the emotions. When this takes place, fear has lost its power over our souls. Here are just a few examples of powerful RSTs:

Existing belief: **I'm insignificant**
RST Truth: **I'm deeply loved by my Creator** Romans 8:35-39

Existing belief: **I'm going crazy**
RST Truth: **God has given me a sound mind** 2 Timothy 1:7

RST belief: **I'm alone**

RST Truth: **God is always with me** Isaiah 41:10

You should memorize the above verses and reinforce them every time the fear dominates the mind. This must be done with RSTs or it will not work. You should know your fear and know the truth that strategically applies to that fear, and repeat this truth to yourself repeatedly until the fear subsides into insignificance. The goal is not to be free of fear, but that fear will no longer have a significant place in your life. Once you learn the power of this you will soon be developing your own list of replacements. These don't need to be scriptures to be used as RSTs. For example, I know I'm a reasonably competent teacher, but if I allow insecurity and fear to rule my soul, I will marginalize my impact through teaching. What I need to do if feeling insecure is to RST the truth that I'm a competent teacher with influence. The truth of my life will support that as truth. **(See Appendix 2 for specific scriptures on fear or insecurity)**

Speaking words out loud can fuel negative or positive emotion:

Be careful what negativity you say out loud, because you could create fear for yourself and even anxiety. Your words are powerful. When you speak lies out loud, your heart is more likely to grab them as truth. For example, if you begin speaking in anger, this will fuel your anger to a new level. What happens is we work up our anger, fear, and panic attacks by simply restating lies. I have observed people increase the intensity of anger as they give in to the fears and the lies associated with the fears. As they speak, their anger escalates into rage. I have done this myself. At first it seems reasonable to vent, and before I know it I will be in an all-out rage.

The best thing to do is confront the lies by stating what you know to be true.

Let me give you a vignette of my own fear-based anger that escalated into rage. *In 2008, the economy collapse impacted our household income and we found ourselves in a financially pressed state. I had begun a fear scenario in my mind that went like this: Our children who grew up moving from one house to another without sufficient space and resources have for the first time found some stability in their lives. We have built this house for our large family and we are going to lose it and the kids will find themselves moving once again. The real fear was that I would have failed as a father and a provider.*

The fear was intense. This fueled anger over incidental expenses that seemed unwarranted and I began to feel out of control in handling our finances, and I was looking for a place to put the anger. I started talking one morning to my wife and I began to express my anger over the expenses. The more I talked about our finances, the more I was angry, and the more I expressed my anger the angrier I became. That morning I worked myself into a rage in front of my wife. She knew nothing about my fear because I was ashamed to tell her I was not trusting God. I was angry with everyone and everything, when in reality I was afraid. Fear was the matrix of my angry emotions, and not until I turned the house and our finances over to the Lord did I see the fear and anger subside. This took an intentional RST approach to combat my fear. Truth won in that season, but because I have the bad habit of negative thinking, I have to go back to truth to stabilize and center my heart.

Speaking lies can bring on increased negative emotion, but when you speak positive truth **out loud,** you will reinforce truth in your heart. It is powerful. Go ahead and say out loud, "*God loves me,*" five times. If you are reading this book in a public place, you may alienate the people around you. This is best done in a reasonably private place. I do this often when I'm under great stress. I will quote out loud the twenty-third Psalm. I personalize it and God uses this to comfort my soul. Speaking truth out loud resets my heart toward the power of God. We must speak truth to our hearts and even verbalize these in writing and speaking. This is why journaling truth is so powerful. I already mentioned in Chapter 3, RSTs must be intentional, reinforced and strategic. You need to speak specific truth in the area of your fear, and it must be done many times every day.

Fear and Laziness:

A seemingly unrelated consequence of fear is laziness and unproductivity. That's right, unproductive people are fearful. Have you ever seen a lazy person get motivated for a cause or event they like? Of course, you have. My kids won't clean their rooms or do dishes at our house, but when they are working at their jobs, they're amazing workers. Our two oldest kids, who were living at home, worked in the same restaurant, sometimes on the same shift. My wife and I went to dinner in their restaurant and were seated, served and cared for by the two of them. My wife commented that she wished they would work like that at home. At home they seem lazy, but at work their boss brags about their work ethic. If you have kids or a memory of your teen years, you probably understand this example.

I believe people naturally want to be productive, but have fear blocking that natural inclination. The connection between fear, unproductivity and laziness is seen in scripture:

> "*The sluggard says, 'there is a lion outside; I will be killed in the streets!'*" (Proverbs 22:13)

What causes the sluggard to be lazy? Of the many causes for laziness, none are as strong as fear. He looks at the potential threat and is unable to go to work. This may be a ruse to get out of work, in which case there is another fear driving his laziness. Yes, people are afraid to work. Laziness is not a primary state, it is secondary to something else. What are some of the fears? Let me list a few I have observed and experienced:

The fear of failure
The fear of opposition
The fear of rejection
The fear of imperfection
The fear of not knowing how to accomplish the task

Fear is such a powerful negative emotion; it can rule the life without any provocation or threat. Leaders, if we could take the fear away from our employees, we would get a harder working team. Most bosses think if they can induce fear, this will motivate the staff. The truth is that fear does motivate, but only while there is a constant threat. The human soul works best free from fear. Fear will eventually turn in on the soul and will result in less productivity.

If leaders and parents could inspire instead of coerce their followers or children, there would be a greater degree of productivity. Love is the greater motivator: love for the work, love for the team, love for the company or family and its mission. Love will turn a sluggard into a productive, strong worker. Leaders inspire; they don't intimidate!

Chapter 4 Life Skills:

Fear is the matrix of negative emotions. We need to ask what is causing our fear. Once we find what the fear is, we can fix the problem. Your ability to find what is really scaring you will give you the key to overcoming negative emotions.

Fear, Worry and Anxiety:
Fear is connected to a real threat; worry is the focus and fixation on that threat, and anxiety happens when the threat is taken beyond reality into an irrational level. The reason anxiety is not manageable is because it is based on a lie. The key is to combat anxiety with truth.

Three steps to overcoming fear:
Step 1–You must identify your fear by listing your greatest fears and your view of yourself in this world.

Step 2 – You must take fear to its logical conclusion and ask yourself: Is this manageable? Could I handle this if it happened? Would God provide grace for me in this situation? How much of a real threat is this?

Step 3–You must replace lies with truth. That is RST (Reinforced Strategic Thoughts) what you know from God's Word and what you know is true from your experience. State these truths to yourself over and over throughout the day until your mind is convinced of these truths.

Be careful what you say:
We will be impacted greatly by verbalized emotions either for good or bad. If you speak angry words, you are in danger of fueling rage.

If you speak positive words of truth, you are more likely to have a deeper soul commitment to truth, and thereby more peace and joy.

Fear and Unproductivity:
If you are having a hard time getting motivated, you need to ask: What is the fear? If you find what you are afraid of and then take the three steps to overcome fear (above), you will unleash your natural inclination to produce and be creative.

Chapter 5–Anger and Bitterness

The Secondary Toxic Emotion

"Cease from anger and forsake wrath; Do not fret; it leads only to evildoing." (Psalm 37:8)

Every one of us have been offended by someone or something. But have you ever been so offended that it tears at your emotional stability? It produces such a visceral response you can't be civil to people around you. I'm not talking about an incidental offense; I'm talking about the kind of offense that goes to your core. For example, you are told you are worthless, you are lied about in gossip, rejected or even abused. I'm talking about the kind of offense that changes you. The word *offense* doesn't seem to accurately describe the woundedness of an abused person, however. *Offense* is the word that God uses to describe the first step on the road to out-of-control negative emotions like rage and bitterness. In this chapter, we will take a deep look at the seven forms of anger in Ephesians 4:26-32.

Everyone has said something like, "He made me angry" or "You make me angry," so it must be true. People can make you angry, right? Do you think people have the ability to make you angry? You will hear one opinion that says people "can't" make you angry, and then another that says people "can" make you angry. So, what is it? Well, the answer is, both opinions are partially right. The notion that people don't have an impact on your emotions is just not true. On the other hand, the notion that people can control you is equally untrue.

The problem is found in the oversimplification of anger. It is very true that other people and circumstances can provoke you. However, the only way anger can take root in your life is when you choose to take "ownership" of that anger. This chapter is about the psychology of anger, how and why we get angry.

Linda's Story:

It took several years for Linda and I to identify that she had an anger problem, whereas my anger was obvious. She was most often kind and mild-mannered, so we didn't think anger was the issue. Of course, our blindness was due to our definition of anger. Her way of dealing with others was to always strive to be kind and therefore be liked. She seldom raised her voice and almost never confronted anyone, including me. I was allowed to be immature and moody when I was upset. She apparently enjoyed the break from interaction with me so she could be alone.

In the three decades of a relationship with Linda, I think I saw her provoked to rage no more than a handful of times. She seemed even-tempered, and I would never have thought that anger was one of her driving emotions. The truth of the matter was, her bulimia, depression and some of her other negative emotions were attached to her anger, which was founded in her fear. Linda spent much time trying to avoid people when it was not on her terms. She would be okay with social interaction when it was a controlled environment, but even the social interaction that was within her control felt risky. She really didn't like to be around people because of her fear that her weaknesses would be exposed. This fear of exposure made her angry with herself, others, and me. We rarely had people in our home and almost never went to people's homes as a couple.

Linda would see me get angry and be disgusted even though I almost never verbally directed my anger toward her. I was angry with her, but I didn't want her to know that. She saw this as my great weakness, and I agreed and was disgusted with myself. We defined anger, not as a state of mind, but as a demonstrative emotion.

Not until we had been married for a few years did the real focus of her anger come to light. She was angry with her mother. It is irrelevant at this point whether or not this was warranted, but it was certainly Linda's focus. She was angry because she was afraid of her mother. She wanted her mother's approval so badly that she would go to extremes to obtain it.

Linda wanted new couches and a new color scheme both inside and outside our home. She wanted a new table and chairs. This was going to be a great expense, but our kids were getting older and it was time to change our décor. We saved and even borrowed and got the job done. I remember thinking how great the place looked. Her mother came for a visit and showed such approval that I was amazed. I had never seen this kind of approval of Linda from her mother. There was no hesitation in her word, no qualification in her compliments. This was such a success I was astonished. Linda had her mother's approval, and though it cost us a lot of money, it seemed like everyone was happy. I really was thankful for Linda and I could see some contentment in her demeanor.

About six months later, we made a long trip to visit her mom and dad. We arrived outside their home, and I was surprised to see that her mother had painted their house the same color as ours. The trim was the same, the shutters, everything. This was only the beginning. I walked inside, only to find their couch, chairs, and décor were the same as ours almost to the detail. Her mother's house was nicer and the furniture was more expensive, but it was the same. I realized, when Linda had gone on a solo trip previously to her mother's house, she determined to match the furniture and décor. This is probably common with mothers and daughters, but Linda admitted that it was unhealthy.

This is one example of many that pointed to Linda's deep need for her mother's approval, which later in her life she would lament: "I never got her unconditional love and approval." She was angry at her mother's rejection and angry with herself for being driven to please an un-accepting mom.

Many theories about eating disorders have been developed. I believe it is often the collision of fear, anger, and control. Because the images for female beauty usually include thin young women, a fearful and angry girl may develop unhealthy eating habits to acquire the perfect body type. The unhealthy eating habits can range from mild to severe, and in Linda's case she was severe in her eating habit of binging and purging, which took place up to twelve times a day throughout our marriage. She lamented that sometimes she would not feel better even after throwing up several times. Throwing up served two purposes for Linda: 1) To control her weight and thereby the world's acceptance of her; and 2) To purge herself of all of her badness. This was something she was conscious of and shared with me. Somehow the purging of food felt like a new start, even though it was followed by an extreme sugar low and a drive to eat again.

It is important to understand that Linda and I assumed, as many do, that anger is not internal but external. In other words, we thought anger was only a problem when there was rage or an outburst of anger. The internalized anger for Linda was deadly.

Learning my rage early in life:
I was angry as a child and didn't know why. I found myself frustrated for seemingly no-good reason. The direction of my anger was almost always turned in. I can remember sitting and musing about how emotionally out of control I was even when I was a preteen. Was it because I was sexualized at an early age? Was it that my parents were imperfect? I have known some people who at an early age had more traumas than I had, but they had substantially less anger than me. What is the difference between them and me? I guess I'm just a high-strung emotional guy. There is nothing I can do about it, so just live with it.

The difference between those who seemed free from anger and me, overwhelmed by anger, was my fear. It took me years to discover the difference, and once found it revolutionized my control of anger. I think I will always struggle with anger, but I'm seeing progress in my life in not just managing but abating anger. However, I have to continually go back to the source of my anger, my fear.

The toxic nature of anger:
At our church we were finishing a remodeling project for our early childhood area. There was some degree of excitement among the parents of young children. The walls had been completed, the carpet was being laid and the bathrooms were ready to be painted and retiled. We found that we had a problem with mold, and this was going to be addressed by professionals to get rid of it. The cost was manageable and the time to fix it would be a few days.

On closer inspection, our contractor noticed that water intrusion through the walls had not been taken care of and needed extensive repair. Because the area was in the basement, we needed to dig outside to seal the outside of the basement wall. The project was a month long and a great expense, but the water intrusion was taken care of and the mold was removed and the children were safe from toxic mold. We had to eradicate the source of the problem, or in a short period of time we would have mold again.

Anger is toxic like black mold. We must address the source of our anger, not simply manage it. There is an intrusion in the heart that fuels the anger. This intrusion is a perceived threat, which is something that causes fear. Yes, that's right: fear is the cause. A few things about anger:

1. Anger is toxic and will permeate the life and destroy emotional health and alienate others.
2. Anger may cause physical problems such as headaches, hypertension, and heart attacks.
3. Anger is fueled by fear. There is some perceived threat that causes the anger to exist.
4. Anger, like toxic mold, will grow without fully removing the cause. Anger management without dealing with the cause is like painting over the mold. It will come through and create more problems.
5. Anger should be taken care of irrespective of the cost. We need to understand the value of getting rid of the anger because the removal of anger is difficult.

Seven Forms of Anger:

In developing an understanding of anger, I have become convinced in my years of working with angry people and struggling with my own anger that anger is caused by our own reaction to events in life. I believe we are responsible for the rage and resentment that reside in our hearts. We have not learned healthy and biblical ways to address the provocations in our lives. In the book of Ephesians,

Paul presents a beautiful treatment of anger from a spiritual and psychological perspective.

As we look at Ephesians chapter 4, we will get an insight on how anger develops, how it grows, and how to overcome it. I will put the original Greek words in parentheses to be able to define the seven forms of anger. Paul presents seven forms of anger:

> *"26 Be angry (**orgizo**), and yet do not sin; do not let the sun go down on your anger (**parorgizo**), 27 and do not give the devil an opportunity. 28 He who steals must steal no longer; but rather he must labor, performing with his own hands what is good, so that he will have something to share with one who has need. 29 Let no unwholesome word proceed from your mouth, but only such a word as is good for edification according to the need of the moment, so that it will give grace to those who hear. 30 Do not grieve the Holy Spirit of God, by whom you were sealed for the day of redemption. 31 Let all bitterness (**pikros**) and wrath (**thumos**) and anger (**orge**) and clamor (**krauge**) and slander (**blasphemia**) be put away from you, along with all malice (**kakia**). 32 Be kind to one another, compassionate, forgiving each other, just as God in Christ also has forgiven you."* (Ephesians 4:26-32)

1. <u>Provocation</u> – (Greek: Orgizo = "to make angry")

> *"Be angry (**orgizo**, provocation), and yet do not sin; do not let the sun go down on your anger."* (Ephesians 4:26)

It all begins here at the point of being provoked. This provocation has many sources but falls into only two categories:

1. Outside (other people or events)
2. Inside (self-provocation)

There is no provocation without fear. Fear is the fuel of provocation. People who are less likely to be provoked are those who have dealt with fears in their lives at a deeper level. People who are not afraid of rejection, loss of control, or loss of power are less likely to be provoked. But everyone can be provoked in life. I have never met a person who is free from provocation. However, I have met many people who have learned skillful ways of hiding their provocation and their anger, but is the answer to simply hide our anger, or is there something deeper and more fundamental we can do?

Legally, provocation is considered in some jurisdictions a defense in a criminal case, usually only to reduce the conviction and the sentencing. In court, a defense attorney typically will look for mitigating circumstances for crimes of those who are facing overwhelming and compelling evidence against them. This is what we do in our personal lives as well, we seek reasons for our anger, and typically these are easy to find. The problem is that once the "reason" is found, we still have not eradicated our anger and bitterness; we have just given an excuse for it.

Understanding the provocateurs' hearts:
There are many motivations in the hearts of those who provoke others. I want to simplify the analysis of why people provoke others into three categories:

1. **Inadvertent Provocateur**: One who is ignorant of the impact of their words on others and has no ulterior motive than to connect with them.
2. **Persistent Provocateur**: One who is not concerned about the impact of their words on others and seeks to use them.
3. **Malicious Provocateur**: One who is aware of the impact of their words on others and uses this to destroy them.

Provocateur	View of their Listener	Goal	Common Impact
Inadvertent Provocation	Ignorant	No personal agenda	Offended
Persistent Provocation	Inconsiderate	Use of others for personal gain	Manipulated
Malicious Provocation	Contempt	Destroy others	Destroyed

I am aware that this is somewhat of an oversimplification, but it may be helpful to get us thinking about the possible reason we provoke others.

Note: Self-provocation can happen when we express anger, which fuels an escalation of negative emotion. When was the last time you tried to unload your frustration and started to see increased anger? The more you express it, the more negative the situation becomes, that is, you experience an escalation of emotions of anger and rage. In some cases, expressing anger maybe the worst thing to do.

2. <u>Personalized anger</u> – (Greek: Parorgizo = "anger alongside," to take ownership)

> *"Be angry (**orgizo**), and yet do not sin; do not let the sun go down on your anger (**parorgizo**), and do not give the devil an opportunity."* (Ephesians 4:26)

Note in verse 26, the difference of the words "angry" is "***orgizo***" (to be provoked) and the word "anger" "***parorgizo***" (to take the provocation alongside) to take ownership of that provocation. Paul is saying there is no sin when you are first provoked, but if you allow time to pass without addressing the offense, it will become your possession and when the provocation becomes something that resides in the soul, over time it will begin to spoil and become toxic to you.

Paul wants us to avoid this road to bitterness. Real emotional trouble starts when we allow a provocation to become our "owned offense." Over time, unfortunately, this will cause us to justify all the negative emotions that come with it, including bitterness and resentment. Fear may keep us from responding in assertiveness to the offender to resolve the offense, and we spin into a declining negative emotional defiance. So you can see the importance of Paul's warning against moving from "*orgizo*" to "*parorgizo*."

Mary's Story:
Mary was fifty-seven years old and a woman of substantial financial means. She was smart and attractive but deeply angry at the world, especially men. When she came to me for help, her concern was that

she could not successfully maintain a long-term relationship with a man. She both wanted a relationship with a good man and was deeply suspicious and angry with men. She was frustrated with the advice she was receiving from friends and family and wanted the input of a pastor.

She shared with me her marital history and about ten minutes into her list of grievances with her two previous husbands, it became clear to me what the problem was. Instead of immediately addressing the issue, I asked her what advice she had received from her friends and family. She started to share how they were lacking in compassion toward her. All of her friends told her she was bitter. She explained she had every reason to be bitter and they just didn't understand. (Here is the problem: unresolved anger and ownership of that anger. Personalized anger is deadly and will not stop destroying until it is removed from one's life.)

I asked her if she would like to have freedom to love well and live with joy. She of course said yes and added, "Why do you think I'm here!" (She was on edge, and I was walking into the dangerous territory called bitterness.) I explained that it sounded to me that those men had provoked her and she had taken ownership of these provocations. She interrupted me to explain once again that she was justified; I acknowledged her and pressed on, I told her the only way she could experience freedom is to hear and believe the truth. She said, "I want the truth and I want freedom." (I was pretty sure she was not open to the road to love or freedom.) But I decided to recklessly press on with her.

I said, "Mary, it is my opinion that you have one of two problems: 1) All the men you have met are jerks and you just have bad luck with men, or 2) You have lost your will for intimacy because you justify negative emotions toward men due to bitterness." (I knew she was struggling to hear what I was saying, so I tried to reach her with a vignette.)

I told her, "I knew a well-known surgeon that had the respect of his community. His wife, for some reason, probably due to his intense work schedule, began to see another man. Her affair resulted in her leaving my friend and marrying this other man. The surgeon was so angry and hurt that his work suffered to the point that he made a drastic mistake and lost his medical license. When I met him, he was living on the street in San Jose, California, begging for food. This brilliant man allowed personalized anger to destroy his life."

At this point in the vignette, Mary looked at me and said, "You think I'm like your friend?" I told her I could see no difference in the justified provocation and subsequent ownership of that anger. Mary was stuck and she knew it. She realized it was not the men in her life, but her inability to process her anger. I referred her to a friend of mine who was an excellent counselor who took over her counseling to take it to the next level. Together they have eradicated much of the anger from her life with truth and the difficult process of going back in some cases to apologize for her actions within her relationships. Today she is experiencing a level of freedom she previously had not known.

We will go to great lengths to justify the ownership of our anger by finding people to support us. Once we own, that is, personalize the anger, we will develop scenarios in our minds to vilify our provokers. In the extreme, we will dehumanize and emotionally destroy them and in so doing lose ourselves in the process.

The teaching of Ephesians 4:26 goes into verse 27 with a sobering warning, "*and do not give the devil an opportunity.*" What Paul is saying in this verse is that you don't simply have a psychological vulnerability, but you are also subject to Satanic attack when you don't release the provocation. The lessons learned in Ephesians 4 should not be underestimated; let's press on.

3. Bitter Resentment (Greek: Pikros, to sour, to become bitter)

> *"Let all bitterness (pikros, bitter resentment) and wrath and anger and clamor and slander be put away from you, along with all malice."* (Ephesians 4:31)

"Time heals all wounds." Right? No, in fact just the opposite is often the truth. When resentment is allowed to dwell in the heart over a period of time, there is an increase in woundedness. The offense is locked in the heart and yet forgotten as a conscious focus. However, the pain resident in the heart drives the life of anger and bitterness. The only way to truly heal is to overcome that woundedness by releasing the offense.

Anger that has been owned or personalized doesn't remain static; it sours, "*pikros,*" becomes bitter. Once it becomes bitter it begins to define us as victims. When a provocation first takes place, it is so intuitive to react and take hold of the anger, but as soon as that anger is held it begins to sour and become bitter. Over time, that bitterness begins to define us.

Have you ever picked up a carton of milk and drunk directly from it, only to realize it is spoiled? You immediately knew you were in trouble because it not only tasted sour, but was clabbered. It made you sick and was a deterrent forever taking that risk again. I watch many people live life with bitterness, and they have even learned to enjoy the taste of soured milk. In some rural areas of the Southern United States, clabbered milk is eaten for breakfast with sugar, nutmeg and cinnamon. I don't recommend acquiring a taste for bitterness. No matter how much sugar you put on it, the bitterness will eventually destroy you.

Joshua's story

Joshua was twenty years old and clearly struggling with bitterness. His stepfather had raped him as a young child. He had been sinned against badly and his heart was broken by the silence and the fear that controlled his life. Having been threatened by his abuser, he was afraid to talk. That fear and anger was an everyday experience for him.

When Joshua shared his story, I asked him what his thoughts were of his stepfather. He said, "I hate him and wish I could kill him." I knew the stepfather had to be dealt with and Joshua needed to be free. Those two things in my mind were separate issues from Joshua's healing. Revenge and even justice would not win Joshua's heart to freedom. My goal was for Joshua to deal simply with the justice side and to work intensely on the freedom side.

I asked Joshua if he had ever thought about forgiving him. He said he was told in church that forgiving meant forgetting and he didn't think that was possible, nor was it something he was willing to do. I tried to clarify the teaching by explaining that forgetting is about not holding it any longer. I explained that a forgiving heart could still be outraged at the bad behavior of the abuser, while deciding to no longer hold it as his own possession. I spent much time with Joshua explaining that he had not lost himself in the abuse, but he had lost himself in the anger and the bitterness of not forgiving. This notion certainly was counterintuitive and was difficult to explain to him.

Eventually, Joshua was able to grab ahold of the truth of forgiveness and is in the process of forgiving his abuser. This road is long and has yielded a certain level of freedom for Joshua.

The only road of freedom from bitterness is the road of forgiveness. The road of justice or revenge will lead to a hollow numbness, not freedom. "Closure," as people call it, is not found in revenge. The abused need to know they are not the first to be provoked, abused or even sinned against. We live in a fallen world, and this happens, and only forgiveness will result in freedom.

The belief by victims is always the same: "If I forgive, I will lose the power over the abuser and the abuse." Ironically, just the opposite is true. When forgiveness is not given, the abuser still has power over the victim. When dealing with something so intense as a predator and the prey, we may tend to justify the prey's bitterness for their abuser and even enable their continued pain. We want to commiserate with their pain. I would suggest that a friend can both commiserate and give solutions. In fact, anything else is not truly a loving response. We must show compassion and understanding for the abuse and yet the maturity to call the abused to freedom through forgiveness.

When anger sours, it becomes the building block for all the future negative emotions. The negative emotions are built in the soul as follows: First, provocation; Second, ownership of that provocation; and Third, the souring of anger, resulting in bitterness. These three produce every form of negative emotion as we see in Ephesians 4:31. The last four forms of anger are the result of bitterness.

4. <u>Uncontrolled anger</u>: (Greek: Thumos, Boiling over)

> *"Let all bitterness and wrath (**thumos**, to boil over) and anger and clamor and slander be put away from you, along with all malice."* (Ephesians 4:31)

The forms of anger in Ephesians 4:31 are inevitable when provocation is owned and held. When the held anger sours into bitterness, it will result in the following manifestations:

The word "*thumos*" manifests itself in seemingly disconnected boiling over. For example, a person is driving along and is cut off, and has a visceral reaction. The moment does seem to warrant the reaction. Oftentimes the feeling of anger erupts when a small event triggers an overreaction, and we don't know where that degree of emotion came from. We focus our anger on the event or person, when in truth it is the personalized residual anger from an unresolved provocation. We may rage verbally or may erupt internally toward the event, but the focus is misplaced. There is something else driving the anger.

What happens in the life of a wounded, unresolved person is a vulnerability to being set off by even the smallest of triggers. They are in a sense a "walking time bomb." These people struggle in their careers and personal relationships because they seem irrational and hostile.

5. <u>Rage and Tantrums</u> (Greek: Krauge, to cry out)

> *"Let all bitterness and wrath and anger and clamor (**krauge**, rage) and slander be put away from you, along with all malice."* (Ephesians 4:31)

When we feel helpless as victims, we begin to cry out for support. In the extreme it becomes "histrionic" (excessive emotional outburst designed to gain attention.) This outcry may be outrageous or refined by social finesse and skillful manipulation. These are typically not malicious people, just wounded and unresolved because there has not been a healthy forgiveness of the heart.

The fear driving this is that they will either be ignored or abused. This is a huge cry for help, and this is where skillful friends or a wise therapist are needed to help them walk the path of forgiveness. I will explain how this works below when we get to Ephesians 4:32.

6. <u>Abusive Speech</u> (Greek: Blasphemia, to speak against)

> *"Let all bitterness and wrath and anger and clamor and slander (**Blasphemia**, to speak against), be put away from you, along with all malice."* (Ephesians 4:31)

When anger becomes so extreme that it is uncontrollable, we seek an outlet for our anger by attacking others. It seems reasonable in the convoluted thinking of a bitter mind that others are posing a threat to our happiness. This person, possibly unknowingly, is lashing out, not in maliciousness but in self-protection.

Friendships with these people are difficult. Typically, the friendships are sabotaged by abusive speech early in the relationship, creating an unhealthy fear in their friends. People with this manifestation often find themselves alone and angry. If relationships last, they are typically unhealthy and fear-based.

Trevor and Jill came to me to talk through their marriage struggles. Trevor explained that Jill could not be satisfied no matter what he did. He explained that she would berate him and yell at him about the smallest things. He constantly felt rejection. He wanted out of the marriage, but felt like God would not honor that decision.

Jill, in not so many words, agreed with Trevor's assessment. She said she was often blowing up at the kids and Trevor for the smallest things. She felt bad about herself and her feelings about herself only made things worse. She struggled to find a way to be more kind, but she couldn't do it. I suspected Jill had unresolved offenses in her past that were reaching into her present relationships. I recommended her to a counselor who could skillfully deal with Jill's attacks on others.

Without getting into too much detail, Jill's counselor was able to help her identify her past offenses, and with his help, she was able to forgive and begin to heal. They are experiencing a whole new level of safety in their relationship.

7. <u>Malicious Motive</u> (Greek: Kakia, bad as in malicious)

> *"Let all bitterness and wrath and anger and clamor and slander, be put away from you, along with all malice (**Kakia**, bad as in malicious.)* (Ephesians 4:31)

As anger reaches its ultimate control of the soul, the life becomes dominated by a victim mentality and this often leads to a need to tear down others to live with one's own failure. Oftentimes the bitter person is not even aware of the extremes of the emotional control over the soul. The soul has been damaged to the point of an unhealthy condition here called "*kakia*." It all started with a provocation that was not dealt with and now has produced a *damaged soul.*

Malice feels justified like the other emotions found in this chapter. The alienation from others, the lack of meaningful relationships, the shallowness of life are a tough way for the malicious person to live. The self-isolation becomes the only comfortable place for this person to dwell. People, in their wounded mind, are just too much trouble.

You have probably seen people who live with the above forms of anger, or you may even have these in your life. Would you know what to say to them? Would you be able to navigate your way out of your own anger? Ephesians 4 is practical in teaching about the resolution to anger and its forms. Here is the road to freedom:

The Road from Anger to Freedom:

> *"31 Let all bitterness and wrath and anger and clamor and slander be put away from you, along with all malice. 32 Be kind to one another, compassionate, forgiving each other, just as God in Christ also has forgiven you."* (Ephesians 4:31-32)

In Ephesians 4:31, the verb is "*let it be put away*." This is passive voice in the original Greek text, which means the subject receives the action. The implication of this grammatical form is that the bitter person cannot just by his/her will decide to remove the negative emotions; there must be some other action that will remove these from him/her. There are three actions that can be taken to have bitterness and all these negative emotions removed. They are found in verse 32.

By looking into the next verse, you see God's formula for removing negative emotions. The verb in Ephesians 4:32 is "be," and is a command with a view of self-help; middle voice in the Greek means to do this on your own behalf. Ephesians 4:31-32 presents two concepts: first, you are stuck in negative emotions, and second, the only way out is the road of forgiveness. If we were to write Ephesians 4:31-32 in conceptual form, it may read like this:

> **"When you show acts of kindness, develop understanding of others and forgive them, the bitterness and all of its negative emotions will be removed from your heart."**

There are three aspects of this road of forgiveness:

1. **Acts of Kindness**
2. **Commiseration (understanding the pain of others)**
3. **Forgiveness**

It's not clear to me in these verses whether these three aspects of the road to forgiveness are done sequentially or concurrently. It is my experience, however, that they will work together as a combined discipline. Let's take each one in order as they are given:

1. Acts of Kindness:
The most difficult thing to accept for someone who has been provoked or abused is to be kind to his/her offender. The flesh screams out to say, "I will lose my control through these acts of kindness." The strategy to attack the abuser is so intuitive it seems the only logical response.

Acts of kindness to a repentant person: To an offender/abuser who is repentant, acts of kindness are easier to give. In the case of a truly repentant offender, the offended person should find ways to show kindness directly to the one toward whom they have been holding resentment. This will dismantle the bitterness that produces a dehumanizing of this individual. The bitter heart needs to see that this is a real person who is not a "force" or a "power" in their life. Personal acts of kindness to this person are the key to overcoming those destructive feelings of hostility and bitterness.

Acts of kindness to an unrepentant person: To an unrepentant abuser it may not be safe for you to approach that person, in which case, you should approach acts of kindness in a different way. In one of my support groups, I asked the group to brainstorm healthy and safe ways in which they could show kindness to someone who had offended or even abused them and has not shown repentance for their bad behavior. This exercise proved to be fruitful. I would recommend that you spend time with a trusted friend and share your feelings about your offender and ask your friend to brainstorm ways that you could show healthy acts of kindness. When we are hurt, we often need an objective person to help us think through these options.

A word of warning: You should be very careful how you handle someone who has abused you. If you were the "prey" and they were the "predator," it would be irresponsible to have exposure to them. You should seek wise counsel, probably from a professional counselor, on how to show acts of kindness to an extreme abuser.

The benefits of showing acts of kindness:

1. **When we act in kindness, we affirm the humanity of our offender**. This is key for our healing. Man has been created for connection with others, and our ability to love the unlovely will greatly impact our emotional health.

2. **When we act in kindness, we take back our power**. The offense and the offender have power, often unknowingly, over the offended. This may last for a lifetime. A great way for us to take back this power is to show acts of kindness.

3. **When we act in kindness, we become free to live**. The wounded heart muddles around in misery through constantly dwelling on the past offense. When we show acts of kindness, it reinterprets the past as an event not an identity, and this will set us free.

2. Commiseration:

This can seem impossible to the wounded heart. The wounded may say, "What do I care about my attacker's past and pain? I was the one hurt by his behavior." The problem is that this could continue a cycle, especially in a family, each generation blaming the past generation and never resolving the root of the pain that drives the offenses.

I saw this pattern of abuse in the life of Bill and his son Richard. Richard was devastated by the harsh treatment by his dad when he was young. As he grew into his teen years, he had spent some time with his grandmother, only to find that she was very manipulative and harsh. Richard, for the first time, began to realize that the harshness of his father came from a wounded heart from an unkind mother. Coupled with this, Richard found his grandfather had abandoned Bill emotionally.

When Richard made the decision to forgive his dad, it was much easier knowing his father's past. He began to commiserate with the woundedness of his father, and he and his father were able to have a loving relationship through reconciliation.

The benefits of commiserating with our offender:

1. **When we commiserate, we acknowledge that our offender is flawed.** The heart of God is one of understanding and acceptance. He is gracious and kind to us in spite of our flaws. We need God's heart to be able to see the bitterness and anger removed from our lives. It is important to understand why someone does the things they do to be free from our own emotional woundedness.

2. **When we commiserate, we allow mitigating circumstances to soften our hearts.** The wounded heart is hardened by anger and resentment. It is self-protective and reasonable to have this happen. However, the heart that is strong and healthy is softened. One of the best ways to get to a softened heart is through understanding why someone does what he/she does.

3. **When we commiserate, we acknowledge our own flaws.** When we understand the way in which our offender has been wounded, we will be reminded of our own flaws and give grace to him. This is crucial on the road of forgiveness and healing.

3. Forgiveness:
Forgiveness is so often misunderstood. As we have said, the wounded will think that forgiveness means perceiving the bad behavior as acceptable. This is not true at all. We need to forgive and release our offender for our own healing, while maintaining a high standard of behavior for others and ourselves. You can at the same time forgive and see the abuse given to you as egregious. We should be able to see the bad behavior for what it is and still be able

to forgive. I have seen the power in my life and the lives of others who have chosen the road of forgiveness over revenge or resentment. Forgivers are always happier than those who don't forgive.

Linda's need to forgive:
Linda was a woman so deeply wounded by her mother, by the time she wanted to forgive it seemed that her very identity wrapped around her anger toward her mother. One of the most difficult problems was the insidious nature of the offenses from her mother. Her offense was subtle rejection and manipulation. If she would have beat Linda, it would have been easier to identify the offense and then forgive. It seemed to Linda there was nothing needing forgiveness. Certainly, from her mother's standpoint there was no need to repent, because in her mind there was no transgression. Both Linda and her mother were stuck in lies that kept them both in bondage.

To the matter of "forgiving and forgetting," we must forgive and not dwell, however, we can remember. The dwelling is the problem. We wear our resentment like a garment and it is like trying to swim while wearing a large fur coat. Life is negotiated and lived best without extra weight from the past. When we forgive, we take the coat off and lay it down. We walk away free, and yet certainly there are times of remembering. When we remember we need to immediately speak truth to ourselves and say, "This offense is no longer mine, I have laid it aside." If we repeat this every time we remember the offense, we will begin to extract our lives from the weight of resentment. Freedom will come in time.

What about God forgetting our sin? It is true that God forgets our sin, however, He is omniscient. He knows everything. He can't unknow your sin. So, what does it mean for God to forget our sin when we repent? God forgets in the sense of not holding it against us as a judge to a defendant. The concept of forgetting is that God is "not counting" our sins against us. Note how it is used here:

> *"that is, in Christ God was reconciling the world to himself, not counting their trespasses against them, and entrusting to us the message of reconciliation."* (2 Corinthians 5:19)

I need to clarify here that forgiveness does not mean reconnecting to your offender. Reconnecting or reconciliation by its very nature means change. There has to be a change both in the offended and the offender to be reconciled. However, forgiveness can be given to anyone irrespective of his/her attitude. To the degree you are willing and able to forgive the unrepentant and unchanged, will you experience freedom emotionally.

The benefits of giving forgiveness:

1. **When we forgive, we are free to live in the present.** When we lay aside the weight of the past, our hearts are more alive. Hanging onto the past is a futile attempt to correct something that should be seen as an event in our past not our identity in the present.

2. **When we forgive, we free the heart to heal.** Healing in the heart will never take place while the offense is still the focus. Ephesians 4:21-32 make it clear that the negative emotions in verse 31 will be removed by forgiveness. This is God's way for our emotional healing.

3. **When we forgive, we function as sons of God.** In Matthew 5:44-45, it says, "*But I say to you, love your enemies and*

pray for those who persecute you, so that you may be sons of your Father who is in heaven; for He causes His sun to rise on the evil and the good, and sends rain on the righteous and the unrighteous." The reality is we have been called to be like God in our treatment of others, even those who have persecuted us. Forgiveness is the powerful way to act in proper relation to our Father.

Chapter 5 Life Skills:

Make a list of your moments of anger. Log them and list the fears that may have produced the anger. List the triggers for your fears. Write down what time of day and what was going on at the time. Note any obvious patterns triggering anger.

Let your mind go back to the most significant negative feelings against anyone in your past: This is not something that needs to be done repeatedly. Once you identify the past offenses and resentment, you may feel you need to go through the process of forgiving as described in this chapter. List the offenses and the names of your offenders. Can you go to this person to resolve the issues? Is this someone who is still a threat to you? Was the offense real? If it is safe and wise to go to them, then go and release them of the offense.

Meet with a trusted and wise friend to help you identify ways you could show acts of kindness to that person against whom you hold an offense: Write down a strategy to show kindness to your offender.

Chapter 6 – Guilt and Shame

Extricating Yourself From the Past

"The sorrow that is according to the will of God produces a repentance without regret, leading to deliverance..."
(2 Corinthians 7:10)

I told my wife once, "I wish I could go back and undue some of my sinful mistakes." She asked, "How far do you want to go back?" I said, "To age fourteen years old." She laughed and said, "Why don't you live what you preach and accept God's forgiveness and leave your shame and guilt in the past and stay here with me?" **Rebuke Accepted**.

In the previous chapter, we discussed the need to forgive those who have offended us and to let go of bitterness. In this chapter, we are going to deal with the difficult task of looking at our own failures and offenses in our pasts. These have a devastating impact on our emotions.

Linda's Story:
When I met Linda, she had struggled with bulimia for several years. She had a difficult time in college, where we met, because the dorm life was so open and there wasn't the privacy she was used to. She turned most days to fasting to minimize her need to purge. This felt good to her but made her quite weak. She later would admit that the control over her weight was a sense of power for her.

At first, Linda felt this was simply a strategy to keep weight off. As time went on, she began to see this as an emotional problem and most devastating was that she began to see it as a spiritual/moral issue. That journey from a weight loss strategy to moral failure is what led Linda to loathe herself and even resent those who saw her failure.

My observation of her struggle was painful because I tried to reach her heart and encourage her to see this as an emotional issue and not a spiritual one. Unfortunately, an ill-advised and moralistic pastor identified eating disorders as the sin of gluttony and told her she was living in sin. I believe this behavior has spiritual implications. However, to deal with this on a moral level would not go into the pain that drove Linda to fear, anger, resentment, and the need to control her life. She needed to go back and discover the pain and resolve it. She needed to extract herself from her past.

(What I'm about to share is both painful and difficult for me. I hesitate to share such personal struggles, but my desire to help others overrides my desire to protect Linda and even my own sense of shame.)

About three years into our marriage, I began to see a strange occurrence. Under the sink, at the back of the shelf in the cupboard, I saw a Tupperware container and pulled it to the front. I noticed it was full of vomit. I was disgusted at the sight. It looked like it was days of vomit. My first thought was to ignore this and act like I didn't see it. This is what I did for an extended period of time. My fear of hurting or shaming her kept me silent for several years as I saw this same thing over many times. I saw the pattern that when there was an increased sense of shame in Linda's talk and behavior, I would see an increase in the storing of her vomit.

As I write this, I'm struggling, and I understand that you may be as well. But what you should know is that shame, when it runs its course, is so destructive that one's self-esteem goes to a level that only the grotesque will identify the life of the shamed. Linda saw purging as releasing her anger and bitterness in an act that in a convoluted way was control. (This sense of control over her weight felt like life to her.) However, when the shame was overwhelming, she would store the vomit to remind herself she was worthless. She saw herself as nothing but useless.

How utterly tragic it was to watch someone I loved living a life of such low self-esteem. Unfortunately, because of my own struggle with insecurity and fears, I couldn't help her in healthy ways. My approach ranged from enablement to abandonment. Both Linda and I lived our lives and our marriage in shame and fear.

A word of warning: Because I'm not a therapist and not trained in eating disorders, I would recommend you filter my conclusions. This is my story and I share it because, at least in my observation, the pattern was obvious and the impact of shame was devastating to Linda and those who loved her. Eating disorders are a serious psychological problem and should be dealt with by professional counselors who specialize in this problem.

Dealing with the past:
Our pasts are filled with wonderful memories and events that are enjoyable to revisit. However, in each of our pasts, there are offenses we have committed and offenses against us. These shape us emotionally and need to be addressed in healthy ways. There are two primary areas of being stuck in the past:

1. **Forgiving your offenders.** As we have already discussed, forgiveness does not mean forgetting. Forgiveness does not mean reconciliation. This may not be possible in the case of a predator or abuser. Reconciliation is an option, not a cure. Forgiveness does not mean the loss of seeing the behavior as outrageous.

2. **Make restitution for your offenses.** To live in the moment, we must resolve our past failures. We will not experience the power of the moment. Life is lived in this moment, not in the past. (More on living in the moment in Chapter 13.)

The distinction of terms related to guilt:
Guilt, shame, sorrow, and related emotions are all about man in pursuit of safety. Adam and Eve's pursuit of safety after their sin resulted in hiding, manipulating, and blaming, and all this was driven by fear. As mentioned in Chapter 4, Adam and Eve had experienced a fundamental change in their nature. For the first time they were experiencing negative emotions. Had God's warning, that through eating of the forbidden tree they would die, come true? Were they experiencing the joys of being like God or were they experiencing the devastating impact of spiritual death? We know the truth: they died spiritually as God warned. Adam and Eve experienced misery for the first time in their lives.

This created fear, guilt, shame, and many other negative emotions. Their attempt to cover up is a forerunner of what we do. We spend much of our lives trying to hide our failures in shame. This is not necessary when we could be experiencing meaningful freedom from our pasts. For the purpose of clarity, I'm listing some important words and some working definitions for each:

<u>Guilt</u>: Guilt says, "I did something wrong."
Guilt is the emotion that occurs when a person realizes or believes accurately or not that he or she has violated a moral or ethical standard, and bears responsibility for that violation. There may be a false guilt that comes with unfounded sensibilities and standards. Guilt is a healthy emotion when based on truth, which will lead

to repentance. However, guilt that is based on self-deception will frustrate and lead to increased failure.

We must understand the source of guilt. Is the source a false sensibility from childhood or false teaching from our church or education? When we feel guilt apart from truth, it most often will lead to misery.

Shame: Shame says, "I am wrong."
Shame is a sense of social rejection or stigma over one's behavior, real or perceived. Shame always involves others, whether in truth or in the mind of the one with shame. Note: Guilt can be private, but shame "always" involves others. Man was never designed to live with acute or toxic shame. Shame is a destructive emotion when unchecked.

For our purposes here, we will break shame into two categories:

1. Mild Shame: There is a sense in which mild shame is helpful. Mild shame may keep people from socially unacceptable behavior. For example, it is unacceptable to speak loudly on your cell phone in a public place. People with mild shame understand this and change their behavior. Other examples: dressing modestly in public, public swearing, publicly arguing with your spouse, or talking during a movie, and things like these. I'm not sure that shame as I see it is the correct term here, but people will use it this way. For example, "Have you no shame?" can be heard when a parent wants to call their child to socially acceptable behavior.

2. Toxic Shame: Shame that is toxic is my greatest concern. Toxic shame is when our guilt turns social and then permeates our lives and shapes our identities. We perceive that people know our flaws and we feel condemned or rejected. When shame becomes toxic it has begun to permeate our hearts and our souls to the extent that our self-worth is denigrated. We feel we are hopeless in getting our reputations back. For example, one with toxic shame may think or say, "The genie is out of the bottle and everyone now knows how worthless I am." When you feel guilt, it is private; when you feel this intense shame, it is out of your control and you feel hopeless. The truth of the matter is you can overcome toxic shame. As we address the matter of shame here, we will only deal with this concept of toxic shame.

Shame feels like death; I mean social death. It is the feeling that you are totally misunderstood, rejected and alone. You want people to see you as better, not perfect, but better, and now there is no way to fix it. Your guilt drives you continually to your failures and this may send you into a place of feeling your shame is justified and people's view of you is legitimate. Of course, most of this goes on in your mind and not in reality. You feel the only solution is to run from the shame, make a change and "get out of here." Anywhere would be fine. So, you divorce, move to new locations, avoid friends, and withdraw from society. In some cases, people will turn to material things and begin to hoard those things. "These things don't have an opinion of me so I'm safe with them," shame says.

Catastrophizing: Catastrophizing says, "I'm alone and no one is as bad as me"

Shame is the fuel of catastrophizing. (For more on catastrophizing, see Chapter 1). When you feel hopeless from shame, you will in a soft, self-serving way, begin to feel self-pity, and when this self-pity begins to sour, the result is toxic self-loathing. The human heart struggles with this and so we begin a journey of *hiding and hurling*. We *hide* our faults and *hurl* accusations and blame toward anyone who may expose those faults. This is shame's only recourse.

In a convoluted way, defensiveness makes sense to shame because it keeps people away from our flaws. If we can keep people at a distance, we can successfully protect against further shame, so we self-protect. Often, this self-protection is unhealthy and leads to more problems.

The story of an adulterous woman:
A woman who had entered into an affair with a married man was exposed in a church I pastored years ago. The messy and unbiblical method of her exposure led to her acute shame. She felt she had no recourse based on her shame but to lash out against the church. In many ways, I don't blame her.

She, to this day, won't fellowship with other believers because of shame and bitterness. When asked about her situation, she hurls blame at the church and the people who exposed her. I tried unsuccessfully to put the lid on this exposure, but it permeated our church body. The result was no restitution, no change for the future, and division. Shame is tough because it may be founded in sinful or bad behavior.

How do we deal with guilt and shame then? We discussed in Chapter 4 the psychology and spiritual failure of Adam and Eve's guilt and shame, but for this chapter let me remind you of God's approach to the first instance of shame in human experience:

Man sinned; there is no doubt about it. Man felt guilt that is appropriate, given the fact that man did what he was told not to do. However, for Adam and Eve there was more than guilt; there was fear that drove their sense of shame. God had a plan for their shame, and He has a plan for yours as well. Notice the skill of God in dealing with His creation. (I know that sounds strange to refer to "God's skill," but it leads us to understand how we might be skillful in dealing with sinners.)

When man sinned, he felt shame, hid himself with fig leaves, and blamed his wife. God's solution to Adam's shame was to:

1. **Pursue Him**, "*Adam, where are you?*" (Genesis 3:9)

2. **Lovingly expose his failure**, "*Have you eaten from the tree of which I commanded you not to eat?*" (Genesis 3:11)

3. **Provide for the redemption of man through a blood sacrifice**, "*The LORD God made garments of skin for Adam and his wife, and clothed them*" (Gen. 3:21). The death of this animal, we learn in scripture later, is the type of the ultimate sacrifice for sins, the Lord Jesus Himself.

For shame to be addressed, we need to be safe and honest. We must have confidence in the individuals walking the journey with us into wholeness. This is a messy business, and we need mature people with us in the process.

There are a few words associated with the term *guilt* that need a brief explanation:

<u>Remorse:</u> This is regret over your behavior. If remorse is unresolved, it will often turn to self-pity and self-hatred.

<u>Sorrow:</u> This is feeling badly about your behavior. This is usually brought on by being exposed or caught. It can be nothing more than shame.

<u>Contrition:</u> This is an intensified combination of guilt and sorrow and acknowledgement of responsibility for your own actions.

The limitations of penance:

It is intuitive to man to pay a penalty for his bad behavior. Religion has come up with a form of penalty called "penance." Penance is an imposed punishment to deal with ones' sins and offenses. On an emotional level this will help to make a guilty person feel better; however, it is not a biblical concept or a permanent solution to guilt. There must be true repentance for this to happen.

Two biblical examples will help us to understand the need for true repentance, Judas and the Corinthian Christians:

The Judas Syndrome:

> *3 Then when Judas, who had betrayed Him, saw that He had been condemned, he repented and returned the thirty pieces of silver to the chief priests and elders, 4 saying, "I have sinned by betraying innocent blood." But they said, "What is that to us? See to that yourself!" 5 And he threw the pieces of silver into the temple sanctuary and departed; and he went away and hanged himself.* (Matthew 27:3-5, KJV)

Judas had a fundamental failure to understand repentance and the deliverance found there. His shame overwhelmed him and led to his failure and ultimate death. Here we will trace his struggle to overcome his shame:

Step 1: Sorrow and shame. When Judas in Matthew 27:3 realized his behavior had gone farther than he anticipated and saw that Jesus was condemned, the shame was overwhelming and he had intense sorrow. When we as humans see someone sorry for what they have done, we tend to release them, forgive them, and even restore them. If, however, we don't detect an appropriate amount of sorrow or contrition, we will see them with contempt. In Judas' case, after the sorrow came the shame.

The word translated "*repentance*" in the King James Version of the Bible is better translated "*felt remorse,*" as in the New American Standard Bible. The original Greek gives some insight here. The word is "*metamelomai,*" meaning a change of emotion or passion. The word for repentance, "*metanoeo,*" not used here, means to have a change of mind. The emotions of Judas were real, even though he had no change of mind. This was why he had no change of direction or behavior. He panicked in his regret and couldn't find restored life.

All the passion in the world will not create lasting change; there has to be a change in what one believes.

Step 2: Confession. One of the common hoops we put people through before we forgive them is that we require them to confess their responsibility. Judas could not have gone farther in his confession to the priests and elders. He clearly takes responsibility for his actions against Jesus when he says, "*I have sinned by betraying* *innocent blood*." You would think this would free Judas from his guilt and shame. However, Judas had started down the wrong path, not by repenting of his sin, but by simply feeling sorry for his failure.

Seldom will an individual who starts with sorrow end up free from shame. Again, there must be a change of mind in what you believe.

Step 3: Restitution: Judas took another seemingly healing step. He gave back the pieces of silver. Well, if you look carefully, the priests and elders weren't having it, so he threw the pieces of silver into the temple. Judas was seeking to absolve himself through an ill-conceived plan of restitution. The problem was, he truly had not had a change of heart. He felt badly about his betrayal and the consequences of his behavior. He needed to receive forgiveness from God, but had no idea how to obtain it.

Step 4: Failure and death: Judas was convinced there was no way for God, or anyone, for that matter, to buy back his situation, and therefore he would simply end the pain: "*he went away and hanged himself*." His suicide attempt was so clumsy that the hanging resulted in a fall that caused a gruesome death (read Acts 1:17-19).

Judas never experienced the redemption he would have liked. The problem was in his view of himself and his sin. He was sorry he was caught (*metamelomai*) but there was no change of mind about his sin or God's forgiveness for him (*metanoeo*).

A journey started on the wrong path will either result in a correction of course or failure. First steps are important and lead to redemption or continued shame. Judas started with shame and ended up with shame, as proven by his suicide. We need to understand our sin and its impact on our lives. We also need to understand the character of God and His heart for redemption. Once we understand these two things, we can move toward God and find His grace.

Notice the contrast in my next example, the Corinthians. Judas was on a course of death; in contrast, Paul gives to the Corinthians a proper understanding of how they had redirected their course and found "deliverance."

True sorrow that leads to change:

> "*8 For though I caused you sorrow by my letter, I do not regret it; though I did regret for I see that that letter caused you sorrow, though only for a while 9 I now rejoice, not that you were made sorrowful, but that you were made sorrowful to the point of repentance; for you were made sorrowful according to the will of God, so that you might not suffer loss in anything through us. 10 For the sorrow that is according to the will of God produces repentance without regret, leading to salvation, but the sorrow of the world produces death.*" (2 Corinthians 7:8-10)

Okay, dig in with me here. Paul wrote a tough and important letter to the Corinthians, which we know as 1 Corinthians. In the letter, he rebuked them and even resorted to some name-calling. Paul in 2 Corinthians 7:8 says he was conflicted emotionally about this letter, but of course realized the letter was crucial for their journey toward wholeness and deliverance from guilt. Paul began to rejoice, not for the emotional distress, but that their emotional distress was turned to repentance (*metanoeo*), a true change of mind.

Paul gives the process of the journey toward deliverance or salvation in 2 Corinthians 7:10. "*For the sorrow that is according to the will of God produces repentance without regret, leading to salvation, but the sorrow of the world produces death.*"

Paul gives a distinction here between godly sorrow and worldly sorrow. Godly sorrow leads to deliverance through repentance, but worldly sorrow leads to death, because there are only bad feelings without turning to God in repentance. Meaningful change comes only when the sorrow drives us to repent, that is, a change in what we believe. The failure to repent leads to death. **Remember: All of the sorrow or shame in our lives will not produce freedom.**

The practical lesson in all this, for our emotional health and balance, is to understand that only through a true change in what we believe can we be free from our past and our guilt, which is a driving force behind a lot of emotional problems for many.

You or someone you know may be struggling with depression that is rooted in a failure to find the grace of God in forgiveness. Judas was a man whose fear and hopelessness resulted in his suicide. If he could have only come to understand the grace of God, he would have been free like the Corinthians. You too should come to see the power of repentance and redemption in God's grace.

The previously taught TNTs (Trigger Negative Thoughts) are often rooted in our inability to resolve our pasts. We may have guilt or even shame over things that took place years ago. It is always safe to resolve the past. The following are the five Rs that will result in freedom from your guilt and shame.

The Five Rs of overcoming guilt and shame:
1 Repent, 2 Return, 3 Restore, 4 Release and 5 Resolve.

1. Repent: <u>Change your mind about your sin and God's character</u>
God calls us to repent. This repentance involves a change of mind about who we are and who God is. We must understand the devastating impact of our sin and turn from it.

> *"14...each one is tempted when he is carried away and enticed by his own lust. 15 Then when lust has conceived, it gives birth to sin; and when sin is accomplished, it brings forth death. 16 Do not be deceived, my beloved brethren."* (James 1:14-16)

I have for years taught the four lies of sin. They are:

1. I can handle this sin.
2. This sin won't affect me.
3. I won't be controlled by this sin.
4. This sin will make me alive.

We must rethink the impact of sin in our lives and to our emotions. Sin is deadly, as it says in James 1:15. Just as you are subject to the law of gravity, you are subject to this spiritual law: **sin leads to death in the soul**. Your emotions, your will, your vitality are deadened by sin.

You should not be surprised by the depression, anxiety, fears, and other negative emotions when your soul has been deadened by sin. God wants you to have joy and freedom, and you will only experience this through true repentance. God doesn't want you to repent as a matter of simply acquiescing to a moral code; He wants you free from death so you can have abiding joy.

The danger would be to think of ourselves as worthless because of sin. That's why the second part of the repentance is crucial to our emotional health. We need to change our view about God. God is holy and therefore we should be holy. This is a call, not just to holiness for holiness' sake, but so we can have intimacy with a holy God.

To simply understand His holiness as a motivator to our own holiness would be devastating. The gospel is the truth about God's provision of holiness through His grace. God does call us to holiness, but also gives us the way to be holy. The powerful hope of believers in Christ is that even though we are sinful, we have forgiveness by God's grace.

2. Return: Journey back to our offense

The road to deliverance from guilt and shame always goes through a journey to our pasts. This journey needs to be done with wisdom. Our pasts can be treacherous places for many of us. We need to be wise and approach this carefully. For our purposes here, I will divide the journey back into two kinds of offenses: unknown and known offenses.

The unknown offense: Being in leadership, I have offended many I am not even aware of. I have had people come to me and express apologies for harboring an offense against me. I'm sure this made them feel better, and I have always tried to be gracious in these instances. However, almost without exception, I felt horrible after their apology. Sometimes we feel guilty about harboring resentment toward someone who has no idea we are negative toward them. It would be selfish and self-indulging to go to an unsuspecting individual and open up an unknown resentment so we are released, not realizing that now they are burdened.

A better approach would be to go to God and repent, and then to begin to show kindness to the individual with whom we had a private resentment. There is so much power in this and it will resolve the guilt you feel.

My need to check my heart and strategy

Today as I have been writing this chapter, my mind went to yesterday and a discussion I had about what I perceived as a predatory takeover of a struggling church by a mega church. I spent an hour or so railing against the lead pastor of the mega church to my wife and judged his character and motives. The fact of the matter is I have no idea what his motives are. I closed my computer for a moment and called my wife to apologize to her for the attack on this brother. I told her I would call him and apologize, and then realized he didn't need to be contacted; I needed only to go to those impacted, my wife and the Lord, which I did. I began to show intentional acts of kindness to this brother.

The known offense: When I was in my twenties, for a brief time in a church, I took an offense against one of the pastors on staff. I was associated with his detractors and became one myself. I began to gossip about this pastor's shortcomings, harming his reputation. My feelings were reported to him.

I paid a high price for my gossip and lack of love for that pastor. Instead of learning from it, I felt superior as a victim and a martyr for the cause of Christ. A few years passed, but I couldn't get past it. I finally realized what was seen as bad behavior was actually sin. I went to him, and even though I was clumsy in my approach, I apologized and received his forgiveness. I felt a freedom that had been lost in those years.

3. Restore: <u>Make amends or repayment when possible</u>
Restoration is a crucial part of the journey out of emotional bondage due to guilt. I will just give two examples here.

My need to make restitution:
I will return here to the story of my gossip and my apology. I knew damage was done by my attack on this fellow pastor to the church where he still served. I decided I must make restitution. I wrote a letter to him and to the board, officially apologizing for the sin. I didn't just want to get it off my plate, so to speak; I wanted him to have restoration if possible.

The letter was sent, and I do think was used to restore the pastor's good name to a certain extent. The letter was used in a way that may have enabled further bad behavior on the part of the pastor; however, for this I had no obligation. I needed to be free and to restore the best I could that which had been harmed.

My father's need to make restitution:
My father, back in the 1940s, was a student at Multnomah School of the Bible, now Multnomah University. He was studying for the ministry and was truly hurting for money. His dad had given him a car, but it was beginning to wear out, and he desperately needed a reliable car. The problem was his transmission was going out and often the car would not go into gear. The motor and body of the car were in great shape.

He came up with a plan to deceive a used car dealer into trading in his car for a good used car. (For those who knew my dad, this story seems impossible because he was such a man of integrity.) *My dad took his car up to the top of the hill above the used car dealer lot and let it roll into the lot without having to grind the gears or worry about the transmission. The used car dealer was impressed with the condition of my dad's car and gave him high value on a trade-in. My dad drove off in an excellent car he received in exchange for his car.*

Years passed, and my dad by his own testimony shared this story at a pastor's conference and said he couldn't get past it. My dad said, "Every time I would get close to the Lord, the memory of cheating this unsuspecting used car dealer stood in my way of closeness to God." He got tired of the feeling of guilt and the regret and so he figured the cost of repair and the interest over the years and went to restore what he had stolen from the used car dealer.

When he arrived at the location of the used car lot, he was shocked to find the dealer had long since gone out of business. He could have walked away and said, "Oh well, I tried." He was concerned about the negative emotions he was carrying and really wanted to be free; he had come this far, and he was going to find a way to make restitution. He did some research and found nothing of this man or his business, so he made, as he said, "One of the most important decisions in my closeness with God."

The used car dealer knew my dad was a student at Multnomah when he traded the car in, so my dad figured the best way he could make restitution was to go to the school. He asked for a meeting with Dr. Aldrich, who at the time was president, and told him the story and apologized for the damage to the school's reputation. The money was given to the school for training other men for ministry. That was a day of redemption for my dad's emotions; he had been set free from that bondage.

This will take great courage and should be well thought through so you are truly free. This is a crucial step in the journey to emotional freedom. Now to step four:

4. Release: Receiving forgiveness from God and others

I don't know how many times I have heard people say, "You must forgive yourself," or "I won't be happy until I forgive myself." The problem with this is that it is not a biblical concept. Self-forgiveness is not the issue; receiving forgiveness is. We need to learn to receive forgiveness from God for our freedom.

1 John 1:9, *"if we confess our sins, He is faithful and righteous to forgive us our sins and to cleanse us from all unrighteousness."* The confession is simply saying what God says about our sin. We come in agreement with God. It is so refreshing to be forgiven by God, a new start, a fresh perspective, and best of all we have freedom.

Being forgiven by God is one thing, but the real problem is that others may not forgive us. You must do all you can to be forgiven, but at the end, it is up to the person. Their maturity determines if they will forgive you or not. Should you be held hostage to their immaturity, or can you move on?

Karrie's story:

Many years ago, my oldest daughter, Karrie, found herself in a difficult marriage and was struggling with her life and feelings of emptiness. She, by her own admission, made many mistakes along the way and ended up divorced from her husband. She remarried and had long since apologized to the people she had hurt in the process, including her former husband.

However, there were some long-term friends from whom she felt a level of tension and wanted to draw close. She went to one of her important friends and explained how sorry she was for her part of the wrong in her divorce and wanted to be forgiven by this friend. Her friend explained that she didn't want to be close friends and said she didn't trust her anymore. Karrie explained that she understood her inability to forgive her, but she needed to spend time with people who agreed with God in His forgiveness, she needed to be with supportive friends who would encourage growth. That relationship was put on hold for the day that her friend would truly forgive and release her.

We need to experience forgiveness from God and others and spend time with those who will be redemptive in their love for us. A few years passed and that friend came to Karrie and apologized for the lack of forgiveness, and to this day remains a good friend. Reconciliation takes time; however, the resolution of guilt took place long before the friendship was reconciled. God's forgiveness had profoundly transformed Karrie and she would not let anyone take that away.

5. Resolve: <u>Leave the offense in the past through RSTs</u>
As we have said before, we must give voice to truth. This happens when our minds dwell on the redemptive voice of God. Giving voice to truth is a decision and a learned practice. In Chapter 3, we learned about RSTs (Reinforced Strategic Thoughts). Once you have taken the first four steps in overcoming guilt and shame, you must be ready to reinforce this through RST or you will slip back into the negative emotions associated with shame.

This is one of the most crucial steps for emotional wholeness, but also one of the most difficult. As we said, God does forgive and you need to receive the release from guilt; however, the truth must be reinforced over and over. Look again at 1 John 1:9, but this time with a strategy for reinforcement: *"if we confess our sins He is faithful and just to forgive us our sins and to cleanse us from all unrighteousness."*

Say it to yourself:
"I'm forgiven."
"I'm cleansed."
"I'm free from guilt."

Say it out loud:
"God is faithful and I'm forgiven."
"My sin is gone."
"I'm clean."

Repeat these RSTs over and over until the guilt is overruled by truth. Let your heart believe this truth, and you will have a release that is deep, meaningful, and permanent. Years after being forgiven and feeling free, there may come into your heart a strategic attack of Satan to trip you up. You will need to repeat only this final step of RST. Own your forgiveness, don't let anyone take it away. It is from God.

A word about the process of the five Rs:
I believe the best way to approach these five Rs is to go in order as they are given. For example, if you try RSTs about being forgiven before you have restored the wrong, your heart will not accept the forgiveness.

First: Repent before God
Second: Return to the offense when possible
Third: Restore where harm was done

Fourth: Release your heart from guilt
Fifth: Resolve through RSTs

Mary's Story:
Mary was a beautiful, young single lady who always did the right thing. Well, not always, according to her. She got pregnant, and in shame-induced desperation got an abortion. When I met her a few years later, depression, grief, and guilt had all but destroyed her. She asked to speak with me after the service one Sunday, and we sat on the first row of chairs. I could see she was struggling with deep pain and couldn't talk for a moment. Finally, when she raised her eyes to look at me, she blurted out the issue on her heart; she said, "I killed my baby." At the time I was shocked and did everything in my power to hide it. I sat for a minute with silence and waited for her to speak. I truly didn't know what to say.

After a minute, she said it again and began to fill in the details of her life. Abortion is a cruel enemy to the mother. It constantly comes to the heart, accusing. I prayed while she told me her story, and I wanted to help her to be free. I knew it would be difficult, but the formula for overcoming guilt is pretty much the same no matter what the offense. I asked her if she wanted to be free from guilt and she said yes.

Over the next few weeks, she took my advice and started the journey of emotional recovery. The first right step she took was true repentance. She came to the reality of what she had done to God and to her child. This created more guilt than she had ever known. She had denied the problem to her conscious mind while unconsciously holding herself in contempt, and had intense self-loathing. Repentance cleared the way for the next step, which I instructed her should be immediate.

The next step would take some creativity. Her boyfriend had been complicit in the abortion and yet she needed to clear away the residue of guilt before him. She called him, though they had not had contact for some time, and said, "I want you to know that I take responsibility for the abortion and I'm sorry that I was not stronger to choose life." This was the first time she admitted to him she was responsible. He was clumsy in his response, but it didn't matter; she believed in her mission toward wholeness. The second part of her journey through this step was to write a letter to her child who was in heaven. She wrote the most loving letter of apology with sincerity and love. She explained that she had chosen to end her child's life out of selfishness and told the child she loved her. (The gender was unknown, but she sensed her child was a girl.) As you read this, you may think what I instructed her to do was cruel or morbid. But what you must understand is that the self-loathing destroying her was crueler than my recommendation to write the letter, and I knew she needed to be free.

The next thing she did was to restore. I encouraged her to get involved with a local pregnancy care center run by some wonderful people who counseled young women who were considering abortion. You see, you can't restore what is completely gone, but restoration can be realized through telling her story to women who might make the same mistake. There is a certain level of catharsis in this act, but my thinking was that she was restoring her respect for our Creator and honoring Him as God in speaking for the life of the unborn.

It was now time for her to release herself. She was doing a little better, but the next two steps, release and resolve, were crucial for her permanent emotional healing.

We talked about how God had forgiven her as she had confessed and repented of her sin. Now she had to receive and resolve this guilt. She began to replace her lies with truth.

She used to say,
"I'm a killer,"
"I'm evil."

She began to RST:
"I'm a child of God, loved and forgiven."
"I'm free and I'm accepted by my Father."

To this day, Mary uses these RSTs to hold off the lies that produce the guilt of shame. It is now her joy to help young women choose life and love them with tenderness when they don't have anywhere else to go.

You say, "Oh to be free and forgiven." You must take the right steps to freedom. Don't wait, start right now. Take your next right step.

The fruit of repentance:
One of the misconceptions about repentance and confession is that it is an acknowledgement of wrong with no change of direction. As we have stated, the very word translated "repent" in the original language of the New Testament means "to change your mind." By now you have read enough to know that if you change your mind, your beliefs, you will change your behavior.

We see in Matthew 18:23-35 a powerful story about forgiveness and what happens when someone truly repents. In this compelling story about mercy, a servant sought forgiveness of his master for a debt he owed. The master forgave his debt, only to find out later that this servant was unwilling to show mercy to others who owed him a debt. The master also had heard his servant had even been cruel in his withholding of forgiveness, and so the master went to this servant and withdrew the forgiveness.

The point of the story was about the importance of the fruit of repentance. If you receive mercy, you should show mercy to others. I believe when one truly repents and is given mercy, he will have at least four fundamental changes:

1. A change of attitude
2. A change of behavior
3. A change of self-esteem
4. A change of heart toward others who need mercy

When you have been set free by God's mercy, this should translate into a mission of love, tenderness and mercy to sinners out of gratitude. If this love isn't there, you may need to evaluate the depth and sincerity of your repentance.

Chapter 6 Life Skills:

Go to those you have harmed and apologize for your offense and make restitution.
You should avoid going to people toward whom you have felt negative, and expose your unknown feeling to them. This would be self-indulgent and would create more problems for them.

When those you have harmed are unavailable, go to the Lord.

If guilt is persistent, take a piece of paper and list all your offenses that make you feel guilty.

Ask: Have I made restitution for these? Ask: Have God and man forgiven me for these offenses?

Focus on those offenses for twenty-four hours while fasting and praying. Receive God's forgiveness.

At the end of the twenty-four hours, destroy the paper and verbally claim release from them.

Begin to apply the Five Rs this week and over the next several weeks

Repent: Change your mind about your sin and God's character

Return: Take the journey back to the offense

Restore: Make amends or repayment when possible

Release: Receive the forgiveness of God and others

Resolve: Leave the offense in the past through RSTs

Chapter 7: Depression, Anxiety and Panic Attacks:

Developing Peace of Mind

"For even when we came into Macedonia our flesh had no rest, But we were afflicted on every side: conflicts without, fears within. But God, Who comforts the depressed, comforted us by the coming of Titus." (2 Corinthians 7:5-6)

The worst place for a depressed or anxious person to be is in their own head. If you have ever experienced this, you will know what it means to be stuck in the dark place of your mind. It feels like torture. You want relief, but it seems to elude you constantly.

Depression, anxiety, and panic attacks are emotional states that have the same root cause: fear. When fear becomes a daily experience, these thoughts will often morph into anxiety and even panic attacks. When fear is combined with hopelessness, it will result in depression.

Word of warning: What I will be sharing has to do with non-organic depression. I strongly recommend if you are experiencing depression, panic attacks, or acute anxiety, you should seek professional help. You need to get a full physical and explain to your physician what you are feeling. You then should seek professional counseling, which can be very helpful. This chapter is not meant to be a replacement for professional help, but an aid to those who have lost hope in the journey.

Linda's and Tim's Story:
When Linda and I were first married, I noticed that she had a fear of intimacy, which coupled with my deep insecurity caused us to function emotionally independent from each other. We accepted a certain level of distance and independence as our norm. This was a strategic error on our part. We needed to be close and honest with an authentic love. However, we pretended to be satisfied with a mild

distance and lack of intimacy. This, of course, was a vulnerable place for our marriage.

For Linda, the vulnerability was emotional depression. I was in over my head and didn't know it. Linda from time-to-time exhibited signs of depression and even suicidal tendencies. I tried to encourage her with truth from the Bible and just didn't know what to do about this. Most days when Linda was especially low in spirit, I would call home from work to encourage her, but also with a secondary motive of making sure she had not harmed herself. This was on my mind more often than I would like to admit. Of course, I could catastrophize like nobody else. Whether valid or not, I was living in fear of finding her after a suicide. Her desire to be free of life was clear and I wasn't sure to what lengths she would go to get out of life's misery.

I had an intense fear of Linda committing suicide or that she would divorce me, rendering me alone and unfit for ministry. How would I raise my daughters? How would I live? In my mind, I had no other marketable skills than ministry. Would I be more miserable alone? Or would I be happy as a single dad? These fears and questions kept me stuck and too afraid to challenge Linda's life too strongly, so I developed a strategy of containment. Containment is a tolerable but empty way to live because you never live with confidence and you live with mediocre intimacy, as a married couple or parents. We were miserable in our hiding and were afraid to take the appropriate and wise actions necessary to change. When life finally played out, to some Linda was the victim, to others I was the victim. In reality, we were both defeated by fear, anxiety, and depression. Linda was afraid to embrace recovery from her habitual behavior and I was afraid to recover from my anxiety.

Linda's primary negative emotion was depression, whereas my primary negative emotion was anxiety; in both cases, we were immobilized by our emotions. We didn't move forward, but seemed to contain the problem socially and to a certain extent domestically.

I loved Linda and she loved me, but we were so emotionally immature, we couldn't live out our love for each other. I had given up on our relationship and turned to other things, work and many other distractions.

(Over the years this had been a great source of regret and pain in trying to find forgiveness, because I knew this was my failure. I had failed God, my children and Linda. When I found significant freedom through Christ's forgiveness, I was able to move on without revisiting the past over and over, torturing my soul with shame and guilt.)

Back to our story. After twenty-six years of marriage, I decided I had to make a change. My life was out of control, and I was tired of living this lie. I was living a life where "godliness" was put into a category of my life, not my whole heart. I had walked away from the Lord with a constant desire to draw close, but feeling shame and spiritual darkness. I realized I would rather take the risk than to continue. I submitted my thoughts to a counselor and I approached Linda with a plan for full reconciliation. I gave her five terms of reconciliation.

Because I knew reconciliation involves change on both sides of the relationship, I asked Linda what her terms of reconciliation were. I asked my counselor and he agreed that my terms of reconciliation were reasonable, measurable and doable. I carefully approached Linda with these terms and told her I believed without them we could never truly be husband and wife, but with them we could have a real marriage. I asked her if they were reasonable and fair. She said yes, but told me she wasn't sure she was willing to meet the terms.

These discussions of terms went on for weeks. She was clearly not excited about having to deal with our problems; for that matter, neither was I. She had become satisfied with our "strategy of containment." The lie of our marriage was comfortable for her, but I couldn't live with it any longer. I knew this was going to be tough, but I did think she would fight for our marriage and our walk with God. What I didn't realize was that the stronghold of depression had an overwhelming grip on her heart.

I found out through observation of Linda and my own research that depression has a cumulative impact. I wondered if I had waited too long to reach Linda's heart; it seemed to me she was broken by hopelessness. She had become stubborn in her depression, but didn't express malice, only fear. She was not going to budge. I gave her a year before we would separate if she didn't meet the five terms. We met each week on Monday to evaluate how we were doing. Those meetings didn't go well; containment had turned to dissension. I had thrown down the gauntlet and it was over in her view.

When the one year was up, without much emotion and with no conflict, Linda moved out of the house. She had found a place and I helped her move the furniture she wanted, and she seemed happier than she had been in a long time. What appeared to be happiness was actually relief. She didn't have to contend with this plan to change. I want to be clear: I knew the extent of my failure and felt responsible before God. I had failed to manage my house well, and I had been willing to allow our marriage to exist in emotional separation for years.

The week Linda left, I told the Elders of my church what had happened and was as transparent as I thought I could be. They put me under their leadership for counsel and tried unsuccessfully to get Linda into accountability.

The Elders kept me on as pastor, without a break, which in retrospect may have been a mistake on their part and mine. Nevertheless, I continued in ministry under their loving grace. Within a few months, Linda filed for divorce, and there it was, over.

The cumulative impact of depression:
Depression is cumulative and will continue to grow as we succumb to the emotions that support and fuel it. The longer we wait to deal with the problem of depression, the more difficult it is to address. In the case of Linda, we waited for years to deal with the depression because we were too focused on the bulimia. We naively thought if we could change the behavior, everything would come together emotionally.

Depression must be dealt with as soon as it starts to impact the life. All of us feel moody from time to time, especially in response to negative circumstances. However, people who are experiencing acute forms of depression will feel this even when there is not a negative situation. Their negative emotions supersede circumstances, and they can't even enjoy moments that would otherwise inspire happiness.

Depression is a feeling of hopelessness brought on by a real or perceived loss. Some key factors causing depression are long-term anxiety with a sense of loneliness and isolation, stressful experiences, and sleeplessness. There are various levels of depression, but in its most acute form it is an extremely painful experience.

Most people are unaware they are experiencing mild depression. They falsely think if circumstances change, it will change their mood. In the short run this is true, so the person never deals with the core thinking that causes the depression, and therefore depression hibernates until the next emotional crisis. However, when the depression comes back due to negative circumstances, it is much worse. Eventually, depression will increase in intensity and mild depression will develop into a full-blown clinical depression.

The characteristics of emotionally healthy people:
At first, having a bad reaction to negative circumstances seems like an acceptable response, but it is self-indulgent. It is crucial that we learn to respond to life with appropriate thinking. The truth is that many people who have been through harrowing circumstances have come through without depression or anxiety. What I have learned from years of observation and counseling is that several things contribute to a healthy mental response to negative circumstances and are safeguards from depression:

1. **Adjusted expectations**: Emotionally balanced people adjust their expectations of themselves and others. They don't lower their values but understand they live in a fallen world with flawed people, and consider this when expectations of others arise. People who tend toward depression have expectations of themselves and of others that are way too high. Life is constantly a disappointment that feeds the negative emotions. (More on this in Chapter 11)

2. **Positive RSTs**: To healthy, emotionally balanced people, their RSTs are almost always reinterpreting life through a positive grid. They learn to love well because they think well. Depression doesn't have a place to grow in the heart

of a person who practices RSTs. Depression can only be fought on the level of thinking. Reinforced Strategic Thoughts are the only way I know that a person can make fundamental changes that last. (Go back to Chapter 3 to review RSTs)

3. **Strong connection with others**: Depressed people tend to withdraw from others into their own thoughts. The further they decline into depression, the more they isolate themselves, which tragically increases depression. Emotionally balanced people are well connected to others and have meaningful relationships. When God created man, He said, "*It is not good for man to be alone…*" (Gen. 2:18) We should remember this, stop looking for perfect friends, and love well those whom God has brought into our lives.

   It might be helpful to make a list of qualities of a perfect friend, then see if you can find this person. When the search fails, it is time to be honest and accept the flawed, yet beautiful people God has brought into your life.

4. **Appropriate boundaries**: We all have people in our lives who are demanding and needy. I mean, the kind of people who will take us to the point where we have nothing left. We have to be careful to limit the access of these people in our lives, or they will deplete us. Healthy people know how to limit the negative impact of these people through appropriate boundaries. (More on this in Chapter 10)

5. **Living with purpose**: Depression develops in a life that is misdirected or has little purpose. Depressed people are often hanging on to a notion that life is about them. The

disappointments of life are overwhelming and there is a sense of hopelessness that is pervasive. One of the most powerful ways to change this sense of hopelessness is to find a purpose bigger than yourself to apply all the energy you can. (More on this in Chapter 12)

6. **Stress management**: Depression grows in a life of stressors. Stress is a major catalyst for the development of depression. Of course, without some stressors in our lives, we would probably be totally unproductive. However, when a stressor moves us to distress, the overload, if not dealt with, will eventually lead to depression. (More on this in Chapter 9)

7. **Exercise and nutrition**: There is no doubt that nutrition impacts our emotions. I have taken most sugars and processed food out of my diet. I eat a diet of fresh fruit and vegetables and for the most part, grass-fed meats. This seems to be the best diet for my emotional stability. This, along with regular exercise, keeps my body working properly and is a great asset in the fight against anxiety and depression.

Overcoming Depression

Depression will not disappear through "trying" to make it go away, "willing" it to go away, or even "praying" it to go away. Many depressed people have found themselves frustrated while well-meaning but ignorant ministers and counselors have told them to try harder and pray more to alleviate the depression. Some pastors have even made it a moral issue. This increases guilt and shame and is not helpful to the desperate.

I heard a great illustration while attending a pastor's meeting at Point Loma Nazarene University. John Ortberg was speaking and asked the audience, "*How many of you could get up tomorrow and run a full marathon?*" Almost no hands were raised. He then asked, "*How many of you if you really tried could run a marathon tomorrow?*" A few raised their hands. The final question he asked was, "*How many of you, if over the next several months you trained for the marathon, could do it?*" Most of the audience raised their hands. The point was clear: trying to do difficult or impossible things will often lead to failure, whereas training will prepare us for success.

Training, not trying, is the key to successfully alleviating negative emotions, even the extreme of non-organic depression. I mentioned the characteristics of emotionally healthy people, but for simple beginning steps I give the following to those who want to begin a journey out of depression. **The approach is T.C.A., which is Think, Connect and Act:**

Think:
Depressed people don't know how to process life properly. They have poor thinking skills. By this I don't mean they are dumb; in fact, most depressed people are highly intelligent people, but they tend to go down the road of sloppy mental responses to life. Maybe because of their intelligence, they create their own scenarios and move away from truth. In any case, they must train themselves in truth. Every time there is a decline in thinking toward negativity, they should apply RSTs with tenacity. Memorizing truth from scripture and meditating on these is crucial for recovery. (See Appendix 2)

Connect:
One of the major problems depressed people have in common is disconnection from others. They tend to have either no relationships or only shallow, non-meaningful relationships. They do life alone.

The depressed should intentionally pursue meaningful relationships with trusted and healthy people. Depressed people feel they must self-isolate because others will not be able to tolerate their negativity. It is crucial to push past these fears and find connection.

Act:
Every human being is here for a purpose. We all need to serve something bigger than ourselves. Depressed people usually are so self-focused they have little to no purpose in life other than survival.

I usually try to get them to approach this step in small ways at first. I encourage a once-a-week goal of doing a random act of kindness to someone. It can be very small at first, then increasing this, leaving less time to focus on self. This step should be accompanied with a prayer to God of thankfulness for being used to do something for Him.

Bethany's Story:
When I first talked to Bethany about her depression, she was living with so much hopelessness that she was unable to function beyond the four walls of her apartment. The tragedy was that she was unable to leave her apartment to even take her children for a walk. A distant mother who eventually committed suicide had raised Bethany, which profoundly wounded her heart. She was angry and afraid of her own potential suicide. She blamed everyone for her pain and would lash out at anyone who got in her way. Remember, fear, anger, and guilt

are the matrix of negative emotions, and Bethany lived with these moment by moment every day.

She had two children; the oldest was eighteen months and the youngest was six months old. She was living with her boyfriend who was an alcoholic. Her day consisted of nothing more than television, junk food and minimal care and nurturing of her children. She would for hours a day allow her children to sit in dirty diapers and cry. She was so depressed that her focus was only on herself. The kids were an annoying responsibility, beyond her ability to handle. I suggested as a starter that she get out of her dark apartment every day for a walk and spend ten minutes in scripture. I gave her specific passages to read. She was unwilling to attempt either of these.

It became clear the situation was neglectful and abusive to these children. I knew this problem had to be addressed. The only responsible thing I could do was to get the kids in a safe home while she recovered from her depression. My wife and I worked with another family to take these kids in temporarily so we could first protect them and then begin to reach Bethany. In the few days we took care of the kids before they were placed in a home, we noticed signs of physical neglect (e.g., malnourishment, severely scarred bottoms from hours of sitting in their own feces.) and emotional neglect (the children showed signs of anger, and other than that they were emotionally disconnected). These kids were on the road to emotional problems that would have a devastating impact in their futures.

Bethany moved in with us temporarily to get on her feet. She was incredibly entitled and selfish. But love (especially from Kimberly) was profound in giving her strength to slowly believe she could move forward. The process for her recovery proved too much for our home; however, God had a plan.

The kids were safe and now it was time to work on Bethany. She showed almost no signs of missing the kids and was clearly relieved to be on her own. What happened over a period of time was one of those things only God could do. Bethany started a business, which included some strenuous physical activity. This caused her to drop weight and get in shape. She lost about 100 pounds, which improved her self-esteem. She was able to have a job that got her out of her own depressed world every day. She had some income, so she was able to get her own apartment and started developing friendships. She still struggles with her anger and sense of entitlement but is making progress. The road to recovery will be a difficult process for her, but she has made strides toward healthy thinking.

Bethany is beginning to "Think" differently, striving to "Connect" with others and has done a few "Acts" of kindness that are beginning to improve her disposition and protect her from deep depression. I think we tend to see emotional stability as black and white. Well, in the case of Bethany, and all of us, for that matter, improvement is success and moving forward is the win.

The kids are now permanently in the home where they were placed, and they could not be healthier and happier. Bethany is able to stay in contact with the kids and she knows they are in a safe home.

Anxiety:

Anxiety is more than fear; however, it is fear-based. Probably the best way to describe anxiety is "fear run amok," that is, fear out of control. When fear becomes irrational, anxiety is the result. Anxiety is fear intensified or exaggerated. I heard a speaker at a counselors' conference describe anxiety something like this:

A man was sitting on a plane ready for takeoff. He was forced to go on a trip by air travel, something he had successfully avoided, out of fear, for over twenty years. But this trip was to see his ill mother and he needed to get to her side quickly. As he sat waiting for the plane to pull away from the terminal, he was gripped by fear. He tried to distract himself by reading a magazine.

Just then he felt the plane push back from the terminal and start to taxi toward the runway. His fear was increasing. He looked around and saw no one worried, just reading magazines. He pretended not to care about the plane, but the fear increased as he heard the engines start to roar. With a huge amount of shaking the plane started rumbling down the runway and with a loud bump they were in the air.

The fear seemed to be in his throat; now all he could think about was the plane crashing. He tried to focus away from his fear by reading his magazine once again, but then with a huge explosion the aircraft lost power and the plane started to lose altitude. The captain yelled over the speaker and said to prepare for a crash landing. He looked up and saw no one was even worried at all, just him.

He closed his eyes one more time and then opened his eyes to look outside and saw they had not pulled away from the terminal yet. All this took place in his mind. Fear drove him to a fabricated scenario that didn't exist.

Note: Fear turns to anxiety when we leave reality to embrace our own fantasy.

Overcoming Anxiety

When your fear takes over your thoughts, you will catastrophize to the level that you may not be able to cope with life. In Chapter

3 we discussed the power of the Philippians 4 passage. Here I want to expand upon those concepts and give the six powerful steps to overcome anxiety:

1. **Prayer**: When prayer is seen in its real purpose, the anxious person goes to God with a request in the context of thankfulness for it. Here is what I mean: Philippians 4:6 says, "*...with thanksgiving let your requests be made known to God.*" Each one of us from time-to-time longs for a change from what is to a more comfortable place. When prayer is understood in the Philippians 4 context, we have made the request with a profound gratitude for what is. The request is not made with a demand for change but a grateful heart that acknowledges that life is not perfect and yet that life is in the hands of a loving God. We release the change into the hands of God.

   The most important thing about prayer is intimacy with God. There is something powerful about being in the presence of God. He is there... He cares... He sees you... He sees your need... and most of all He loves you.

2. **Thanksgiving**: This thanksgiving must be intentional. We decide to be thankful. We focus on what is and say, "This is enough." We must not let what we desire steal away our focus on God's provision for what is. It is a matter of trusting God for what He has already provided. Once we are in this frame of mind, our request is humble and truly in the hands of God.

3. **Request**: The request should be for purpose, not simply comfort. When requests are made, we often attach

expectations to the request. This can be dangerous. In some theological circles there is an understanding that when we believe God for something, we will have what we want. I think the key is to believe in God, not our request. Note the difference between the two formulas:

Request + Demand Outcome + Unsatisfied Results = <u>Increased Anxiety</u>

Request + Thanksgiving + Focus on God = <u>Peace of Mind</u>

"6 *Be anxious for nothing, but in everything by prayer and supplication with thanksgiving let your requests be made known to God. 7 And the peace of God, which surpasses all comprehension, will guard your hearts and your minds in Christ Jesus.*" (Philippians 4:6-7)

The very purpose of praying in Philippians 4 is undermined by our expectation and demands for God to act on behalf of our desires. God gave us Philippians 4 to address anxiety. This will only happen in the context of thanksgiving. You will experience meaningful peace when your thanksgiving is so pervasive that you can't even remember what you wanted.

4. **<u>Focus</u>**: As was stated in Chapter 3, our focus is a matter of RST Reinforced Strategic Thoughts. In Philippians 4:8, Paul puts it like this: "*dwell on these things.*" This means to calculate the needed thoughts and reinforce them in your focus.

5. **Worship**: When we see God as present and considerate of our needs, we will see anxiety melt away. One of my favorite verses is Isaiah 41:10, *"Do not fear, for I am with you; Do not anxiously look about you, for I am your God. I will strengthen you, surely I will help you, surely I will uphold you with My righteous right hand."*

   God is present, powerful, and ready. Trust Him. It would be helpful to memorize this verse and bring it to your mind when you are beginning to feel anxious.

6. **Submit to God as provider**: In Jesus' Sermon on the Mount, found in Matthew 5-7, He calls all His followers to trust Him by prioritizing the most important thing in life, the pursuit of the Kingdom. Within this pursuit, God will provide for every need.

   "31 Do not worry then, saying, 'What will we eat?' or 'What will we drink?' or 'What will we wear for clothing?' 32 "For the Gentiles eagerly seek all these things; for your heavenly Father knows that you need all these things. 33 "But seek first His kingdom and His righteousness, and all these things will be added to you. 34 "So do not worry about tomorrow; for tomorrow will care for itself. Each day has enough trouble of its own." (Matthew 6:31-34)

Panic Attacks:

Panic attacks, for those who experience them, can be harrowing. You just don't know what is going on with your body. Panic attacks are described as a sudden attack of terror, intense fear, or feelings of impending doom that strike without warning and for no apparent reason. These episodes of terror are brief and intense and are always over in ten to thirty minutes. They are brought on by fear and anxiety. Here is how it works:

The panic attack is brought on by the body responding to anxiety with adrenaline, which produces physical symptoms of heart pounding, sweatiness, excitability, dizziness and numbness of limbs from hyperventilating, and sometimes chest pain. Because there is no real threat, the mind reacts to these physical symptoms by creating scenarios that are irrational. The reaction is usually fear of going crazy, being seen as crazy, fear of acting out in bizarre fashion, or even in some cases fear of dying from a heart attack.

My panic attack:
A few years ago, I was under intense pressure and stress. For the purposes of this book, it is irrelevant why, but much of the stress was self-induced. I was sitting in a theatre with my wife and I began to feel as though I couldn't breathe. Unknown to me, I was hyperventilating. I started feeling dizzy and was beginning to have a strong pain in my chest. My fingers and lips were feeling tingly. I was sure I was having a heart attack. (I was in the throes of a full-blown anxiety attack.) I turned to Kimberly and said, "We need to leave, I think I'm having a heart attack." She was startled, and this jolted me to look inside of myself and begin to examine what was really going on. I began to breathe from the diaphragm, slowing down my breathing and focusing my thoughts on more positive things. Within about sixty seconds, I was feeling fine.

I have had this kind of attack three other times that I recall. They are unpleasant but somewhat harmless. What happens after this kind of attack is that there becomes a fear of future anxiety attacks.

Where will this attack happen? Will I make a fool of myself in front of others?

Anxiety attacks can be on many different levels. For example, there is immobilizing anxiety that limits behavior, such as flying in an airplane, driving to work or the grocery store, travel, spending money, and even letting go of possessions, as in hoarding. There is social anxiety that limits contact with others in social settings. In some cases, it can lead to agoraphobia (fear of open spaces). For those who have severe panic attacks in trying to accomplish regular life activities, the following section should be helpful. It is also helpful to have a knowledgeable counselor take you through the process of immersion so you can overcome the fear.

Overcoming Panic Attacks:
Even though panic attacks for the most part are harmless, they are uncomfortable, and the fear of reoccurrence can be overwhelming for some. We must learn tools to deal with these so they lose any power over us. Here are six things you can do to make sure panic attacks don't overwhelm you.

1. **Accept the attack**: When we realize what is happening, the attack has lost almost all its power. We must perceive it for what it is: a harmless reaction to fear. When we realize we are not going crazy and we are not going to die, we gain power over the anxiety attack. I encourage people to accept the attack and just roll with it. That is, when you realize the attack is taking place, let it run a short life (a few minutes to a half hour) and you will survive as though it never happened. Tell yourself, "I'm safe and this cannot hurt me," or "My body is telling me to slow my breathing and relax."

2. **Practice RSTs**: Reinforced Strategic Thoughts are crucial in this process. Speaking truth about the anxiety attack will dismantle its power. "This will pass," and "This can't hurt me," and "I'm not in danger." Repeat these and you will calm yourself. The most helpful RST of all for me is "God is with me." During the panic attack, catastrophizing is common. We need to reorient our thinking to truth. Use the same tools found in Appendix 2.

3. **Practice Diaphragmatic Breathing**: The anxiety attack is a physiological reaction to fear. Your breathing has become shallow and you are hyperventilating. The immediate cure for this is to breathe into your diaphragm. Breathe: Inhale, count to four, then exhale slowly and count to six. Do this repeatedly and the symptoms of chest pain and numbness will go away.

4. **Focused relaxation**: Focus your attention on each body part and begin to relax the muscles in each limb. As you learn the relaxation technique, you will master that skill and be capable of using this in any situation you feel fear. Because this is primarily a physical symptom, it will speed up your recovery time substantially from a panic attack.

5. **Take Action:** Now that you have gone through steps 1-4, you should change your environment for a few minutes, if possible. I find that to get up and walk for several minutes gives me a stabilizing of my body to normal. The key here is to get up and move.

6. **Thankfulness to God**: I know this seems strange, but it is powerful. Immediately, when the panic attack begins

to subside, you speak to God with gratitude for His protection and His presence. This reorients you to the real source of power in your life. For some the panic attack can be followed by another panic attack. This prayer of gratitude usually is enough to take our attention off ourselves to God's presence.

Chapter 7 Life Skills:

Overcoming Depression:
Use T.C.A.:
Think: Memorize specific scriptures from Appendix 1 and think on truth.

Connect: Develop at least one meaningful authentic relationship with a trusted friend. Don't wait until you feel better; do it now.

Act: Do something today for someone else. Small or large acts of kindness will take your mind off of self and put meaning back in your life.

Overcoming anxiety
Prayer: Come before God in humble adoration and find intimacy with Him to be satisfying.

Thanksgiving: Give thanks for what is. Do this until the vision of what you want is very dim.

Request: Make the request in full surrender to the will of God. Tell Him, "Whatever You want for my life is sufficient, God."

Focus: Dwell on all that is good. Make a list of all the good you see around you and in your life. Read that list over and over until the list is "top of the mind" for you.

Worship: Speak to God's provision and His character. Who is God? What has He done? State it over and over in your mind. Speak to God about His greatness and power over your life.

Submit: Speak specifically to God's care for you and tell God whatever He provides is enough. Tell Him repeatedly that you are satisfied with His provision today. Submit to His care of you and seek nothing other than His Kingdom and His righteousness.

Overcoming Panic attacks

Accept the attack: Roll with the attack. Know that it is harmless and will be over in a few moments. In doing this, you will remove its power.

Practice RST: Apply Reinforced Strategic Thoughts from Appendix 2. Choose those RSTs that apply to your specific fears, and repeat them over and over until they are first on your mind. If you make a list you can read at any given moment, keep it in your purse or wallet so they are readily accessible.

Practice Diaphragmatic Breathing: Breathe from your diaphragm, four seconds inhale and two seconds exhale. This slowing of your breathing will bring relief to the physical symptoms of a panic attack always.

Focused relaxation: Relax your muscles, limb by limb. You can do this in almost any environment. When the body is relaxed, your vulnerability to panic attacks recurring is greatly diminished.

Take Action: Get up and move. Change your environment.

Thankfulness to God: Express gratitude to God for who He is and what He has done. Make a list of God's faithfulness to you, so it is available to you.

Chapter 8: Obsessive Irrational Thoughts:

Steps Toward Quieting the Mind

"We are destroying speculations and every lofty thing raised up against the knowledge of God, and we are taking every thought captive to the obedience of Christ."
(2 Corinthians 10:5)

When we find ourselves in "emotional defiance" (Chapter 2), the mind begins to create scenarios that are irrational. Some people would assume this is only relegated to the "crazy." However, this is not true. Sane people may find themselves experiencing irrational thoughts that are confusing and deeply troubling. In this chapter, I hope to give the meaning and source of these irrational thoughts and how those who experience them can overcome.

Warning: I can't stress this enough. If you are having irrational thoughts, you should seek counsel from a therapist. A good therapist can help you navigate your way through these irrational thoughts to a healthy perspective. This chapter is meant to share my view of how these irrational thoughts develop and steps to alleviate them.

Linda's Story:
I had just finished preaching and was exhausted from three morning services. I was on my way home and noticed a missed call from Linda. I hadn't talked to her for a while, so I was curious what she wanted. When I got home, I listened to the voice mail and was struck by a sense of finality in Linda's voice. When she said goodbye, it seemed as though it was a final goodbye. I started making some calls to talk to her, but no answer. I called Karrie, our oldest daughter, and asked if she had heard from her mother. She said that she had missed a party they were having and hadn't heard from her. I hung up with a feeling of shock at what may have happened and because I tend to catastrophize, I took a moment to pray and then went with

my instincts. After repeated calls to Linda's cell phone, I took a risk and I called the police and asked them to check on her home, which was a forty-minute drive from my house. I told them if she didn't come to the door, I suspected she was in danger; "Please do whatever it takes to enter her home." I explained that she was depressed and I was concerned about her hurting herself.

The police arrived at her house and were able to get in through the front door. They found her on the floor, unconscious and yet breathing. I arrived just as they were putting her in the ambulance. I certainly was not prepared for this event or the events of the next eight days. I knew this was a crucial time in Linda's life and she needed my love and compassion more than ever. I asked the Lord to give me wisdom.

Because we had been divorced for several years, I had difficulty getting the kind of access to her that I would have had if we were married. However, she asked for me when she regained consciousness. They pumped her stomach and removed the drugs she had swallowed (ironically, they were a combination of prescribed drugs, one of which was an anti-depressant). In my ignorance, I thought she would be relieved that I had called the police. She was not. She was angry, but as usual she tried to be kind in her anger with me. This was not a cry for attention but a bona fide attempt to take her life, and now I had disrupted that.

The next several days were the most eye-opening into her decline into emotional darkness and irrational thoughts. When someone is willing to walk in the darkness, their life becomes dominated by that darkness. She had lost touch with what was important and what life could be. Life had become about her pain and feeling abandoned by God and people. This was the Sunday before Thanksgiving and the day our first grandchild was dedicated to the Lord. Linda was never happy about being a grandmother. She loved Ryder, our grandson, but really didn't want the world to see her as old enough to be a grandmother. I believe this was a major factor in her suicide attempt. Another factor was the breakdown in some of her relationships, especially a romantic relationship with a young man who had terminated their romance. Unfortunately, she saw this as a rejection of her for the one thing she couldn't change: her age. She was significantly older than him and he couldn't see his future with a woman the same age as his own mother. Linda was devastated.

I went to the hospital Monday, Tuesday and Wednesday. On Thursday, Thanksgiving Day, she was released from the hospital and reluctantly went to her cousin's house for the Thanksgiving meal. Each day at the hospital was torture for me. I felt helpless to reach her heart. Linda had changed; she had become committed to ending her life. She had lost any will to live and she didn't mind telling this to the psychiatrist or me. She had become irrational in her view of purpose and meaning in life. There was nothing to live for and the pain of her world had caused her to see nothing but that pain. Linda, even though outwardly kind and gracious, was callous toward me and toward truth. She knew God had given her life in Christ, and she just wanted to be in heaven.

My conversations were about our children and about our marriage. She said one thing to me in the hospital on Tuesday that tore into my soul like nothing I had ever felt. She said, "Tim, you have always been kind to me and you have always taken care of me and the girls, but why did you stop loving me? Her only complaint was, "You stopped loving me." I had no answer to give her. But she was right. Years before, I had stopped loving her. I knew why, but couldn't bring myself to speak of my efforts to protect myself from her while she was so vulnerable. I told her the truth, that I would always love her and I did love her even at that very moment. She said, "You know what I mean, why were you not in love with me anymore?" To this day, I hear those words over and over in my mind. The truth of the matter was that I had fallen out of love with her because I didn't trust her with my heart. Being a needy young man and deeply insecure, I didn't find the support my immature soul craved. I just felt it would be irresponsible and dangerous to share this with her while she was lying in a hospital bed in front of me.

In those moments of our most crucial conversations, I wanted to speak words of life. I knew she was hurting from her breakup with her boyfriend. I tried to reach her heart with the love of God. I reminded her of something I had said hundreds of times, from the pulpit and to her in private, "If we could hear the voice of God, you would hear Him say, 'Linda, I see you… I know you… and I love you.'" I begged her to seek God's love and purpose for her life. She was adamant that she was done with life. The legal time for her to be held against her will was up. They had to release her from the hospital.

After Thanksgiving, she came home and started down the road of isolation and thoughts of darkness. Lies were filling Linda's heart, and she was in an extremely vulnerable place. I was struggling with my own thoughts of "What if." I felt like a failure and yet wanted to reach her.

On that next Sunday evening, I received a call from one of her former boyfriends who had remained a loyal friend to her. He was a young man who was ill-prepared for what he had just found; Linda had taken a combination of drugs and alcohol, enough to end her life. He walked in to find her lifeless body on her couch.

Fortunately, I was able to reach our youngest daughter before she arrived at her mother's home. The years following Linda's death were some of the most difficult for my girls. Their hearts were broken. They felt a combination of loss and anger. Life would be different for them. For the family left behind, picking up the pieces after a suicide is beyond difficult; it is impossible without God.

Linda had fallen prey to lies that made her irrational and defeated. She was hopeless as she looked at a future that only held aging and fading beauty. Linda's very core had been shaken by self-deception. The greatest problem was what she believed. She believed life was best when young and beautiful. This trap was at the core of Linda's misery throughout her whole life, and led to her inevitable suicide.

Obsession Cycles:
Our hearts are driven to safety. In fact, we are constantly in pursuit of safety. Problems arise when we have issues in life that create fear in the form of threat. For example, you think you will be exposed for some bad behavior in your past, such as a sexual affair. So, the threat drives us to seek safety.

This safety pursuit may take us in strange directions with flawed strategies. Then seemingly out of nowhere, an irrational thought pops in our minds. The thought may be as extreme as violence toward others. Where do these thoughts come from? These thoughts are unconsciously used to distract us from our real fears. In most cases, these thoughts are extremes and pose no real threat. Unfortunately, as we contemplate the irrational thought, we begin to take it seriously as if it is a real threat and it scares us. The more we try not to fixate on the thought, the more we find ourselves obsessed.

Uncontrollable Threats:
There are two kinds of uncontrollable threats: real and perceived. We don't have to have a real threat for it to have power in our lives. If we believe something is a threat, it is emotionally a threat.

Examples of real threats: Arrest for a crime we committed, exposure of bad behavior, getting caught for theft, marriage failure, and loss of job for underperformance.

Examples of perceived threats: Being killed in an airplane accident, attacked by a mugger, being sexually assaulted, cancer, catastrophic illness and catastrophic financial failure. Even though some of these are possible, there is no current evidence that they are a real threat.

These thoughts pose threats to our safety, and we want to avoid these. So, what happens is that we develop thoughts that are controllable; these are the irrational thoughts some people experience.

Irrational Thoughts:
Everyone has irrational thoughts from time to time. However, the difference is that some people tend to catastrophize, and they believe the irrational thoughts. The irony is that they were meant to make us feel safe because they are controllable scenarios, and yet now they are making us feel out of control.

Examples of controllable thoughts: "I will harm others or myself," "I will act in sexual deviancy," "I will lose my sexual identity," "I will act crazy in front of others," or "I need to wash my hands repeatedly." (Obsession about numbers of chairs, tiles on the floor, or clean hands are all attempts to control our environment and threats around us.)

Julie's story:
Julie, who has so much that is right in life had found she was struggling with anxiety over her irrational thoughts. These thoughts consisted of irrational fears of going crazy in public, harming her kids, and even some that included sexual deviancy. When she came to me, she was desperate and wanted answers for these problems. She was afraid she was crazy, and she was devastated.

As I sat and listened to her explain her irrational thoughts, I was struck by her avoidance of the real issues going on in her life. I asked her about her marriage and she responded with a quick "everything is perfect." I said, "Perfect? How could everything be perfect if you are struggling emotionally so much?" She said they were having sexual problems and yet she thought they would resolve it if she could get her "act together."

Through a couple of discussions, I found out she was involved in an affair with another man and he was demanding that she leave her husband and be with him. She was afraid this was going to come out to her husband and she would lose her husband and her kids. She was not in the affair for a long-term relationship, but to fill the insecurity she felt about herself.

Julie had an "uncontrollable fear," the exposure of the affair. This drove her psychologically to develop "controllable fears," sexual deviancy and harming her kids. She unconsciously knew she would not go to the extremes of her fears, so they were controllable, and yet they had become so frequent that she thought she was going crazy.

I explained to her that she had one option if she wanted to be whole emotionally. She needed to stop the affair and tell her husband. She, of course, was scared to do this, so we developed a plan that included me sharing this tragic news with her unsuspecting husband and helping him to process the information. While she was in the room, we explored their love and some of the breakdown in their marriage. I was able to see this couple reconciled and her "irrational thoughts" subsided and are now completely gone. They have since moved away from our area and yet have given me updates that they are doing well.

Richard's Story:

Richard was a pastor under tremendous stress. He had taken a lead pastor position at an established church and was trying to bring to it some new life. The opposition to his leadership direction was fierce. The people had personalized, spiritualized, and even moralized their traditions. Richard knew he was going to have to change much of the outdated traditions of the church to reach the people in the community. He tried to teach and communicate well the needs for the change. However, when the changes were enacted, the long-term members were harsh in their criticism of him.

Richard was polite but determined to make the changes. He knew it was going to be a long road and so he set his heart to love the church through the process. However, something started happening to Richard that he couldn't explain. He started having "irrational thoughts." These thoughts were fears that he was going to hit people. This may sound silly as you read this, but to Richard it was making him feel as though he was going crazy. Richard had never hit anyone in his life and was not a violent man. These thoughts would come at the strangest times. For example, during a casual conversation, he would find himself thinking about hitting the individual with whom he was talking.

Richard didn't know what to do about these thoughts. He thought there was something wrong with him. He was right. Something was wrong, but it wasn't that he was crazy; it was that he was bearing too much stress. When we talked through these irrational thoughts of violence, these thoughts, Richard concluded, were simply due to stress. He knew he, being a non-violent man, would not act out. I explained the theory of "uncontrollable threats" and "controllable threats."

He was encouraged to speak to his board to let them know the stress he was under and why. He didn't share the irrational thoughts, only the stress he was under. He was afraid to share this with the board because he didn't want to appear a weak leader. Great leaders feel stress and must learn how to handle the stress.

When Richard did finally share with his board the stress he was under, they began to help take up the leadership with the people. Richard's stress was diminished and the "irrational thoughts" of violence completely went away.

Stress is an uncontrollable fear and is dangerous. We need to develop skills to handle stress (see Chapter 9, Stress Management).

Cheryl's Story:
Cheryl was a woman with a sensitive heart who loved her husband deeply. In 2005, she lost him to a heart attack, and she was devastated. At first, she was able to cope with her pain, but as time passed, she began more and more to obsess about her loneliness.

For some reason, she felt better when she purchased items. When she brought home the purchases, she felt a temporary sense of relief. This continued for several years until her house was filled with unusable items. She had become a hoarder. She had developed an irrational connection between these items and her husband, and was unable to let them go.

In 2010, the Health Department where she lived evicted her from her home because of the unsafe environment. She couldn't even walk through the house any longer. She was unable to let go of her irrational connection and lost her house altogether for a period of time while she got help and the house was cleaned up. In Cheryl's mind, she was trying to control her grief by controlling items she placed in her home.

Hoarding is a complex pathology. I don't mean to oversimplify the constructs that create this problem; however, it serves to show the dynamics of irrational thinking that is seeking to control the uncontrollable.

Controlling irrational thoughts:
You will always have some irrational thoughts, but you can learn to diminish their power. The two primary ways that irrational thoughts develop is through:

1. Uncontrollable fears
2. Too much stress.

The thoughts for some people, when put in perspective, become almost humorous because they see them as self-manipulation.

These are not the same as catastrophizing or worrying thoughts. These come from a time of anxiety and the inability to deal with perceived uncontrollable threats in our lives.

Remember: These thoughts are fears. You are not in danger of committing these acts. The point is that you need to control, and these extreme scenarios are what you have developed to be able to control your life.

Linda's irrational thoughts of suicide:
Early in Linda's life, she began to fantasize about suicide. Back then there was very little danger of committing an act of suicide. But when depression was a part of everyday life for so long, the cumulative impact was one of hopelessness and the suicide became a real threat to her.

Note: It is important to seek counsel if there are thoughts of violence toward others or self.

Here are a few ways to dismantle the power of irrational thoughts:

1) Acknowledge the thoughts for what they are: Controllable Scenarios.
Irrational thoughts have power only in the context of darkness. Once exposed to the light of day, they will most likely seem ridiculous. You will see that you are in control of the thoughts.

2) Find the root of the problem:
What am I afraid of? What is uncontrollable in my life? My marriage? My reputation? My addiction? My past? You need to be honest about what areas of your life are threatening your happiness. You may have to go and apologize or come clean with someone about your secret offense, such as a sexual affair.

3) Evaluate the irrational thoughts:
Ask yourself: Will I really do this? Is this really a threat or am I seeking to control my world? Trying to stop thinking the thoughts is usually futile. Actually, you should think it all the way through and see it is a controllable lie that poses no threat. Once you see it is a false scenario, you will be on the road to freedom from the fear of the irrational thoughts.

4) Talk to a counselor:

When you share with a counselor the irrational thought, it is hard to defend it as a legitimate fear; this will help you see its powerlessness. You should be careful here not to share casually with a friend; most people don't have the skill set or the capacity to understand and accept the irrational nature of your thought. You should seek out only the professional help of a counselor.

5) Practice true biblical meditation:

Biblical meditation is a focus on the truth of God's Word. **Meditation is essential to mental and emotional health.** Typically, Christians see meditation as a spiritual exercise for spiritual depth, and it is. However, meditation in scripture is clearly a method of bringing emotional stability. Here are a couple of examples:

> "*Tremble, and do not sin; Meditate in your heart upon your bed, and be still. Selah.*" (Psalm 4:4)

> "*6 When I remember You on my bed, I meditate on You in the night watches, 7 For You have been my help, and in the shadow of Your wings I sing for joy. 8 My soul clings to You; Your right hand upholds me.*" (Psalm 63:6-8)

Meditation in scripture is different than an Eastern approach to meditation. Biblical meditation is a focus on God's revealed truth. Eastern meditation can give temporary relief from anxiety and emotional imbalance in our lives. The problem of meditation that places our thoughts on things that are not true is that we open ourselves up to lies. We need a transformed mind, not an empty mind.

> *"And do not be conformed to this world, but be transformed by the renewing of your mind..."* (Romans 12:2)

Biblical meditation is about focus on scripture. This practice has saved my mind from irrational thoughts and given me peace that is stabilizing. You must first have the Word of God in your heart, and then you will be able to bring it up to ruminate on it (Hebrew for meditate means to ruminate). Ruminate is what a cow does when it eats. The cow ruminates by softening food within the first compartment of the stomach, then regurgitates the partially digested food, known as cud, and chews it again, to get every bit of nutrition from it.

When we take in the Word of God initially, we gain some insight and value from it. But similar to the cow, we need more time with it to get all the nutritional value. We need to "ruminate," that is, refocus on the truth in relation to our lives. This is meditation in a biblical sense. This is almost a lost discipline in the church, but is essential for spiritual and emotional growth and stability. Notice the teaching of chapter 1 of Psalms, about the impact of meditation:

> *"1 How blessed is the man who does not walk in the counsel of the wicked, nor stand in the path of sinners, nor sit in the seat of scoffers! 2 But his delight is in the law of the LORD, and in His law, he meditates day and night. 3 He will be like a tree firmly planted by streams of water, which yields its fruit in its season and its leaf does not wither; and in whatever he does, he prospers.* (Psalm 1:1-3)

Meditation in Psalm 1 gives a promise of strength and impact. When you focus on truth through meditation, you will have strength like a tree by the rivers of water:

1. You will have a constant source of nourishment.
2. You will have regular seasons of fruit bearing.
3. Your leaves will not wither; you will be healthy.
4. You will be prosperous in all things

Meditation on scripture will bring incredible benefit to your life. The opposite to this man is one who walks in the counsel of the wicked. God wants our lives to be filled with joy and blessing, and the only way for this to be realized is through biblical meditation.

As we discipline ourselves to meditate, we will see a steady change in our dispositions and our emotional stability.

(See Appendix 2 to find scriptures that can be used in specific areas of your life for meditation.)

Asaph's journey into irrational thinking:
In Chapter 2, I talked about Asaph's "alarm reaction." He sought to get on the other side of his unhealthy emotions by behavior and environment modification, which didn't work. What worked is that his journey out of unhealthy emotions was "exchange modification" (replacing lies with truth). Let's take another look at his journey from the perspective of his journey into irrational thinking.

In Psalm 73, Asaph was transparent about his journey into emotional darkness. He was both spiritually and emotionally irrational. Please read Psalm 73:1-28 so you can see this incredible journey into darkness and then into restored stability.

There are several things that should be pointed out here about Asaph's journey. First, Asaph reached a point of almost complete emotional failure due to an inappropriate focus on comparing his life to others (Ps. 73:2-3). Comparing our lives to others is a dangerous place to put ourselves. The fact that we can't control others is a major cause of irrational thoughts.

Second, Asaph inappropriately thought purity of heart and good living would keep him from experiencing pain in life (Ps. 73:13-14). The whole goal of life is to bring glory to God, not comfort to our lives. This game of trying to manipulate God into working for our ease of pain because we have behaved well will lead to further frustration and feeling that life is out of control. This is what happened to Asaph.

Third, Asaph had placed himself in a vulnerable place by wanting the wicked to be harmed and his life to be eased. He created a life out of control (Ps. 73:12-20). Asaph found in God's truth that the wicked would be punished, but even this didn't help. Note that his knowledge of the future of the wicked drove him deeper into irrational thinking: Psalm 73:21-22, "*When my heart was embittered and I was pierced within, then I was senseless and ignorant; I was like a beast before You.*"

Fourth, the correction of Asaph's emotional stability only came when he properly understood God's presence was all he needed (Ps. 73:23-28). Life is not about our ease of living, and our emotional stability will be at risk while we live with this expectation. The whole of life and emotional stability are found when we esteem the presence of the Lord properly. Notice Asaph's final conclusion in Psalm 73:28, "*But as for me, the nearness of God is my good; I have made the Lord GOD my refuge, that I may tell of all Your works.*" If we could learn the importance of Asaph's journey, we could find tremendous freedom in the presence of God in our lives.

Chapter 8 Life Skills:

Follow the five ways to quiet the mind:

1. Acknowledge the thoughts for what they are: controllable scenarios.
2. Find the root of the problem.
3. Evaluate irrational thoughts.
4. Talk to a trusted friend or counselor.
5. Meditate on truth to displace fear.

Memorize 2 Corinthians 10:4-5

> *"4 For the weapons of our warfare are not of the flesh, but divinely powerful for the destruction of fortresses. 5 We are destroying speculations and every lofty thing raised up against the knowledge of God, and we are taking every thought captive to the obedience of Christ."* **(2 Corinthians 10:4-5)**

Spend at least fifteen minutes in meditation on the Word of God in the morning every day.

Chapter 9: Stress Management:

The Difference Between Good and Bad Stress

"But the Lord answered and said to her, "Martha, Martha, you are worried and bothered about so many things; but only one thing is necessary." (Luke 10:41-42)

According to the National Health Resource Network, 75 percent of the general population experiences at least "some stress." The network goes on to give the warning that stress contributes to heart disease, high blood pressure, strokes, and other illnesses in many individuals.

Of the top four causes of cancer, many lists place a weak immune system at the top. The immune system is adversely impacted by negative stress. Stress should be seen as a killer and must be addressed by all of us. Those of us who are wrestling with negative emotions have a greater need to deal with stress because this is a major driver in our ongoing negative emotions.

We must know the difference between "stress" and "stressors." It is possible to be stressed when there is not an external stressor. We can fabricate our stress by developing scenarios that don't exist. In this chapter we will look at both the good and the bad sides of stress.

My life of stress:
I have to be honest; the truth about my stress is that I have more stress than I do stressors in my life. I have found the combination of stress and my inability to accept that I can't change or control some things has put me in emotional conflict.

My issues of control cause increased stress even when there are few stressors. Fear will rise up in an insignificant situation and I will begin to catastrophize it, and it becomes uncontrollable and insurmountable.

In recent years this has been evidenced in the way I handle my large family and my ministry responsibilities. I really want to be at peace, but struggle to get on top of everything. Knowing the difference between "stress" and "stressors" and "good stress" and "bad stress" has helped me greatly.

Stress and the stressors:

Stressors are triggers that create pressure on your body and mind, whereas stress is the emotional, mental and physical response to the stressors. The stressors are external and the stress is internal. We can work on both of these areas, but the greatest control should be directed at the stress and not the stressor.

We can apply quality life tools and principles to our stress, whereas there are practical but limited controls we can put on our stressors. I will give tools to deal with both later in this chapter.

Stress is a physical and psychological response to perceived demands and pressures from without and from within. To respond to these demands and pressures, we mobilize physical and emotional resources, which produce stress hormones to increased levels in the body. Consequently, we will experience various impacts in our lives from stress. The impact of stress on the life:

Physiological impact: When stress is perceived, the body produces cortisol. When we experience chronic stress (stress that is ongoing with very little relief), the damage can be extensive. The presence of ongoing cortisol in the system due to stress eventually can lead to even more serious illness, such as heart disease, cancer, diabetes, or thyroid dysfunction. It is important to address the stressors and our reactions to these stressors.

Psychological impact: The mind often seeks relief from stress in unhealthy ways. Some of the unhealthy ways people tend to deal with stress are: anxiety and panic attacks, depression, obsessive compulsive disorders, drug addiction, alcoholism, or even sexual deviancy. The reason these are pursued is because they give a sense of relief or control. For example, if I can't control my public image, I may develop an obsession with neatness or cleanliness, which gives me back a sense of control of my life.

Emotional impact: With persistent stress, one may experience: explosive anger, frustration, feeling overwhelmed, lack of motivation, fear, poor mood, unhappiness, sleep problems, difficulty thinking, short-term memory loss, and in some cases, you may feel detached from life or feel you are living in a dream state.

As you can see from this list, it is crucial that we address stress and the stressors in our lives.

The two kinds of stress:

Most people see all stress as bad stress. However, the truth is if we didn't have some stress in our lives, most of us would be unproductive. Stress is a great motivator. Any discussion on stress must start with clarifying the two categories of stress: Eustress and Distress.

Eustress: This word comes from the Greek prefix "Eu," meaning good, and stress. The idea is that there is stress that is manageable. The characteristics of eustress are the following:

1. The stress is manageable.
2. The stress is controllable.
3. The stress is within your personal emotional parameters.
4. The stress produces motivation for action and optimum performance.

Remember: Without some good stress, we will most likely underperform or not perform at all.

Years ago, I ran a gas station in Jackson, Wyoming. I had a master mechanic working for me named John. John was working on a car one day and was frustrated because he couldn't find his torque wrench. I asked him why he didn't just use one of the other wrenches. I could tell I had asked a dumb question by the look on his face. He explained reluctantly that the torque wrench showed the exact pressure he would need to put on a bolt to the manufacture's specification. I said, "I would think you would know how much pressure to put on the bolt with your experience (my second dumb assertion)." While we were talking, John found the torque wrench and showed me how to use it. John explained that in auto mechanics the pressure on a bolt must be great enough for the bolt to hold without stripping the threads. If it is not tight enough, the bolt will rattle loose from the engine vibration. In this story, I was the "tool."

I was thinking sometime later that this is the way life is. We need enough stress in our lives to be motivated to function at our optimum level. However, if there is too much stress, we will be broken. Finding that balance is key to our emotional and physical health. The question then becomes: "How do we find the right amount of pressure and what do we do when the stress is pushing us beyond our ability to cope?"

A word of warning: Everyone is different in his or her levels of stress tolerance. One person can handle a great deal and others can handle very little. You should not gauge your stress based on the stress tolerance of others.

Distress: This is the stress that is an overwhelming pressure to the point of emotional, mental, or physical exhaustion. The characteristics of distress are:

1. The stress that is caused by loss of control.
2. The stress that causes overwhelming fear.
3. The stress that is beyond manageability.
4. The stress that causes one to be stunned into being unproductive.

Distress may cause: irritability, anger, anxiety, depression, fatigue, tension headaches, stomach aches, hypertension, ulcers, heart conditions and others.

I have seen many individuals become distressed, and their lives become almost intolerable. We will develop some life skills to deal with this kind of stress, but first let's look at some of the triggers, stressors that may cause distress.

A few of the stressors (triggers for stress):
Financial pressures: Most of the time, financial pressures are due to lack of good financial management. I would suggest that if you are experiencing acute financial pressure, read the book, ***The Total Money Makeover***, by Dave Ramsey[2]. I love what one guy said about financial management: "Sell your crap, pay off your debt and live."

Living beyond their means has led many to unbearable stress. The best way to deal with this is to make some clear life choices for your own freedom. Is that house or that car or that trip worth the stress you will experience?

[2] The Total Money Makeover, Thomas Nelson, 2003.

Relationship difficulties and relationship changes: Having relationships is the best part of life. Relationship with God and man is what life is all about. However, when we go through relationship change, we experience stress. Marriage, divorce, the birth of a child, or the death of a loved one are among the greatest stressors in life. Some of these are uncontrollable, and we need to know how to overcome the stress we experience when difficulties happen.

Career pressures: I can't tell you how many people I have watched over the years reach a point of devastation because of being "downsized." We need jobs for income, and jobs give us a sense of self. When our jobs or careers are sidetracked, we can experience a great deal of stress.

Heavy workloads: When workloads become so great that you can't keep up, the stress can be unbearable. We need to learn to manage our time and figure out what is truly important. If we are working in an environment that is too demanding, we may need to make a change before we burn out.

Health and aging: Inevitably, everyone gets old and most everyone experiences health problems. Some of these can be avoided, but not all. We experience stress when confronting life-threatening or disabling health problems. One of the things I have noticed at my age is that I begin to see my career in terms of the years I have left, and this creates stress. The stress can be avoided with proper faith and life skills.

Note: These are the stressors in contrast to stress. Some people have challenging lives and don't get distressed. You may not be able to modify all the stressors in your life, but you can learn to overcome stress.

Overcoming Distress:
Man needs rest. The purpose of God resting after He created man was that He wanted man to rest. God wasn't tired and didn't need a break. God established a sacred principle of rest and focus on God, called the Sabbath. This rest is crucial for man's happiness and existence.

I love this statement in the midst of troubling times: God said to His people in Isaiah 30:15, "*For thus the Lord GOD, the Holy One of Israel, has said, 'In repentance and rest you will be saved, in quietness and trust is your strength.' But you were not willing,*"

I will give two primary ways to deal with stress: **keep the Sabbath and C.O.P.E.**, a life skill I developed for myself and in my counseling of stressed people. The more important of the two is keeping the Sabbath. God means it when He directs us to keep the Sabbath for our own good.

<u>**Live within the Sabbath rest:**</u>

> "*8 Remember the Sabbath day, to keep it holy. 9 Six days you shall labor and do all your work, 10 but the seventh day is a Sabbath of the LORD your God; in it you shall not do any work, you or your son or your daughter, your male or your female servant or your cattle or your sojourner who stays with you. 11 For in six days the LORD made the heavens and the earth, the sea and all that is in them, and rested on the seventh day; therefore, the LORD blessed the Sabbath day and made it holy.*" (Exodus 20:8-11)

Jesus wanted to make sure all realize the Sabbath was to accommodate man's limitations in a finite reality. Here is what Jesus said in Mark 2:27. *"Then he said to them, 'The Sabbath was made for man, not man for the Sabbath.'"* To make this a legal responsibility is to miss the point of the holiness of the day. Jesus was not ignoring the requirements of the Law, but was placing emphasis on the need of man and God's love for him in creating a day of rest.

There are two important parts to observing the Sabbath:

1. **Rest**: The Sabbath was a means for rest in our body and soul. This is a break from activities that are stressful and demanding.

2. **Celebration:** The Sabbath was a memorial of the creative act of God. When we properly observe the Sabbath, we will focus on God's creation and His sovereign power and control. This focus will create a sense of awe and protection. The benefit for us is that we are focused on God's control over our lives and the circumstances that affect us.

The first aspect of the Sabbath rest is essential for healthy minds and bodies. We need to rest minds, not just our bodies. When we fail to take time off of work, we are constantly running the risk of developing chronic stress. When we are on overload for an extended period of time, we will inevitably develop many of the problems mentioned at the beginning of this chapter. God is fully aware of this and has called us to live the Sabbath rest.

The second aspect of the Sabbath rest is a focus on God's creative power and His sovereignty. When we weekly focus on God's power and sovereign care, we reset our worried minds to faith in our Almighty Father who loves us. When we look at creation on that Sabbath, we see God's handiwork, and five things are realized:

1. God is all-powerful.
2. God makes things for His glory.
3. God is in control.
4. My life is small and I should see my problems and challenges as small.
5. My life is a part of creation and therefore exists for the purpose of bringing God glory.

If we could live this out, we would experience great joy and pleasure in the process of life and avoid greatly the distress of circumstances out of our control. I recommend the Sabbath be observed beyond once a week in the life of a distressed individual. Here is what I recommend to people I work with who are experiencing a great amount of stress in their lives:

1. **Take a fifteen-minute break every three to four hours at work.** Use this time to reflect on God's sovereign power. Appendix 1, at the back of this book, will be helpful in gaining truth to focus on during this break. Meditation will be key to make this work well; see Chapter 8.

2. **Take a full day off work every week**. Spend times throughout the day reflecting on God's creation. It will help to get outside and in nature to do this best; stop and observe small things like plants and small animals and small children. Also observe large things like the sky and clouds or the stars at night. You are a part of something so big, and God loves you personally. This will help you reset to God's gracious care of your life. You are safe in His care.

3. **Take a full weekend break every quarter**. It would be good to spend time evaluating your creativity at this point. What things have you created in the past quarter? Celebrate those accomplishments. The Sabbath is a celebration of the best, God's creation. You are created in His image; be creative and celebrate it each quarter. The benefit is that we learn to enjoy the process of life and see God's work in and through us.

4. **Take time for a two-week break every year**. I mean two weeks in a row. Don't piecemeal your break. Give yourself time to relax and rest from the pressure of life and work. A couple of years ago, our friend Lori Wilhite, the founder of "Leading and Loving it," sent my wife, Kimberly, a message on a pastor's need for vacations. Her husband, Jud, is the pastor of one of the largest churches in America, Central Christian Church in Las Vegas, and he has committed to taking time off in the summer to refresh from his demanding responsibilities. I had always skipped vacation time except for a few days here and there, but realized I was not really relaxing. Because of their influence, I became so convicted that I started taking three weeks in a row for vacation. Nothing falls apart while I'm gone, and I come back stronger than ever. Sabbath is essential for all of us. If there is any way for you to take at least two weeks off, please do it for your health and your family.

Practice C.O.P.E.

When your stress level exceeds your ability to **C.O.P.E.**, you need to restore the balance by reducing the stressors or increasing your tolerance, or both. You will know you are overwhelmed by stress when, for example, you overreact in anger, frustration, fear, or worry, or you are moody and withdrawn. Practice C.O.P.E. (Contentment, Organize, Prevent and Express)

Contentment: Reinterpret life with a heart of gratitude.

To **C.O.P.E.** with stress, you will first need to accept that not all things matter that much. This for many people with problems of stress is one of the core problems we face. We take everything too seriously. A friend of mine in Lovell, Wyoming, Wes Meeker, used to say to everyone, "The main thing is relax." Wes had some physical challenges that have buckled other men, but Wes was always great to be around because he enjoyed the simple things of life. As a young man, I always wanted to be like Wes, who knew and lived contentment.

If you are ambitious, you should look more to the process than to the outcome. Setting goals is valuable, but learning to celebrate the process is essential to emotional health. Find balance between ambition and contentment by being thankful for the process. Much of stress is due to the desire to succeed and the frustration of not being able to make it happen.

Here are three ways to that help you to be content:

1. Adjust your expectations: Every time you feel as though you need to produce more or be more, stop and say, "Where I am is enough," or say, "Today is enough." If you compare your situation to others, it will only increase stress. (More on adjusted expectations in Chapter 11)

2. Reinterpret success: Success for anxious people is always "more." More than others and more than our own

achievement. The unhealthy person almost never gives place for the celebration of incremental achievement. If you are going to experience contentment, it will be through an intentional celebration of moments of accomplishment. The end goal is important, but celebrated achievement along the way becomes crucial for emotional health.

3. Eternal perspective: We often look at the crisis of the moment as if it is everything. These moments and the crisis pass. We need to look at the stress in the scheme of all eternity or at least a lifetime. Ask yourself, "How will this impact all eternity?" or "How important will this be in ten years?"

Organize: Often stress is avoidable by organizing our commitments. We may be driven out of false guilt or a need to impress to take on things that are not necessary for us to do. We must be willing to alter our commitment and set margins in our lives. We must put our commitments and responsibilities into priorities. We need to revise and moderate our commitments when possible.

One of the best ways to organize tasks and responsibilities comes from Stephen Covey. He teaches the ABC prioritizing system. Here is how it works:

Create three lists of priorities:

The "A list" is the list of priorities that are both "urgent and required" and are placed as a top priority.

The "B list" is the list of priorities that are "important but not required," and they are placed as a secondary priority.

> The "C" list is the list of the priorities that "are not directly related to our goals or our responsibilities," and are placed on a wait list.
>
> To be honest, when I make these lists, I usually never get to the "C list." However, when I don't make the ABC lists, I often will do C activities as if they are a higher priority.

Once you organize and execute your priorities, make sure you celebrate your accomplishments every day. To alleviate stress, the caveat is "every day." At the end of each day, spend time celebrating the day's accomplishments.

We so easily get overwhelmed and stressed with tasks that, if organized, would be manageable. The best time spent will be time to make the ABC list. You will then accomplish more of the right things, and you will alleviate stress in your life.

Prevent: Stop stressors before they take over.

Much of the stress we experience could be avoided if we applied some prevention in our lives. We must know the triggers for stress and write them down, along with what causes our reaction. I recommend you keep a stress journal and look for times of day where you experience more stress. Write down events that cause you stress and even people who cause you stress. In your journal you will begin to see patterns of stressors and reaction.

Take control of your environment as much as possible. Here are a few examples: If you have stress getting the kids out the door in the morning for school, start earlier. If you are chronically late for work and traffic is a constant excuse for being late, leave earlier.

If you arrive fifteen minutes early, you can relax and get ready for your day. Or if you are experiencing financial stress due to overspending, you should evaluate if it is worth spending more than you make.

Sometimes stress comes from the fear of being exposed for things that you have done wrong. You need to evaluate what you want out of life when making decisions that will not be according to your values. Don't compromise yourself, and you will avoid the stress of fear and regret over guilt and possible exposure.

If there are things that can be exposed, it may be beneficial for you to expose it yourself to take away its power. It may be helpful to talk to a trusted friend to process if this should be done. It may be that you only need to expose the transgression to someone who can hold you accountable.

Express: Assert yourself when appropriate.

You must be willing to state your concerns to others and set boundaries. Much of the stress we experience is due to the fear and failure to speak truth about what we truly want. Asserting yourself is different than being aggressive. Aggression loses sight of what you really want.

Recently, I was in a movie theater, and a cute young child was running around making noise. This little girl was more and more distracting to the people in the theater. The only one who seemed to be unaware was her father. In retrospect, I wish I had gently asked him to take care of the situation. I could have said, "You probably are unaware of the impact your daughter is having on the people in the theater but, would you mind having her quiet down a little?"

I'm not sure this would have worked, but I will never know because what I did do didn't work. I waited too long, and by the time I spoke to him, I no longer was in tune with what I really wanted, which was to watch the movie without a screaming child running around in front. Instead, I wanted him to know he was wrong and that was exactly what I said to him. This provoked him and he was so upset I thought he was going to hit me.

What we need to do is respectfully ask others to change their behavior. When someone is constantly late or doesn't do their work, we need to point out the need and encourage positive change. A helpful book I recommend is, ***Crucial Conversations***, by Kerry Patterson[3].

Communicate your feelings openly. Tell your boss you are struggling with the time-sensitive demands. Don't say, "You are demanding." Rather say, "I feel frustrated getting all my work done with the time demands." What this does is express the need and doesn't attack the boss. If you regularly have problems finishing appointments on time, state your limits in advance. Tell your appointment the limits of your time: I have five minutes, ten minutes, or I have to be finished at 3:00 pm. This will make it less awkward when you need to close the meeting; time is the culprit, not you.

The Story of Martha:

It seems to me one of the most poignant stories on priorities in scripture is the story of Martha and Mary in Luke 10. They both made a choice and only one found favor with Jesus and ultimately freedom from the stress of life.

3 Crucial Conversations, Tools for talking when stakes are high, Kerry Patterson, McGraw-Hill Books, New York, 2012.

> "38 *Now as they were traveling along, He entered a village; and a woman named Martha welcomed Him into her home. 39 She had a sister called Mary, who was seated at the Lord's feet, listening to His word. 40 But Martha was distracted with all her preparations; and she came up to Him and said, 'Lord, do You not care that my sister has left me to do all the serving alone? Then tell her to help me.' 41 But the Lord answered and said to her, 'Martha, Martha, you are worried and bothered about so many things; 42 but only one thing is necessary, for Mary has chosen the good part, which shall not be taken away from her.'*" (Luke 10:38-42)

This story is about two well-meaning women who had vastly different priorities. Martha chose to focus on the responsibilities of a host. This is probably what many of us would choose. Let's look at a few of the mistakes Martha made in her choices:

First, Martha chose to obey her deficit need to perform. This caused her to miss the most important thing in life: Luke 10:40 "*But Martha was distracted* (drawn away) *with all her preparations* (serving)..." Martha missed the value of Jesus being in her home. Mary was sitting at Jesus' feet and listening to Him, while Martha was distracted by her work and her need to perform. Martha falsely perceived the relationship with Jesus was about doing things for Him. This false construct has led many to value service over worship. This is the trap that many of us fall into. If we were honest, this perception is based on our own arrogance and need to control what people think of us. This is a major cause of stress. We value what people think and prioritize our lives around our public image.

Second, Martha chose to seek control of her environment. Martha showed her emotional immaturity by demanding that Jesus rebuke Mary. What Martha actually told Jesus was, "…tell her to help me." This word "help" as recorded in the original Greek is *"sunantilambanomai,"* which is a big word, meaning in this context, "Mary should work together with me instead of what she chose." The word "help" means more than help; it means to abandon her choice and come join Martha's choice.

Martha's problem was not just that she cared too much what people thought of her, but she also felt a need to control the world around her, in this case, Mary. Martha wanted the world to comply with her standard and choices. Think about the stress that puts one under. Because Martha needed to pressure people to comply with her, she was always going to feel the stress of needing to control the uncontrollable. We will experience overwhelming stress when we put our expectations on the behavior of others.

Third, Martha chose to play the role of God. Martha rebuked Jesus and charged Him with lack of concern. She was asking Him to use His authority to rebuke her sister for not helping with the chores. When we come to the place where we demand action from Jesus, we put ourselves at risk of overwhelming stress. Here is how it works:

1. We rebuke the Lord for His lack of cooperation with our desires.
2. Jesus refuses to cooperate with our inappropriate desires.
3. We are in isolation from Jesus and others. The problem is we still feel we are right to pursue our performance agenda, but we have no help. We have judged others and God as not caring about what we think is important. We feel sorry

for ourselves and experience the stress of our own perfectionistic dysfunction.

If only Martha could hear the heart of Jesus and experience the peace that comes from setting aside the lesser (work) for the greater (worship), she would have avoided the emotional conflict.

The power of waiting for the supernatural:
One of the most difficult things for me to do is wait. The drive inside me is like a lion that can't get enough. I'm constantly in a hurry even when I have no place to go. You may relate to this. If you are a driven person like me, you may have the same trouble waiting.

However, many who appear to be patient may just be apathetic, suppressed or have given up. The person who "waits upon the Lord" is neither driven nor complacent. The person who waits upon the Lord is looking outside of the natural realm; they wait for God to act. Isaiah 40:28-31 shows the contrast between man's limited strength and God's omnipotence and how waiting on God produces a supernatural power.

> "*28 Do you not know? Have you not heard? The Everlasting God, the LORD, the Creator of the ends of the earth does not become weary or tired. His understanding is inscrutable. 29 He gives strength to the weary, and to him who lacks might He increases power. 30 Though youths grow weary and tired, And vigorous young men stumble badly, 31 Yet those who wait for the LORD Will gain new strength; They will mount up with wings like eagles, They will run and not get tired, They will walk and not become weary.*"
> (Isaiah 40:28-31)

Are you sure you understand the metaphor here? God is promising you will be able to fly without effort. There are two aspects to what is being promised: 1. We will be able to fly, and 2. You will fly without effort. I weigh 220 pounds, and I'm pretty sure I can't get off the ground.

If you have ever felt like life is too hard, you may be in a cyclical pattern that many hard-working people experience:

1. Work hard.
2. Run out of energy.
3. Become hopeless.
4. Eventually try and work hard again.

This cycle can be devastating over time. It feels like there is no progress and you can't go on. God is promising in Isaiah 40 a supernatural strength; that is, the ability of the weary young man and the stumbling strong man to go on when others would fail. It all starts with waiting.

We live in San Diego, which is a large city with rapidly decreasing open space. However, where our house sits there is an open area that is owned by the city. It's a valley far below our home. This gives us a wonderful view of downtown, but more importantly gives us a view of birds that ride the thermal wave coming off the hillside up from the valley floor. The eagles will come out of the trees and fly into that thermal and rise up above the valley floor, wings spread, with only minor adjustments every so often to change angles. They fly effortlessly, and it seems almost supernatural because they hang there for an extended period of time.

Watching these birds soar reminds me of Isaiah 40:31. When man is out of strength, he feels the strength of God under his wings and soars without effort. This breaks the effort cycle. You don't need more effort; you need to wait upon the Lord and He will give you strength.

Waiting is tough for all of us. I always thought only driven people were impatient and couldn't wait, but I have realized over years of counseling that not only the driven person struggles to wait, but the complacent person also struggles. Here is some advice to the driven and the complacent:

Advice to the driven: If you are driven, you probably have the following characteristics: Ambitious, organized, status-conscious, you take on more than you can handle, you're impatient, proactive, and obsessed with time management and you don't understand why others won't get to the point, and feel about productivity like you do. With this list of character traits, think about how much stress you are under, not to mention how others are stressed around you.

God has called you to wait. You may say, "I don't have time to wait; I have too much to do." The problem is that life is not the sum of your activities and productivity. God wants to do things through you that you could not do in your own strength. You will need to be intentional about waiting, as in Psalm 46:10, "*be still and know that I am God*." You are limited in what you can accomplish, and you need to trust the Lord. Wait! He will show up like the thermal rising and you will soar.

Advice to the complacent: If you are complacent, you probably have the following characteristics: suppressing emotional expression, you aren't motivated by the demands of life or others, you may not manage time well, you are often late for appointments, and most devastating, you tend to give up. Complacent people tend to feel hopeless and helpless.

God has called you to wait. Your response is, "It's my nature to wait," when in reality, you have given up and don't feel that God will ever do anything, so why try? God wants you to be productive even when you are out of resources. "*He gives strength to the weary.*"

Waiting and giving up are mutually exclusive. When you have given up and are hopeless, you have taken your eyes off the supernatural power of God to do what you can't. Waiting for you is going to have to be an intentional focus on divine power and God's desire to work through you. So, wait upon the Lord. He will come; don't give up, He is there, ready to cause you to soar.

Chapter 9 Life skills:

Make a list of triggers in your life (Suggested list below:) After each one, write what an optimum situation for this area would look like. Then put down the steps that must be taken to achieve this optimum lifestyle:

Financial pressures

Optimum Life: (Debt-free, spendable money, generosity.)

Steps to achieve optimum life:

Relationship difficulties

Optimum Life: (Kids, Spouse, Friends)

Steps to achieve optimum life:

Career pressures

Optimum Life: (Realistic career goals)

Steps to achieve optimum life:

Heavy workloads

Optimum Life: (What can be delegated? What can be eliminated?)

Steps to achieve optimum life:

Unrealistic expectations

Optimum Life: (How can I change my expectation without compromising my purpose?)

Steps to achieve optimum life:

Health and aging

Optimum Life: (What dietary changes do I need to make? Exercise?)

Steps to achieve optimum life:

Set a reasonable Sabbath schedule: The point of the Sabbath schedule is to secure time for rest and reflection upon God's creative power.

Daily: Schedule for a fifteen-minute break every day.

Weekly: Schedule for one full day every week.

Quarterly: Schedule for one full weekend off every quarter.

Annually: Schedule for two full weeks off (Better three, if possible) every year.

Practice C.O.P.E.:

Contentment: Reinterpret life with a heart of gratitude. Focus on what you are thankful for by keeping your thanksgiving journal.

Organize: Often stress is avoidable by organizing our commitments. Create your ABC list and be diligent to follow it every day:

A list: urgent and required, top priority list.

B list: important but not required, secondary list.

C list: Are not to directly related to our goals or our responsibilities, wait list.

Prevent: Stop stressors before they take over. Once you know what your stressors are, make a list of causes that bring about those stressors. Once you have this list, begin to prevent these causes by taking evasive action and making wise decisions before they turn into stressors.

Express: Assert yourself when appropriate. We often fall into the stressor by not speaking to our real need. We need to speak up and have the uncomfortable conversation to avoid a world of ongoing stress.

Memorize Isaiah 40:31

> *"Yet those who wait for the LORD will gain new strength; They will mount up with wings like eagles, They will run and not get tired, They will walk and not become weary."* (Isaiah 40:31)

Chapter 10: Setting Boundaries:

Understanding the Power of Influence

"Death and life are in the power of the tongue, and those who love it will eat its fruit." (Proverbs 18:21)

In everyone's life there is some "white space," you know, the space between one activity and the next. This is crucial for life to be lived well. If the space is too great, we are unproductive and may fail to experience the power of a purposeful life. If the space is too small, we will fall into the burden of burning out, being stressed and having an increase in negative emotions.

I have always struggled with the cliché "Less is more." It seemed to me that more is more. And if anything was important it was "more," more of everything. I remember thinking how incredibly talented Neil Young was when he would play the guitar and the harmonica in the song, "Heart of Gold." However, in contrast to that, picture a man on the street corner with a jar who has simply added one more instrument: Harmonica, guitar and cymbals between the knees... well, you get the picture, "less is more."

I remember when I laid out my first newsletter as a young man, with no publishing experience. I had written what seemed to me the genius musing of a wise young pastor. Setting aside the idea that my musing turned out to be not so genius, I looked back at a file of my old newsletters from the 1980s and found that first newsletter. I laughed as I saw so many obvious mistakes.

Some mistakes were grammatical and some were theological, but the most obvious mistake was the layout. The layout had two tragic flaws: First, I had used too many font styles and sizes for the newsletter to look professional. In those early days of the personal computer, I made the mistake of thinking the contents of a newly acquired font package should be used in one newsletter; you may remember that temptation. Second, I put too much on each individual page. There were no open spaces on the page. It was filled to overflowing with text and not so cool pixilated graphics. I was so proud at the time I published it, but in retrospect I am shocked at the flaws.

The reason space is important in publishing is the way the mind sees information and processes it. Publishers know there is a greater impact when the mind can assimilate information. If the page is too full of text and pictures, the impact is lost or at least diminished. This is true in music where a pause is powerful in bringing emotion and impact to the performance. Without "rest" in a musical piece, the presentation would decline into a series of notes without impact. In public speaking, the audience would be worn out and unmoved if the speaker was like a machine gun of information. Space is essential to impact in most areas of life.

Value is measured by impact, not by volume. For someone like me, life has been about producing as much as you possibly can until you die. Stress and frustration will be a part of anyone's existence when life is based on this false value; i.e., **life = production**. Production is important in life, but it does not secure impact and value. The problem is that we may not want to have what we consider to be waste in our lives, so we don't want times without productivity.

The great tragedy is how the lack of "white space" impacts us emotionally. We need to have "margin," the space between the text and the edge of the page.

Solomon said in Ecclesiastes 3:1, "*There is an appointed time for everything. And there is a time for every event under heaven.*" We need to embrace the seasons as they come and adjust to them; however, some of the negative influences in life can be and should be avoided.

I want to spend this chapter discovering how we can minimize the negative impact that other people and too many activities have in our lives, while learning to be productive and to truly love others. We will discover how to create "margin" in our lives, as well as how to set boundaries so we can experience optimum health emotionally. First, let's look at the impact people have in our lives.

Karrie's Story:
I remember the moment I first saw my firstborn, Karrie. I watched as her mother gave birth and I was so happy to see her that I couldn't stop laughing and crying at the same time. We didn't know she was a girl until she was born, so I was happily surprised. That day is one of my favorite days because I became a father for the first time. Karrie and I have always had a bond, a kind of beautiful understanding that for me was what I always wanted with my children.

Karrie was a fun kid and always made me laugh. Her affection was like life to me. Her wit and engaging personality were amazing, and I couldn't get enough. As she grew into her teen years, she exhibited some rebellion, but those moments were only temporary setbacks in our relationship. Along the way, Karrie began searching for something she wasn't getting at home. She wanted so desperately to be nurtured and loved. I was more the mentor and disciplinarian in her life. I think in some ways I needed her to fill the void of companionship in my life and confused the purpose of my role as a dad.

In her search, Karrie had fallen into friendships with those who wanted to experiment with drugs. She became deeply involved in a dual life of drugs and church. As a pastor and counselor, I should have seen her behavior as drug-induced, but totally missed it. For several years Karrie lived out a life of drugs and friendships that were unhealthy. I don't blame the friends she had for her drug use. I realize now that our dysfunctional home was the place where her heart was wounded and she was driven to find fulfillment in unhealthy ways. We talk about it now, and Karrie recounts being under the influence of drugs and telling her friends about the love of Christ. She had a wounded heart but still loved God and truth. She also loved her friends and wanted them to know Jesus, even though she was not personally living out her faith.

After graduation from high school, Karrie was standing at a cross-roads in life. The choice she made at this point was crucial for her future. This is the case for most kids growing up and questioning their purpose in life. Back in the summer of 1992, Karrie drove me to the airport to drop me off to catch a flight. She knew I was considering my future and I was thinking about moving from our city. That day was one of the most painful days I have ever had. Karrie walked me to the gate (this was long before the 9/11 restrictions) and she stood there and looked into my eyes and said, "Please, Daddy, get me out of here." Those words hit me like a ton of bricks. The Lord impressed upon me the urgency of her request. I knew these were deep and painful words for Karrie. I knew I had to leave Northern California to save the little girl that just eighteen years earlier was my most prized gift, precious and innocent. Some of that innocence was gone, but her preciousness to me was never stronger.

I got on the plane that day and was desperately asking God to help me save Karrie. I thought, too, that my broken marriage could be helped with the change. Forty-five days later, I moved my family to San Diego. Karrie immediately connected with friends who loved God and accepted her. She was now on a new journey; the course had been corrected and the change in her was permanent. The change was so demonstrative it was staggering. She found her love of the Lord and freedom from drugs. After a few incidents of failure, she is now many years sober. The beauty of those friends in our new church was a lifeline to my little girl. She was alive again.

There is no other way to put this than the "power of influence." She wanted to be whole. She wanted to live well. She simply needed the right people in her life. A few years later, Karrie started a ministry she called "Freedom Movement." The transformation to victory proved to be a lifelong journey. Even though there have been some mistakes in life, she has had an unwavering desire to correct her focus to the Lord even after great failures. This commitment to the Lord has been because of the people who were in her life. Karrie and I have enjoyed a special bond that is better than the best of friendships. In this chapter, I want to share how you can maximize your relationships for growth.

The power of words:
Proverbs 18:21 says, "*Death and life are in the power of the tongue, and those who love it will eat its fruit.*" The meaning of this is simple and profound. The words people speak have power, the power to bring life or death to the listener. The caveat is that the greater the love for the speaker, the greater the impact of their words on the listener.

People you love will influence your heart. For example, a negative word from a parent to a child arguably has the greatest influence in that child's life. We love our parents, and when they speak "words of death" we are devastated because we eat the fruit of the tongues of the ones we love. The verse says, "*and those who love it* (the tongue of the speaker) *will eat its fruit*." When you love the speaker, they impact your life. If you don't love the speaker, the impact is marginal. The key here is to value those who speak life.

Limiting the negative speech from people in our world is strategically wise. One of the most important ways to live free from negative emotions is to limit the access of negative words in our lives. I would call this "influence boundaries." This is an oversimplification, but based on Proverbs 18:21 there are two types of people in your life: lifegivers and killers. Your ability to recognize these individuals in your life will greatly help you limit the negative and accentuate the positive. We need to recognize both and set boundaries on killers and open our hearts to life-givers.

The Two-Teams Concept:
I see relationships in life with a view of those who speak life and those who speak death. I put people in two teams: those who are on my team and those who are my opponent's team in life. The other team is comprised of those who may or may not want to harm me, but for sure they are more interested in their own win. These are not the enemy; simply put, they are on the other team.

This two-team concept is not about who will receive my love. It is rather to whom I will grant access to my heart and who will be the greatest influencers in my life. The two-team concept helps me to see love not as a calling to allow unhealthy relationships in my life, but as a calling to give to others. We are to love well, while at the same time protecting our hearts from those who could do great damage to us.

We must be careful not to see people as an enemy to be opposed or a commodity to be used. People are to be respected and loved. We should "esteem others as more important than yourself" (Phil. 2:3). But this doesn't mean your resources should be depleted to the point that we become ineffective.

We also need to find the balance between understanding our limits and unhealthy self-protection. If we take the concept of two teams too far, we could easily fall into a life of paranoia or become overly judgmental. I freely admit that I tend to be defensive. This concept could feed into that so I must be very careful to see those on the other team in a balanced light.

Here it is, plain and simple: you must understand the value someone brings into your life. You need to understand who brings energy and who depletes you.

What the two-team concept is not:

1. A cause for paranoia
2. The development of a judgmental spirit
3. An excuse not to love unconditionally
4. The perception of people as tools to be used

What the two-team concept is:

1. A way to categorize people as to the impact they have in our lives: life givers or killers, Proverbs 18:21.
2. A way to gauge limits in our lives.
3. The way to set boundaries on the influencers.
4. A way to secure relationships that are crucial to growth.

Those on your team, life givers:

These are people in your life who are above the encouragement line, and they bring added value. You will want to maximize your time with these people. There are three kinds of "life givers" in our world: The Fan, the Teammate and the Coach. These are individuals who speak real life into our hearts. When you listen, you will be encouraged and make the changes necessary to grow. People speak into our lives from the standpoint of their own experience and personal relationship to us. This metaphor of sports may help to understand the impact of life givers on our emotional stability.

Your Coach: The coach in your life is the one who teaches you, guides you, holds you accountable and moves you into deeper growth. Your coach is someone with whom you will want to spend maximum time. You will learn new life skills and your coach will speak truth into your life. When you are trying to figure things out, this is the person you go to. You may have more than one coach in your life at any given time. The coach speaks from experience and knowledge of life.

Who: Your coaches are often your teachers, professors, mentors, pastors, group leaders, supervisors or parents. You need to know that just because someone holds one of these positions in your life, it doesn't guarantee they will be a good coach. You need to look to the results of their impact in your life to estimate their value.

Results: When you are around your coach you will be "equipped" for life. **The need for growth and change in your life will become inevitable.**

My coaches have been the men in my life who have meant the most to me. Other than my own family they have influenced me the most. I remember my first coach as a kid. It was in Little League. I was a small kid and the coach seemed like a giant to me. I thought this guy was a professional baseball player, but later realized he was a volunteer, probably one of the dads.

After three at bats in a row of striking out, I was discouraged. I went to him and said, "I'm not a good player, am I?" He put his arm around me and said, "Tim, all you need is a little help and you will be great." He started working with my batting skills. I never really was great at fielding the ball, but I became a really good hitter. He gave me confidence through his instruction, time, and love. I remember he was a big guy who would give the boys on our team attention, instruction, and love. I think these volunteer coaches are heroes.

You need those people in your life who will coach and mentor you so you will be equipped for life.

Your Teammate: Your teammates are many and they are always in the huddle with you. Your teammates support you because they are invested in your life. They want you to succeed because of their personal love for you. They listen to your input and acknowledge your worth. They are right next to you as life unfolds. These are the ones with whom you are doing life.

Who: Your teammates are friends, siblings and colleagues. Again, don't assume these roles in your life will guarantee these are your teammates. You need to discern their value in your life.

Results: When you are around your teammates you will be "comforted and strengthened." **The need for growth and change in your life will become clearer.**

Teammates in my world were my friends and support system. We joked together, worked out together, traveled together, and competed together. We loved the sports we were in and it pulled us into a special world of connection. As young kids we were able to console each other after losses and celebrate together after wins. We debriefed the reasons for wins and losses. We competed "with" each other and "against" other teams and aspired to become mature athletes together. These guys were the glue that held my life together outside my family.

Life without teammates would not be possible. We need this camaraderie and friendship. They bring added value to our lives. They "strengthen" us and make us better.

Your Fan: Your fans will speak inspiration into your life. Their value is limited by their involvement. They are on the sidelines, watching your life. You will enjoy being around these people because you are constantly inspired. This is an important part of growth, but sometimes you will find that even when you are not doing well, you will be encouraged to continue on in your life without really changing and growing.

Who: These are people who like your posts, read your tweets and think you're awesome. They watch you and speak into your life when you do well. They also may encourage you when your actions are not the best. This obviously is dangerous because it will impede your growth into maturity and change. These are people who may have varying relationships to you, but in distinction to your teammate are not alongside you in the game of life. They are on the sidelines, watching with curiosity and interest. They yell from the sideline, "Do well, we are watching and we believe in you."

Results: When you're around your fans you will be "inspired." This is crucial for survival in a difficult world. These are the people who could become your teammates, as your relationship grows closer with them. **The need for growth and change in your life will become easier.**

It was 1994 and I was sitting in the stands almost right on the fifty-yard line. I watched as the Chargers ran onto the field and the fans went wild. The Chargers had won their previous five games in a row. In a press conference that week, our coach had called for the "twelfth man" to show up for the game (the twelfth man is the fan.) After the coaches and players, the fans are the most important component of the win. The twelfth man was going to make a difference that day.

Junior Seau was an exciting linebacker with an incredible energy for his teammates and the fans in the stand. He would get the fans excited as he called for us to yell during the opposition's count. They could barely hear because we were so loud. The fans got the Chargers going and the Chargers got the fans going. That relationship is crucial in our lives. We need fans to help us stay "inspired" in life.

Those on the opposing team, killers:
These are people in your life who are below the encouragement line and bring little or no added value. You will want to limit the time spent with these people. There are three kinds of "killers" in our world: The Opposing Fan, the Opposing Players, and the Opposing Coach. These are individuals who speak death into our hearts. When you listen, you will be discouraged and will fail to make the changes necessary to grow. Just like the people on our team, these people speak into our lives from the standpoint of their own experience and personal relationship to us.

Opposing Fan: Those opposing fans can be heard cheering for others. They may even be yelling insults against you. Their interest is in their team or themselves. The problem is that we may not know that is what is going on in our relationships with them. Oftentimes we have relationships with others and don't discern that they are not interested in our growth, but are centered on their own interests. The damage they do to our hearts is minimal because we are not overly invested in their lives.

Who: The problem in identifying these opposing fans is that they may be our well-meaning but immature friends or siblings. Usually, these people don't speak against us but talk about themselves or gossip about others. These people are identifiable because they talk about people and not life skills or inspiring truth.

Results: When you are around the opposing fans, you will become "discouraged." They are not necessarily antagonistic toward you; they are simply interested in their own team and will discourage you by the lack of positive input into your life. **The need for growth and change will be impeded.**

I was playing basketball for my high school in Jackson, Wyoming. Our team was pretty good that year, and we were going to play a team that for some reason had these tall players. They were from a little town called Lusk, Wyoming. I think it was the first time Lusk was in contention for the state championship. We arrived at the gymnasium and the crowd was going wild.

We came onto the floor, and it was almost completely silent. Then, when the Lusk boys hit the floor, the crowd roared like I had never heard and didn't stop until the game was over. The opposing fans intimidated us and we couldn't think straight.

They didn't have to yell at us; they simply had to cheer for their team and leave us to fail. When someone is more interested in his or her win, you can become demoralized. You will become "discouraged." We lost the game that night.

Opposing Players: The opposing player is on the field of life hitting us hard, stealing the ball and fighting to win their own game. Sometimes the people on the opposing team are not attacking us but are simply trying to win their own game. Because they are immature and self-interested, we may not see them as an opposition to our growth, just flawed. They may be people who seemingly can't do anything on their own. They will tend to avoid responsibility for life, but will ask you to meet their needs. They are entitled and see no problem in taking from others. They are life stealers and will drain us of our vitality.

Who: The opposing players are comprised of just about anyone in our lives who is immature and selfish. They could be friends, parents, teachers, and siblings. We will know them by the self-centeredness and lack of interest in our growth.

Results: When you are around the opposing player, you will be "weakened." It will seem that your vitality is being drained from you. **The need for growth and change will become a battle.**

In my junior year I went out for football to show my brothers that I was tough. I had always done track and basketball. The first thing I noticed was how hard the opposing team hit. I never liked football. I guess I wasn't that tough. I remember being rocked so hard one day I wanted out of the game. I told the coach I was hurt, but in reality, I was scared and intimidated.

When the opposing players hit hard, they can steal your joy for the game, your ability to think, and your desire to win. If you are spending maximum time with the opposing team you will be greatly "weakened" in life.

Opposing Coach: The opposing coach has no desire for your win or for your health. In fact, he will do everything to defeat you. He will beat you down and take your vitality. He will kill your growth and maliciously undermine your emotional stability. In effect, he kills you.

Who: Malicious people who sometimes are deranged and beyond selfish and seek to destroy. Sometimes they are insidious and their destructive impact is hard to discern. You're getting beat up and don't know it.

Results: When you are around the opposing coach, you will be "destroyed." It is essential that you don't have much exposure to this person in your life. **The need for growth and change in your life will become seemingly impossible.**

Many of us remember the outbursts of Coach Bobby Knight of the Indiana Hoosiers, as the epitome of emotions to win. He would go crazy when things didn't go right. You may remember the chair-throwing incident. This is what most people think of as a coach who intimidates us as the opposing team. In reality, a more difficult coach to face in basketball would be John Wooden, who was much more strategic and balanced.

John Wooden was the most formidable coach in college basketball. He was wise and knew how to get a win for his team. It may not seem fair that I would put John Wooden as the example of the opposing coach in this metaphor, but I want you to know that when you are facing an opposing coach, he may not be out of control like a Bobby Knight. You may be facing the likes of John Wooden.

When you face a skilled and an in-control coach, he can leave you "destroyed" and your hope for a win decimated.

We need to master the influence in our lives through time allotment. When we say no to others, we are not saying no to love. We are saying no to negative impact. When we are saying yes to others, we are not playing favorites. We are saying yes to positive impact.

The Two-Team Concept is about answering the question: Who should get the most time on our calendars? Time is limited and we have to be wise when we choose with whom we will spend it. When we begin to understand the impact people have in our lives, we will begin to set our calendar accordingly.

The following chart should help to understand the people in your world:

People in your life	Connection	Impact on you	Added Value
Coach	Seasoned Counselor	Ignites your vitality	Equips X3 Plus
Teammate	Vested Participant	Shares your vitality	Strengthens X2 Plus
Fan	Spectator	Catches your vitality	Encourages Plus
Line of Encouragement and Vitality			
Opposing Fans	Reckless disregard	Drains your vitality	Discourages Negative
Opposing Players	Competition	Destroys your vitality	Weakens X2 Negative
Opposing Coach	Strategic opponent	Undermines your life	Destroys X3 Negative

The distinction between "margin" and "boundaries."
The way I will use these terms is a simple distinction as follows: Margin is the control of my life's activities to create appropriate space to allow for rest, whereas boundaries is the control of others intruding on my margin. This is really a matter of scheduling out time and activities. The way we set our calendar needs to reflect our value for margin, white space that gives us rest and clarity. We become more effective and more attractive with margin in our lives.

When I create margin, I'm limiting my activities to a tolerable level. When I set boundaries, I'm stopping others from negatively intruding in my life. That is to say, margin is the restriction of myself, whereas a boundary is the restriction of others.

Creating Margin: (Protection from self)
This is not about being a victim; this is about controlling your limits to live maturely and responsibly with your resource: time, money, emotional stability.

We need to live free from "shoulds" and "should haves" that are not based on true values and responsibility. False responsibility may be nothing more than our way of seeking perfection and control, and in so doing we live without control. We may feel guilty about not meeting someone's needs, and we are driven to try to do for everyone. The "shoulds" are those things we feel we should do, but may not be our responsibilities.

Remember Stephen Covey's ABC organization approach I mentioned in Chapter 9; we need to put on our list of responsibilities only those things that rise to the level of important, urgent and our responsibilities. The other things we commit to may be detrimental to our lives.

Andy Stanley puts our responsibility in this way: when he speaks to his staff, he tells them, "***Do for one what you wish you could do for all.***" That is great advice, not only to the overworked pastor, but also for anyone who tends to over commit or maybe better said, "wrongly commit."

We need to ask the following questions before we commit:

1. Is this the best use of my time?
2. Is this something only I can do?
3. Will this injure me emotionally or spiritually?

4. Can this be delegated to someone else?

Setting boundaries: (Protection from others)
For the sake of your emotional stability, you need to learn to say no to people. The failure to do this will lead to stress you can't afford. Here are some specific ways to communicate to people your limits:

1. **Let others know you are limited in resources and may not be able to meet their needs.** This should take the form of a kind but clear declaration; for example, "I'm sorry, but I'm not going to be able to meet with you." Or "I don't have the availability in my schedule." Don't explain it, just give the simple statement and allow them to process this. When we put too much explanation in the statement, we sound defensive.

2. **Give others reasonable choices with consequences**. In some cases, they will persist. Don't allow it to be about power. You have the power over your schedule in most cases. If you make this about power, you may lose yourself in the struggle. Be clear that you can't continue under the present conditions. Try to give him/her reasonable options for his/her needs to be met, another person they can go to, or another avenue to have a job accomplished.

3. **Give others time to change.** Don't expect a positive response from "below the line people," that is, the opposing team. They may have become used to you always saying yes and may personalize your unwillingness to continue. Let them process and then come back to reassure them this is about your need for boundaries. This may not be

acceptable to them, but the truth has been stated and they will adjust.

4. **Be prepared to enforce your limits**. Setting boundaries is useless if not enforced. If someone is unwilling to respect your boundaries you will need to give reasonable consequences for that lack of respect. It's important to set consequences that are reasonable, enforceable, and within your authority. Remember, your goal is to have margin in your life, not to devastate others.

5. **Don't use setting boundaries as an excuse for selfish living**. God has called us to sacrificial giving. We should be careful to give within our means. It may be helpful to ask the following questions:

   1. Am I not giving out of fear?
   2. Am I not giving because I'm lazy?
   3. Am I not giving because of lack of love?
   4. Am I being pushed beyond my ability to meet the need?

   Note: This is not about controlling others; it is about controlling your influences. This is about living within reasonable tolerances for a healthy and productive life.

Two kinds of boundaries:
We need to make a distinction between two types of boundaries, Flexible and Rigid. Clearly there are times where our boundaries are not rigid, and this should be understood going into a discussion with others about boundaries. This chart will help to give the characteristics of the two kinds of boundaries:

Level 1 Flexible Boundary	Level 2 Rigid Boundaries
Negotiable	Nonnegotiable
Tolerable	Intolerable
Reasonably sacrificial	Unhealthy sacrifice
Healthy needs	Unhealthy demands
Productive	Unproductive
No Compromising	Compromise values

You should have a clear understanding in your own mind what kind of boundary you are setting before the conversation takes place. A helpful exercise is to list on a piece of paper the demands that come without the boundary. Take the list and put one of the characteristics from the chart next to the demand. This will then help you to analyze the nature of the boundary and it will become clear what kind of boundary it is.

Jesus and margin:

In Mark 6:30-32, Jesus gives some great instruction about boundaries. This was more than a call to rest, it was a call to boundaries. Look at these verses:

> *The apostles gathered together with Jesus; and they reported to Him all that they had done and taught. 31 And He said to them, "Come away by yourselves to a secluded place and rest a while." (For there were many people coming and going, and they did not*

> *even have time to eat.) 32 They went away in the boat to a secluded place by themselves.*

Note that Jesus told them to do two things: First, come away, and second, rest awhile, that is, experience the white space of life.

Just because someone has a need doesn't mean you have an obligation. This sense of obligation will destroy your growth and steal your joy. You should acknowledge, as Jesus does, that not every need will be met by you.

In the classic book, ***Crucial Conversations***[4], the authors talk about how to deal with emotions in our conversations. We need to learn to be assertive before aggression takes over. Most of us who struggle with toxic emotions tend to move between "silence" (that is shutting up and saying nothing) and "violence" (that is, the tendency to lash out to win or punish) instead of setting reasonable boundaries. Because we are trying to prove our worth, we tend to be overcommitted and then resent the demands of our commitment.

Without setting boundaries, it will usually lead to aggression internally or even externally. Set the boundaries, be clear and kind, and you will find others will adjust and you will live emotionally balanced.

---

[4] Crucial Conversations, Tools for talking when stakes are high, Kerry Patterson, McGraw-Hill Books, New York, 2012, pages 59-61

Chapter 10 Life skills:

Evaluate the people in your life: Who is on my team? Who is on the opposing team? How much time is spent with these people? Create a chart of people and add a column for time spent with them. You will be able to gauge your emotional health in large part by the exposure these people have in your life.

This should be done on a regular basis to truly be helpful in reallocating your time for your own emotional health.

People in your life	Connection	Impact on you	Added Value	Who and how often are they on my calendar?
Coach	Seasoned Counselor	Ignites your vitality	Equips X3 Plus	
Team-mate	Vested Participant	Shares your vitality	Strengthens X2 Plus	
Fan	Spectator	Catches your vitality	Encourages Plus	
Line of Encouragement and Vitality				
Opposing Fans	Reckless disregard	Drains your vitality	Discourages Negative	
Opposing Players	Competition	Destroys your vitality	Weakens X2 Negative	
Opposing Coach	Strategic opponent	Undermines your life	Destroys X3 Negative	

Write down the boundaries that need to be set in your life. Be specific. Write down what you should say to the person who needs to be confronted; be clear and loving without giving excuses.

Make a list on a piece of paper the demands in your life. Take the list and put one of the characteristics of the demands:

1. Flexible boundaries:
   Negotiable, Tolerable, Reasonably sacrificial, Healthy needs, Productive, No compromising

2. Rigid boundaries:
   Nonnegotiable, Intolerable, Unhealthy sacrifice, Unhealthy demands, Unproductive, Compromise values

Analyze the nature of the boundary, and it will become clear what kind of boundary it is, and hold your ground strongly.

Memorize Proverbs 18:21

> *"Death and life are in the power of the tongue, and those who love it will eat its fruit."* **(Proverbs 18:21)**

Chapter 11: Perfectionism and the Need to Control:

Living With Appropriate Expectations of Self and Others

"My soul, wait in silence for God only, for my hope is from Him only. He only is my rock and my salvation, my stronghold; I shall not be shaken." (Psalm 62:5,6)

The need for control is strong in us. We want safety and for many of us this means control of our world: the people, the economy, our health, our careers, our reputation and our image, just to name a few areas. One of the problems is in our world there are many things that are uncontrollable. So, we develop strategies, flawed though they may be, to try to control the uncontrollable.

In Chapter 8 we discussed how some people go to the extreme of obsessive irrational thoughts. Most of us don't struggle with these thoughts all the time, but we do in many ways seek to control our world. The best way to deal with this is to change our focus and adjust our expectations, which will relieve much of the pressure from our lives. My goal in this chapter is to explore the strategy of adjusted expectations to combat our perfectionism and need to control.

Linda's Story:
It was not until after Linda's suicide that I truly realized how the need to control was fundamental to her strategy for survival. Nothing was more profound in relation to her struggle than an entry in one of her journals. She wrote, "I have thrown up five times and I still don't feel better." What did this mean?

To those who have little experience with eating disorders, this may seem strange. However, from my observation, Linda was really doing two things: First, through purging, she was addressing a practical solution to her body image distortions by getting rid of calories. This was an issue of control. Her ability to stay thin through binging and purging was her ill-conceived strategy to be loved. The second issue she was addressing in her note about purging was by throwing up she was purging "badness" (her word) from her life. That's right; when she would throw up, she believed her "badness" would leave her. She then was able to control the evil that she perceived was inside her.

In a therapy session I attended with Linda, the therapist gave a vignette that hit on Linda's struggle. We sat stunned as he shared this story:

> *"There was a professional woman who was fastidious about house cleaning and felt stuck. She would obsess about her house while at work. There were times that she would have to leave work for her lunch break and make sure that her house was clean enough. This carried on for some time and it only got worse where she would be forced to leave work several times to check on her house.*
>
> *After a great deal of therapy and soul searching, she concluded that she was driven to perfection because she felt her mother never accepted her. She knew her mother loved her but she just was never accepted.*
>
> *One day she had left to go to work after having cleaned the house extensively and began to wonder how the control could have been given to her mother. In an unusual act of defiance, she turned her car around, went to her bed and pulled back the comforter and threw the pillows on the floor and said out loud,* ***"Hell No, Mother!"*** *She got back in her car and had the most focused day at work ever. Every time she thought about the pillows on the floor, she laughed.*

> *Eventually, she got the courage to talk to her mother and through a series of well-orchestrated therapy sessions, she and her mother were able to reconcile their relationship. The woman began to heal and to this day is free from an obsession about her home's cleanliness."*

Linda's therapist looked directly into her eyes and said, "It's time for you to take the power back from your mother. You need to control your own life." He had uncovered the obvious truth; Linda was fighting her mother every day, trying to win approval, trying to break free from her mother's control.

Out of pain we didn't explore this as we should have and we never were able to see Linda extricate herself from the perception of her mother's control. I want to be clear: for the most part, her mother was not seeking control. This was a matter of Linda's perception. The years of her mother's disapproval led Linda to believe her mother wanted control. If Linda could have gotten a grip on the control issues, her life would have turned out differently.

When the need to control reaches the level of obsession, it can destroy our lives by turning us upside down emotionally. The drive toward having a perfect world, that is, perfectionism, is about control. To really get to the heart of the issue, we need to go through a process of understanding: First, we will look at the need to adjust our expectations. Second, we will explore how we fit into this world we find ourselves in by discussing "spatial awareness." Third, we will look at the locus of control (location of control) and how this impacts our emotional stability.

The problem with expectations
The higher our expectations of self and others, the more vulnerable to emotional excesses we become. We not only have expectation demands on people, but we also have expectations on life and even on God. Stress and anxiety are usually connected to our expectations. If we could learn to adjust our expectations, we would make great strides toward emotional stability.

There is a big difference between "lowered expectations" and "adjusted expectations." When we lower our expectations, we are accepting a lowered quality of life and mediocre living. With lowered expectations we will not pursue growth or achievement; we will settle for less than the best. Life will be less than fulfilling, and we will rarely if ever experience exceeding joy. Happiness will be found in a kind of ascetic life of self-denial, which is not a resilient life-giving happiness. What we really need to do is adjust our expectations and experience an abiding happiness.

There are four things that constitute an adjusted expectation:

1. Redirected source.
2. Redirected values.
3. Redirected outcomes.
4. Redirected prayers.

Redirected source: Our expectations always have a direction. The direction of most people who experience frustration and anxiety is toward things out of their control. What the wise person does is look to the one who has the power over circumstances today and in the future. We need to look to a loving, sovereign God.

Here is how David put it in Psalm 62:

> "1 *My soul waits in silence for God only; From Him is my salvation. 2 He only is my rock and my salvation, my stronghold; I shall not be greatly shaken.*" (Psalm 62:1-2)

> "5 *My soul, wait in silence for God only, for my hope is from Him only. 6 He only is my rock and my salvation, my stronghold; I shall not be shaken.*" (Psalm 62:5-6)

In verses 1 and 2 David makes four declarations:

1. I wait for God.
2. My salvation is from God.
3. God is my rock.
4. God is my stronghold.

He then makes it clear that as a result he will not be "*greatly shaken.*" Whereas in verses 5 and 6, where David restates these four declarations but adds one more component, "*For my hope is from Him,*" the result is changed to "*I will not be shaken.*" This simple observation will help us understand the power of "redirected source." When God is your strength, but you are still expecting things out of life, you will make yourself vulnerable to emotional instability.

The distinction between "*being greatly shaken*" and "*being shaken*" is substantial. For example, if you are in an earthquake and you are not "*greatly shaken,*" you could experience some pretty extensive damage. But if you are in an earthquake, and you are not "*shaken*" (at all), the earthquake has no impact on you.

What you must realize is that David is giving a key to making your life strong and stable, emotionally and spiritually. This key is after you have waited, seen God as your rock, salvation and your stronghold, you need to expect only from Him. God becomes your focus of expectation; He becomes your redirected source. He won't fail, whereas others often do.

To properly understand the implications of what David is saying, let's look at the word he used in the original Hebrew for "*hope*." Hope is translated from the word "*tiqvah*," which means expectation. This is significant, because it symbolizes the connection of one thing to another as a cord. In fact, the meaning of the word is both "*hope*" and "*cord*." The idea is that our expectation is connected to God, and we are tethered to Him. This connection will give us hope, but it is with expectation that we look in the direction of God, thereby having a "redirected source" of life, an "adjusted expectation."

Joshua wrote about the deliverance of Rahab from the destruction of Jericho and used the word *Tiqvah* to describe the cord she would use to be saved:

> *"18 Behold, when we come into the land, you shall tie this scarlet cord (Tiqvah) in the window through which you let us down, and you shall gather into your house your father and mother, your brothers, and all your father's household. 19 Then if anyone goes out of the doors of your house into the street, his blood shall be on his own head, and we shall be guiltless. But if a hand is laid on anyone who is with you in the house, his blood shall be on our head. 20 But if you tell this business of ours, then we shall*

> *be guiltless with respect to your oath that you have made us swear.*" (Joshua 2:18-20)

This is such a great picture of the heart of God for deliverance for those who are obedient in faith. But to my point, it is the meaning of the word "*tiqvah*" that is our interest. The word clearly is a cord, the cord of connection between God and our hearts, our expectations, our hope. When we redirect our hope toward God, we set ourselves on the path of emotional stability, "*and I shall not be shak*en."

To put a practical approach to this, we should put our RSTs to work. Reinforcing the truth. You might speak this truth: "God is all I need" or "God is with me and never will leave me." Or "God is my hope and I will trust in Him." These simple truths stated over and over in the midst of turmoil help us to redirect our source of expectation to God, not to what He will provide, but His presence with us. It would be a great exercise to write down as many truths about how God is present in our lives and RST each truth.

On this matter of redirected source, we should understand that our hope should not be in the future of this life but in eternity. Life is manageable today with the presence of God and life will be perfect in heaven. Allow perfection to take place in heaven and be content with the presence of God in the fallen world; He is our strength.

Redirected values: One of the biggest problems with expectations and our emotional vulnerability is an incorrect value system. For example, look at the teaching of Jesus on the contrast between loving God and loving wealth.

> *"24 No one can serve two masters; for either he will hate the one and love the other, or he will be devoted to one and despise the other. You cannot serve God and wealth. 25 "For this reason I say to you, do not be worried about your life, as to what you will eat or what you will drink; nor for your body, as to what you will put on. Is not life more than food, and the body more than clothing? 26 Look at the birds of the air, that they do not sow, nor reap nor gather into barns, and yet your heavenly Father feeds them. Are you not worth much more than they?"* (Matthew 6:24-26)

Jesus is teaching a key principle in emotional freedom. Notice His concern is not that you would have money or be wealthy, but rather that you would not worry, verse 25. Jesus' teaching on the pitfalls of money and wealth is that one would put their expectations on it, not that they would have money.

Paul wrote to Timothy about money and was clear, money is not the root of all evil; it is the *love* of money that is the problem, 1 Timothy 6:10:

> *"For the love of money is a root of all sorts of evil, and some by longing for it have wandered away from the faith and pierced themselves with many griefs (distress)."* (1 Timothy 6:10)

Distress is derived from putting our expectations on something other than faith in God. God is our provider, our sustainer, and He is all we need.

Our life is to be about God's glorification, not our gratification. In fact, Paul stated this concept in this way, "*For me to live is Christ,*" in Philippians 1:21. When we make life about our gratification, we create a vulnerability that God never intended for us to experience.

We need to RST our purpose in life. "I'm here to serve God" or "My life's purpose is to bring glory to Christ" or "God will supply all my needs according to His plan, I'm not worried about anything, I trust Him,"

Redirected Outcomes: The average person will speak of the quality of life as a life that includes four things: 1 health, 2 wealth, 3 families and 4 social belonging. Most would agree there are other factors, such as spiritual maturity and acts of benevolence. But at the core of quality of life, for most people, it revolves around the big four.

We make ourselves emotionally vulnerable when the outcomes of life control our happiness. In fact, we can't find peace without outcomes cooperating with our expectations. The key in adjusting our expectations is to adjust our view of the real important outcomes of life. What is life supposed to produce? How much do I need to be happy? Can I be happy even though I may be experiencing declining health or financial loss?

> "*10 The thief comes only to steal and kill and destroy. I came that they may have life and have it abundantly. 11 I am the good shepherd. The good shepherd lays down his life for the sheep.*" (John 10:10-11)

Many Christians have been caught up in what I call the "Abundant Life Myth," that is, God wants us to have more. In this false view of Jesus' promise to produce the "abundant life," is the idea that Christ came to give us more of the big four: health, wealth, family, and social belonging. The myth that has been perpetuated by well-meaning but misguided leaders is that Jesus will give us surplus or even an excessive amount of provisions.

A closer look at John 10 reveals the abundant life is a promise of simple protection and provisions of a shepherd with his sheep. Jesus was contrasting Himself with the hired hand who runs when danger arrives. Jesus promised protection because He truly was the Good Shepherd watching out for the sheep. The abundant life is not "more stuff" but the simple protection and basic provisions for the sheep by the Good Shepherd. To make it different than this is to miss the promise and to create a false expectation. When the false expectation is a part of our belief system, we are set up for misery.

Redirected Prayers: Christians tend to see prayer as a tool to get what we want from God. Of course, that doesn't work, so we blame God for being inconsiderate or we blame ourselves for not having enough faith.

Here is the reality about prayer: it is a means to communion with God and a means to align our heart with His. Let's look at the Lord's Prayer:

> *"7 And when you are praying, do not use meaningless repetition as the Gentiles do, for they suppose that they will be heard for their many words. 8 "So do not be like them; for your Father knows what you need before you ask Him. 9 "Pray, then, in this way: 'Our Father who is in heaven, Hallowed be Your name. 10 'Your kingdom come. Your will be done,*

> *On earth as it is in heaven. 11 'Give us this day our daily bread. 12 'And forgive us our debts, as we also have forgiven our debtors. 13 'And do not lead us into temptation, but deliver us from evil. For Yours is the kingdom and the power and the glory forever. Amen.'* (Matthew 6:7-13)

Without getting deep into the context and why Jesus was presenting this teaching, notice that our Father knows what we need before we ask, verses 7-8. Jesus is not presenting a way to move God to act on your behalf. Praying according to Jesus should follow a certain pattern. Here in simplicity is the content of prayer:

1. Worship God, verse 9
2. Submission to the will of God, verse 10
3. Request for this day's provision, verse 11
4. Reconciliation with God and man, verse 12
5. Request for divine power to deliver us from temptation, verse 13

We have turned prayer into something it is not, an opportunity to plead with the Almighty to get what He never promised. Jesus said, pray like this, "...give us this day our daily bread..." We should be asking only for what we need for the moment. We are not told to ask for a storehouse full of excess. If we could make this adjustment of our expectations to what we need for this moment, we could live by faith and be free from the "demandingness" of the soul.

The key here is not to lower expectations but to adjust/redirect out expectations. We need to have high standards, and we can even be ambitious in many ways, but we need to adjust our expectations. Here is why we should adjust our expectations: The greater the distance between reality and your expectations, the greater your misery. We will call this the "misery factor." Notice the chart below:

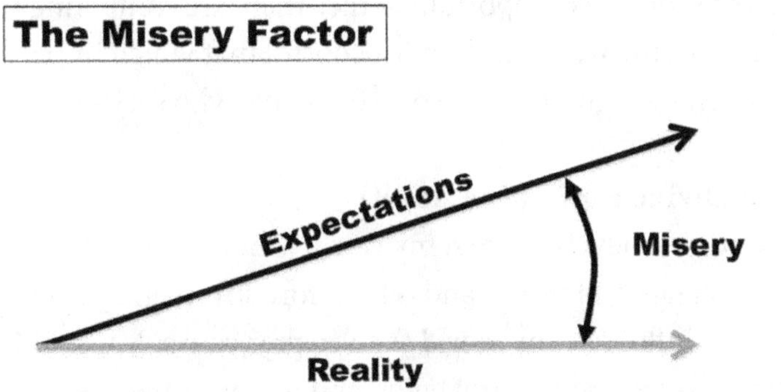

Personal misery is based on the distance between our reality and our expectations

Spatial Awareness and the need to control

The term "Spatial Awareness" is most often used to refer to a person's ability to judge the location of themselves in relation to the objects around them. The term is also used to refer to one's sense of themselves in relation to the world around them, that is, social psychology. Who am I in this world? How do I fit? What is the purpose of people around me?

Maturity can be seen in the transformation of one's spatial awareness. Here's how it works:

Stage 1: Personal world (The infant)

Infants start out with this view: I am the center of all things. The world exists for my needs. Life is about my gratification and me. Others are in my world to serve my needs.

Stage 2: Social world (The Adolescent)
Adolescents develop this view; other people have needs, which compete with my needs. When my needs are heightened, the needs of others become less important to me. There are competing forces for control of my world and I must control that which impacts me. I must learn to negotiate in a world of people who seek dominance.

Stage 3: Divine world (The Adult)
Mature adult's view becomes: my world is not about me but about God who created all things and is therefore sovereign. My purpose in life is to influence my world for a higher cause. My goal in life is to love God with all of my being and to love others as myself.

The chart below shows the stages of growth:

Spatial Awareness		
Stage 1 Personal world (The Infant)	Stage 2 Social world (The Adolescent)	Stage 3 Divine world (The Adult)
Sensitive to self and intolerant of others	Suspicious	Sensitive and tol-erant of others
Entitled	Competitive	Empowered
Takers	Manipulators	Contributors
Fears control	Negotiates for Control	Self-controlled by trust in a sovereign God

Emotional maturity is found not only in our view of ourselves, but also those around us and how we relate to them. We will begin to change our spatial awareness when we see others and ourselves through the grid of scripture.

A passage of scripture that helps us understand our spatial awareness is Philippians 2:3-4:

> "*3 Do nothing from selfishness or empty conceit, but with humility of mind regard one another as more important than yourselves; 4 do not merely look out for your own personal interests, but also for the interests of others.*" (Philippians 2:3-4)

The concept of seeing other people's needs as "*more important*" than your own needs is counterintuitive. A life without concern for your own needs is not a new standard. This is the old standard, "*love your neighbor as yourself.*" Look at verse 4 and you see that your involvement with the needs of others does not negate the awareness of your own needs. Spatial awareness is not seeing yourself as unimportant, but rather intentionally seeing yourself as a contributor to the needs of others in this life.

A second passage that is helpful in understanding spatial awareness is Matthew 20:26-28:

> "*26 It is not this way among you, but whoever wishes to become great among you shall be your servant, 27 and whoever wishes to be first among you shall be your slave; 28 just as the Son of Man did not come to be served, but to serve, and to give His life a ransom for many.*" (Matthew 20:26-28)

Greatness has always been about achievement and success in the minds of man. Jesus, however, has redefined greatness as service for others. A man with mature spatial awareness is one who sees life as giving and meeting needs, not self-gratification. Matthew 20:28 says even Jesus, "*The Son of Man came to serve.*"

When we are able to redefine the meaning and purpose of life to service, our spatial awareness changes, and we begin to experience real emotional healing through service. With this view we would say, "I will enjoy life when I serve and love well."

The Parable of the Fools' Gold:

> *A boy found a rock on a hillside where he had been told there was gold. He saw this small rock with its shiny gold color and was convinced that he was rich. He showed it to his friends and they were jealous of his newfound wealth. Before long he decided to take it to have the value determined. When he showed it to the expert, he was told the rock had no value and that all he had found was "fools' gold." The boy had never heard of fools' gold and inquired as to its value. The man said it again: this rock is worthless.*
>
> *The boy was ashamed and afraid that his friends would find out he had mistaken a worthless rock for real value. He spent his life trying to hide the lack of value from his envious friends. Most days he was successful.*

Thinking that you have found something of great value may be an illusion. What do you really have? What have you really accomplished? What is really important? We don't ask these questions; we ask, "What does man think is valuable?"

Life has only real meaning in serving others. For those struggling with negative emotions that dominate the mind, rethinking value in life is essential to emotional balance. Drop the fools' gold and invest in real meaning in your life.

Locus of Control (LOC)

Locus of Control (from the Latin meaning location) has to do with our perspective of the location of the control of our life, either internal (in our power) or external (in the power of others, fate or even God.) An external LOC can cause fear-based emotional problems.

In some cases, when our life is out of our control, we will seek other ways to bring about a sense of control. Dave's story will illustrate this.

Dave's Story:

Dave was a pastor who was successful by almost anyone's standard. He had a strong growing ministry, a beautiful wife and three wonderful kids. When people met Dave, they were immediately taken by his intelligence and creativity. He was not only a gifted speaker, he was also a talented musician. There are people in this world who have the charisma to draw people to them; Dave was one of these who had followers who adored him. He was a triple threat: talent, intelligence and charisma.

Dave's need to control others was seen by the people in his church to a certain degree and by his family to the extreme. He had rules in his church that were in some ways oppressive. For example, the people had to dress in certain ways when coming to church. He was against many forms of entertainment and his children had to be homeschooled. The rules were presented as spiritual disciplines but were actually a need/drive. Dave had to control his world. This need to control was pathological. He didn't realize what he was doing and probably thought his intentions were well meaning, but the drive to control the controllable areas of life was an obsession.

His discipline of his children was excessive, including times of confinement in their rooms or in a bathroom. The spankings were more like beatings. The children and his wife lived in fear of Dave. He was miserable and so was his family. The people in his church who saw these things ignored them because of his ability to talk himself out of bad situations and to put a spiritual spin on almost any behavior.

As people began to see problems, Dave felt compelled to leave his church and move to a new location. After years of moving from church to church, it became obvious to those close to Dave that something was wrong, but no one knew the extent of Dave's secret life.

Because Dave was raised with Christian values, the secret world he was living was especially hard for him to reconcile with his ministry. The theological paradigm he grew up in was one of ranking sins. That is, there were acceptable sins and unacceptable sins. One of the most rejected sins was homosexuality. The church he grew up in implied that if you were homosexual, you were not a Christian.

Dave's earliest memories of sexual desire were homosexual. And now, here he was a pastor, preaching family values, and yet he was tortured over his sexual drive. If his wife discovered his true sexuality, he feared he would be divorced and lose his family. If the people in the church found out about his struggle, he would be publicly shamed and out of the ministry.

To make matters worse for Dave was that he was not trying to restrain his appetite for sexual encounters. He was not struggling with fighting the urge to act out sexually, he was struggling with getting caught for the excessive and his almost daily anonymous homosexual encounters. The fact that Dave was unable to control his sexual appetite was the uncontrollable issue in his life. In Chapter 8, I gave some teaching on the destructive power of "uncontrollable threats" in our lives. As I said, these uncontrollable threats can lead us to irrational thoughts. Similarly, "uncontrollable actions" in the case of Dave led to "controllable disciplines," such as rules in the church and home. This, in a convoluted way, brought a sense of dignity to Dave's out-of-control lifestyle. He would control what he found to be controllable.

Living with this lie took its toll on Dave's life. Eventually, his wife found out about his sexual unfaithfulness and his house of cards came tumbling down. Dave was stuck; in his mind, he had one of two options: gain power over the sexual addiction or denounce his faith. Unfortunately, Dave took the route of denouncing his faith and indulging in further sexual addiction.

The point of this is: when you are living an uncontrolled life, you will seek control of something. This leads to a life of misery. We need to realize that the consequence of an out-of-control life often will lead to excessive control somewhere.

Internal locus of control

This individual who perceives the control believes his/her behavior is guided by his/her personal decisions and efforts. Those with a high internal locus of control have better control of their behavior.

1. They take responsibility for their actions, successes, and failures.
2. They are more confident.
3. They have less stress.
4. They are more proactive and seek to influence through leadership.

External locus of control

This individual believes his/her behavior is guided by other external circumstances. Some with external locus of control may fear there are conspiracies at work against them. Those with high external locus of control have a greater tendency for a life of fear and to feel helpless. They are more likely to become depressed. They look for people and events to provide safety for them.

1. They blame others for their actions, successes, and failures.
2. They are often insecure.
3. They have higher stress.
4. They are passive and yet demanding (often this is not verbalized).

When external LOC is properly seen under the care of a sovereign and loving God, we derive great comfort. Any attempt to change our locus of control should be with proper view of God's sovereignty.

Taking back control:

First, we must understand that LOC is not a constant. It changes from one environment to another. For example, a CEO may have strong internal LOC at work and yet experiences external LOC at home.

Here are some steps toward changing from external to internal LOC:

1. Make a list of your options when feeling helpless. Oftentimes, we have more control than we think. For example, a budget that is written down and followed can change the financial LOC from external to internal.

2. Take your feared scenarios to their ultimate conclusion and write down how you feel about the fear. Then ask yourself if these truly are a threat that is worth the negative emotions you are feeling. Oftentimes, we have catastrophized a situation; and it is not really out of our control it is only in our minds. This is why it is helpful to let the scenario play all the way out, and most often we will see the ridiculous nature of our fear and realize the LOC is actually internal, not external.

3. Submit to God's control in prayer. When we "*cast our care upon God*" (1 Pet. 5:7), we take back the control within the sphere of our safety. That is, even though we may not have control personally, we know God who is almighty loves us and He has control. This will bring strong stability to our lives emotionally.

4. Use RSTs to overcome these feelings of helplessness. "I have options," "God is in control of all things," "God sees me and loves me," "God will never forsake me." Of course, the value of RSTs are the reinforced aspect of truth. You

must repeat this over and over for them to really begin to shape your beliefs.

Perfectionists and control

There is a difference between someone committed to excellence and a perfectionist. The perfectionist has lost himself/herself in the matter of control. The need to control one's environment drives a set of unwanted problems emotionally and socially. When we are committed to excellence, we are still able to see the ceiling of our ability. The problem with a perfectionist is that there are no limits to their expectations. An extreme perfectionist believes there are two kinds of people: 1) perfect people and 2) failures. He knows he is flawed and therefore he perceives himself to be a failure.

Taking what we have learned in this chapter, we should understand the perfectionist tendencies in the following three ways:

1. The perfectionist has high expectation needs and finds it difficult or impossible to adjust his or her expectations.

2. The perfectionist has immature spatial awareness. The perfectionist will tend to see others as in the way of their perfect world. They will also struggle with their own failure to meet the self-imposed need to be accepted as perfect by others.

3. The perfectionist has an external LOC. He or she will see the control out of reach. The need to always strive for better for the "perfect" will cause him or her to live in constant misery.

Overcoming perfectionism through the "LET GO" principle in the Lord's Prayer:

L–Let God be God
E–Expect God's will to be done
T–Thank God for today's provisions

G–Give room for reconciliation
O–Overcome temptation by God's power

Let God be God: "*Our Father who is in heaven, Hallowed be Your name.*" Worshiping God is putting God in His proper place. We in truth say, "God is God and I am not." If God is God, then He can handle the control, and if I'm not, I don't need to control. As well, God is perfect, but I don't need to be because I'm not God. What a relief!

Expect God's will to be done: "*Your Kingdom come. Your will be done, on earth as it is in heaven.*" The problem with the need to control is that we want our will to be done. When we pray properly, we are transferring our agenda from our outcome to His. We become free from this transfer to enjoy whatever God chooses to do.

Thank God for today's provisions: "*Give us this day our daily bread.*" Jesus teaches us to ask for the simple provision of the day's needs. We are constantly striving for more, but to be thankful dislodges the stronghold of selfish ambition. The freedom to be overwhelmingly satisfied with what you have comes from an intentional and reinforced thankfulness.

Give room for reconciliation: "*And forgive us our debts, as we also have forgiven our debtors.*" So much guilt can be avoided by having our debts taken care of, creating room for reconciliation. To release others of their obligations is to have freedom from "justice control." Justice control is what perfectionists strive for in life. Perfectionists are always trying to set things straight, make things right. This is a lot of pressure and creates stress for the perfectionist. When we seek forgiveness of our debts to God, we are reminded of our need, and then when we release others, we release the justice control of life. You don't have to control all the injustices in the world.

Overcome temptation by God's power: *"And do not lead us into temptation, but deliver us from evil."* The sense of obligation to perform for God is intense in most of us. What a relief that when we submit to God, He will lead us away from evil. Our primary goal should be to submit to God, and He will produce strength in the temptation as He leads us away from evil.

Chapter 11 Life skills:

Make a list of things, places or people who cause you fear or a sense of helplessness. Write down what you believe is causing this fear. Divide your fears into two groups: 1) Realistic fears, 2) Unrealistic fears. Spend time analyzing the real threat if you were to let go of emotional control.

Adjust your expectations through redirection:

Redirected source: God is your only source of hope and expectation.

Redirected values: The value in life is Christ, *"for me to live is Christ."*

Redirected outcome: I don't need more; I simply need Christ's protection and provision.

Redirected prayer: My prayers are not about what I want God to give but rather worship of God with a simple request for today's basic provisions.

Spatial awareness and reclaiming your Locus of Control

1. Make a list of your options when feeling helpless.
2. Take your feared scenarios to their ultimate conclusion and write down how you feel about the fear.
3. Submit to God's control in prayer by positively affirming His love and sovereignty in your life.
4. Use RSTs to overcome these feelings of helplessness. "I have options," "God is in control of all things," "God sees me and loves me," "God will never forsake me."

Apply the "LET GO" principle of the Lord's Prayer:

Let God be God.
Expect God's will to be done.
Thank God for today's provisions.
Give room for reconciliation.
Overcome temptation by God's power.

Memorize Psalm 62:5-6

> *"5 My soul, wait in silence for God only, for my hope/expectation is from Him only. 6 He only is my rock and my salvation, my stronghold; I shall not be shaken."* (Psalm 62:5-6)

Chapter 12: The Power of Love:

Putting Attention on the Needs of Others: An Essential Step to Relief

"11 For this is the message that you have heard from the beginning, that we should love one another. 14 We know that we have passed out of death into life, because we love the brothers. Whoever does not love abides in death. 16 By this we know love, that he laid down his life for us, and we ought to lay down our lives for the brothers. 18 Little children, let us not love in word or talk but in deed and in truth." (1 John 3:11,14,16,18)

Most people who struggle with negative emotions tend to withdraw from others as a strategy of self-protection. Ironically, this does just the opposite. We seek seclusion to protect ourselves and we end up getting worse emotionally. Things are made worse because the problem is not others; it is our reactions to others. This chapter is about exploring our divinely given purpose of loving others as a strategy for relief from negative emotions. I call this strategy "Others Focus."

Patt's story:
Patt is my mother, when she was an eighty-seven-year-old, a former pastor's wife, and Bible teacher. She had lost two vital parts of her life: her husband and her eyesight. She was not completely blind, but she could barely make out images due to macular degeneration. Her ministry with my dad, according to her, was one of the most meaningful things in her life. She, at this point, began to struggle to find purpose in life at this age without full use of sight and a husband by her side. With her vision lost, she was unable to read and research as she always had. Unfortunately, in our society, the elderly are put on a shelf and forgotten. It is more difficult, but not impossible, to find purpose in this environment: old and legally blind.

To make matters worse, because her sight was lost late in life, she had developed "Charles Bonnet Syndrome." This is a condition that causes individuals who have lost their sight later in life to see images that aren't there. She will see vivid images of people in her room. These are not scary to her, but they are a cause for distraction. She really thought for a while that she was going crazy. She equated the visions with dementia and was quite concerned, just about to give up on life.

Because of these limitations, she had decided to give up teaching her Bible study in the Christian assisted care facility where she lived. In my opinion, this would have been a huge mistake, and I attempted to turn that around. I began to help her apply RSTs to the situation. We began to spend time daily restating truths about her value, and we repeated these every day. I encouraged her to be very intentional on her use of RSTs to combat the lie that she was beyond value to the Bible study or even society in general.

Purpose may need some creative help along the way. Here is the beauty of this situation; we discovered that if I did the research and taught her the principles (over the phone because we lived miles apart), and if we went over them enough, she would have much of them memorized and she would be able to teach from this reservoir of truth without notes. She would have a staff member at her facility print up notes for those in her class, and she was able to teach. Of course, her memory wasn't strong at her age and she made mistakes, but for these people it was some of the best Bible teaching they would get each week.

In some cases, when purpose seems fragile, all we need is a little creativity. People don't survive well in life without purpose. Unfortunately, most people have a skewed idea of what is valuable and therefore have a false purpose. My mother struggled daily to keep her focus on her purpose, but kept her head above water with the help of others.

The power of "others focus."

When people struggle with negative emotions, it is most often due to a view of self that is unhealthy. In fact, we might say, "One of the major problems in life emotionally is the obsession with self." If there is anything that identifies emotional immaturity, it is self-centeredness. Self-centered people need to work harder at overcoming emotional immaturity because they have made life about themselves. The only way for this to really change is to have an intentional plan for serving others.

Jan's Story:

A woman named Jan was in the church I pastored years ago. She was depressed to the point that she was unable to get out of her home. Not only depressed, but she had become somewhat of a hoarder. She had been a successful businesswoman who was married to a man who cofounded their business. Everyone knew the genius behind the business, the drive and success, was from Jan. Even her husband freely admitted her talent and drive. The one thing that was powerful about their relationship was that he loved her well. This love was one of the driving fuels for her success.

About fifteen years into their marriage, Jan's husband abruptly died of cancer. He was diagnosed and within a month was gone. She began her spiral into depression because of this loss. She certainly was capable of handling the business without him but had no drive. She began to indulge her grief. Grief turned into depression, and depression fueled isolation. Her isolation from others led to many lies she would tell herself. She would say to herself, "God is mad at me," and "God has abandoned me," or "Life is worthless," and "I can't go on without my husband." These lies were permeating her soul and driving her to despair. She was falling deeper into depression. The business had been sold and she was living off the money from that transaction. This gave her the ability to live without having to work.

Her sister insisted she go to counseling after Jan had mentioned to her that she was scared she would kill herself. She was in counseling for some time and medicated for depression. However, Jan felt she needed some spiritual counsel along with the therapy. She had come a long way in getting control of her depression but was still unable to work or connect with others intimately.

I shared the greatness of God's love for her and that God truly cared about her loss. At first, she was not open to this, but I gave her several scriptures to memorize and meditate on. Her next visit was a hard awakening for Jan. I told her she was being selfish and she needed to start helping others to get the attention off of herself. With this abrupt statement, I took a great risk of moving her farther away from health and confirming she was a victim. Because she was strong, I sensed she simply needed an awakening.

Thankfully, even with my clumsy counseling, she joined our jail ministry to women that very week. She began to go every Sunday night to love on the ladies in jail and to share Christ with them. After a short time, she began to emerge from her home for social events and church activities. She began to sell the "junk" she was hoarding and gave the money to the outreach ministries of our church. She had found a purpose for those unneeded possessions.

Jan's recovery is astonishing when you fast-forward a few years. She is now married again and doing what God gifted her to do. She has started a few businesses and is helping to build the community. Jan still does outreach ministry each week to minister to women.

Jan's recovery was through a simple process of her getting the attention off self. I say simple only in the sense that it is easily understood, whereas the process of application feels like torture until it produces the result of love.

To help understand this journey, the following section will put it in three steps.

A.C.T. for "others focus"

How can people who are self-centered move into a life of service and "others focus"? I ask my support groups to follow a simple acronym, ACT:

> **A**ccept that you are self-centered,
> **C**onnect with the needs of others,
> **T**ake the first step.

The journey is one of movement from selfishness to love. Love is the power to free us from negative emotions, especially depression.

When you are self-absorbed, you can't really see past your own needs at the moment. So, taking action is difficult but essential. Let's take a deeper look at each step toward others focus.

Accept that you are self-centered: Yes, I know this sounds harsh. The truth of the matter is no one who struggles with negative emotions, especially depression, is going to improve until he/she admits that self-centeredness is the core problem. This admission is difficult because we don't want to believe we are selfish. We would rather believe we are victims. We will never make a heartfelt change to reaching others with a broken heart of love until we admit our selfishness. We need to also accept that this self-centeredness is not improving our lives but destroying our hearts. It is a detrimental strategy, not a helpful one. Ironically, this is the opposite of how it feels.

We feel that no one will take care of us like we could take care of ourselves, so we don't look at the needs of others, but self-protect as a life strategy. Once we come to the point of admission that we are not victims but that we are selfish, we can begin to overcome our negative emotions. Anger, fear, depression, anxiety, bitterness, worry are all self-defense mechanisms to protect us from the threats we perceive. This being true, it is essential to deal with the self-centeredness to overcome these negative emotions.

Once you make an intentional acceptance of self-centeredness, you must immediately move to correct it by moving to the "C" of ACT.

Connect with the needs of others: The heart of man has an incredible ability to empathize with others when faced with real needs. We need to see their pain so it will soften our hearts, just as in the story about Jan. When she was able to connect with the heartbroken women in jail, she began to commiserate with their pain, and her heart turned to love from selfishness.

When you meet needs without connecting with their hearts, you are using people to make yourself feel better. In most cases, this will not work to heal your heart. One of the most influential men in San Diego over the past thirty-five years is a man called, simply, Father Joe. He has spent his life meeting the needs of the poor and homeless. Over breakfast one day I asked him this question: "What one thing would you tell people about the right way to deal with poverty in San Diego?" His answer was one word, "Time." Time with hurting people touches them in meaningful ways and also changes your heart. We are created in the image of God, and His love will begin to pour through us if we spend time with the hurting.

It is nothing to hand a dollar to a man on the street. But to give your time, this is love that will change your heart. You must invest in others if you want to be free from negative emotions.

The journey is difficult but begins with one step. Let's look at the "T" of ACT.

Take the first step: When we talk about moving from selfishness to love, it is obvious that our motives are going to be mixed at best. We want to feel better and if helping others will produce this, then I'm in. That motivation is selfish. Here is what I'm suggesting: act past your selfishness and let the Lord break your heart for others. I promise you this will happen. The first challenge is acting even when your motives are flawed. The second challenge is taking the first step when everything in you feels it is impossible.

Taking the first step when you are depressed or anxious is difficult because your self-protection seems at risk. That first step is the most difficult but is essential. You have to act by faith here instead of believing your lies. You have to be like Jesus, who said, "*I came to serve not to be served*," (Matt. 20:28). Serving others is so rewarding it feels selfish, but it is a matter of obedience. We obey the love of Christ and reach out to others with a result of the healing of our souls.

Defensiveness: a deterrent from loving others:
When one perceives a threat in his/her life, they will seek to protect in the form of defensiveness. One of my great struggles over the years has been defensiveness. I have developed a habit of indulging

in this thinking and this lifestyle. Being defensive makes us weak. Even though it may feel like we are being strong, it makes us vulnerable to dangerous extremes emotionally and socially. Many of the mistakes, maybe I should say, most of the mistakes I have made in leadership could be attributed to my defensiveness.

Defensiveness happens at the speed of light. You are in the middle of a conversation and seemingly from nowhere you feel and express defensiveness before you can stop yourself. You may be thinking there is no way to stop this kneejerk reaction to situations and perceived negative stimulus. But there are ways to deal with defensiveness that cause the response, a positive response, to be intuitive and natural. Defensiveness is a learned habit based on a flawed belief system. You can change these beliefs and your defensive reactions.

My struggle with defensiveness:
In leadership of a church, I have often found myself in situations that move from mundane to crucial in a matter of one comment. This happens in board meetings so quickly it is stunning. One board meeting I had come with very little on the agenda, and I was looking forward to an easy meeting. We were right at the end of the meeting and one of the Elders mentioned how my preaching had not been as good as in the past and wanted to know why I had changed my style so drastically.

The moment he spoke those words, I could feel my muscles tighten, my heart started to beat faster, and I was ready to fight. I subconsciously and in a split second started an internal narrative that was an overreaction. The narrative went something like this: "This man has an agenda to destroy me and get someone else in here as pastor." In reality, I had changed my style intentionally and for good reason.

Because he was socially clumsy and I was overly sensitive, it was a potential for conflict and a childish demonstration of defensiveness.

Before I could open my mouth and prove that I was immature, our chairman Jack spoke up and said, "I get something out of Tim's messages every week, and I think if we get biblical truth to live each Sunday, it is a success." Still being defensive, and Jack knowing I had priors in showing that defensiveness, he said, "Let's close this meeting in prayer, and we will adjourn."

The problem with this story is that defensiveness doesn't just impact you but others who love you. Your defensiveness will cause people to have to choose sides. You will be known for your defensiveness and others will stand and fight or run from you. In either case, there will not be the closeness with others you would like, and in the case of leadership, this will not foster team camaraderie.

The various faces of defensiveness:
Defensiveness has many different faces. It looks different in the lives of different individuals; however, it is always associated with self-protection. Here is a list of some of the faces of defensiveness: *sarcasm, criticizing, blaming, shaming (attacking and exposing the flaws of others), lecturing, trivializing others, endless explaining, over communicating, withdrawing into silence or pouting.* All of this is done consciously or subconsciously to divert attention away from our own personal flaws.

In some cases, when defensiveness reaches a level of aggression, it produces people whom some refer to as HCPs, "High Conflict Person." It is difficult if not impossible to deal with someone when his/her defensiveness reaches this level. The HCP has the following character traits: all-or-nothing thinking, dominated by emotions, aggressive communication and behavior, blaming others, lack of empathy and the inability to forgive or apologize. If these character traits are driving your communication, I would encourage you to seek professional therapy. Your relationships will not improve until you find the solution to what is driving this mindset. The good news is that with a trained counselor there is hope for real meaningful change.

Defensiveness comes from self-protection and is fueled by self-talk. The self-talk perpetuates the belief that there is a threat. The more we feel threatened, the more defensive we will be. We fuel this threat by speaking it over and over in our minds. We run various scenarios repeatedly until we become fixated on the threat. Defensiveness is nothing more than trying to control your environment and others' perception of you and a desire to feel comfortable with who you are.

Overcoming defensiveness:
Defensiveness has some strange ways of inserting itself into our relationships. There are some people I work with who have a difficult time receiving a genuine compliment. They will try to debate a person who gives them a word of encouragement. This is a softer side of defensiveness but nevertheless real defensiveness. It hurts relationships and doesn't promote growth in our lives. To graciously accept a compliment or word of encouragement is socially important. If you are having a difficult time receiving a compliment, just simply say thank you and process your own insecurity or negative thoughts later.

The other side of defensiveness is the one we usually think of when talking about the problem, that is, the inability to handle high stakes conversations with balanced rejoinders.

The simple answer to defensiveness is to grow emotionally to the extent you are no longer self-protective; however, there are some life skills you can apply to overcome so you are free to love others well.

Defensiveness should be addressed at two different stages:

Stage 1: Before the conflict
Stage 2: In the midst of conflict

Those who try to deal only with their responses during a conflict will eventually fail when the threat is too high stakes to resist the temptation to react. The best approach to handling defensiveness is to deal with the heart, not just the behavior.

Stage 1: Before the conflict:
<u>Identify your triggers for defensiveness:</u>
When am I most defensive? What are the triggers for my defensiveness? Do I have something to hide? Am I living a lie? Am I hiding bad behavior? Do I feel unloved or disrespected? What do I fear?

Every one of us has "buttons" that can be pushed, that is, things we are sensitive about that drive our defensiveness. Those areas usually fall into one or more of the following three triggers:

1. <u>Threat to respect</u>: Fear of not being valued, honored or treated with an appropriate level of esteem. We all want to be taken seriously and not diminished. When we feel we are not being respected in a conversation or event, defensiveness will be triggered. When I refer to respect, I'm primarily focusing on the external aspects of respect. Our

fundamental need to have others affirm our value. This is for the most part social.

2. Threat to significance: People want to see themselves as important and valuable. In fact, a strong driver for most is the need to live with purpose and to have that purpose recognized and valued by others. When we feel as though people are minimizing our significance or we feel less than others, we will fight our way toward significance. This results in some bad behavior due to intense fear of being less than.

3. Threat to intimacy and love: Feelings of abandonment may cause a defensive reaction to harmless misunderstandings. For example, someone may not be attentive to you at a party, when in fact others had distracted them. Friends may not show the kind of consideration you would show, and you feel unloved.

The potential drivers behind our defensiveness are endless. But at the core of all defensiveness is low self-esteem. If we are suffering from a defeated spirit or low self-esteem, we will most likely turn most threatening situations into a personal attack. We need to resolve those issues that are working on our self-image. The pursuit of one's identity in Christ should be of highest importance.

What does scripture say about who I am in Christ?

> *"Therefore if any man be in Christ, he is a new creature: old things are passed away; behold, all things are become new."* (2 Corinthians 5:17)

> *"So you are no longer a slave, but a son; and since you are a son, God has made you also an heir."* (Galatians 4:7)

> *"For our sake he made him to be sin who knew no sin, so that in him we might become the righteousness of God."* (2 Corinthians 5:21)

A good way to find the area of defensiveness is to answer the question, "What makes me feel threatened?" For example, do I feel threatened by the exposure of something I'm hiding? Do I feel threatened by the loss of respect? Do I feel threatened by the loss of control? Make an honest list of the things that make you feel threatened and you will have a list of areas of defensiveness.

Change your beliefs:
Once you discover the triggers for defensiveness, you need to find out what your beliefs are. For example: "When my children leave their clothes on the floor, it proves that I'm a bad mother." When my wife says, "I'm too tired to have sex tonight," she is telling me I'm too fat. These are beliefs and judgments often times unfounded in truth.

It is difficult enough to deal with real issues of rejection without adding attacks that aren't real. Defensiveness is not defending oneself; it is an obsession with the control of others' opinions of us.

Take responsibility:
Defensiveness often takes the form of hurling and obstructing to divert attention away from the real problem. The more we do this the more we foster our defensiveness. When we foster, we don't change. Often people will put the blame for their defensiveness on

others. "He attacks me." "She is unkind." We need to make a clear evaluation of where the defensiveness comes from and make the necessary changes to stop it from arising.

As long as we blame others and get away with it, we will not move forward into maturity. The immature response to threat is defensiveness and we must have the courage to face our own responsibility for it.

Stage 2: In the midst of the conflict:

In the book, ***Crucial Conversations*** [5], much emphasis is given to the definition of dialogue. The point in the book is that people will only contribute to the "pool of shared meaning" when they feel safe. You should know that defensiveness causes safety to be lost in a conversation.

The truth is that we have no idea most times when a conversation will turn from casual to high stakes, and so we must prepare by learning communication skills that keep us on track to really communicate well and free from defensiveness. Here are a few helpful communication skills:

> "*Death and life are in the power of the tongue, and those who love it will eat its fruits.*" (Proverbs 18:21)

Joyce's story:

Joyce was a strong and driven attorney with every intention of making her law firm the number one law firm in the county. She had a plan and everyone knew it, and everyone admired her drive. The problem was that she saw the goal of becoming the number one

[5] Crucial Conversations, Tools for talking when stakes are high, Kerry Patterson, McGraw-Hill Books, New York, 2012, pages 24-28

law firm as more important than working with the people in her firm. Her vision had a deficit; she didn't realize she couldn't do this through intimidation and harsh interaction with her staff. She perceived her staff as assets to be exploited for her goals; after all, she was paying them.

Every meeting with Joyce was a battle; every conversation was about where she was taking the firm. But most of all, Joyce was defensive and couldn't take criticism from her staff. The people who were closest to Joyce who knew the business best couldn't get through to her. Joyce went through staff so often, her firm never made it to the top. In fact, because Joyce couldn't listen to others, she overextended her business and had to file for bankruptcy.

Joyce had preconceived ideas of staff/boss relations and defended her control to her own hurt. She failed because the staff was her greatest asset, and yet she treated them as if they were possessions. Joyce needed to provide a safe environment for her staff to interact so she and the firm could grow and become what she envisioned. Her fear of failure led her to the flawed strategy of control, which drove her defensiveness and resulted in her failure. It is unfortunate when fear is the base of our interaction with others.

The tongue is powerful because people associate our words with our hearts, even when we use words that don't really convey what we feel. There are two parts to avoiding defensiveness in the midst of a conflict:

1. **Listen with patience.**
2. **Speak with compassion.**

1. Listen with patience:

Use clarifying speech: If you have ever watched the *Real Housewives of New Jersey*, you know their dialogue is not real communication. These women talk past each other in very high-stakes situations. They don't listen, and they have decided to take sides. All their speech is for the purpose of reinforcing their prejudice for and against. It makes for fascinating TV, but is deadly for relationships.

When you hear words that offend you, ask for clarification. This, in many cases, will resolve the need to defend because the words were careless and were not communicating the real heart of the speaker. If you can learn to move toward clarification, much of the negative speech and emotions will resolve. This takes listening without judgment, asking and clarifying.

Slow down or step out of the conversation: We often feel trapped in a conversation and don't feel as though we can extricate ourselves from it, so we press on only to find it escalates into higher levels of attack and defense. The truth of the matter is that in many cases we are able to politely slow down the conversation by asking for clarification, as above, or we can even step out of the conversation for even just a moment to think. You might say, "Our conversation is important to me and I want to think about what I'm saying right now; give me a minute to collect my thoughts."

I'm a highly emotional person and need a break from conversations both in my personal life and in my professional life. I find that people respect the need for a conversation break and grant it without hesitation. My wife has been especially accommodating on this, maybe out of self-preservation. But this really works to be able to take intimidation, aggressiveness and fear out of conversations.

The goal is communication and we must be strategic in making that happen.

Redirect the conversation: Redirecting the conversation is simply moving to where you both share mutuality. In an emotional conversation, it is best to have a touch point of mutuality to go to when things get too intense. This serves to bring connection back to the conversation. In many cases, when we become defensive, we stop seeing the other person as human but more as a barrier to our goal. This causes us to treat them and the truth recklessly.

As you are in the midst of a conversation that has gotten emotive, ask what you really want. Do you want to lash out and harm connection, or do you want to be understood? Defensiveness usually causes us to overstate our intentions. For example, if you feel you are not being respected, you may exaggerate your accomplishments, creating potential competition that was unnecessary.

A better way to communicate in a high-stakes conversation is to stop and redirect. Ask, "What do we really want?" "What are our real goals here?" This will redirect the conversation to a happy mutuality and move the conversation to that goal.

2. Speak with compassion:

Remove risk from the conversation:

As I have already stated, fear and good communication don't mix. You must take the risk out of the communication if you are going to bring about meaning in your conversations. Defensiveness drives a need to control by hiding and intimidating. This should be avoided if your goal is meaningful conversation.

The risk can be taken away by speaking with compassion to the other person. See them as human, not an obstacle. Look into their eyes and see the person. If they are upset, look beyond and see the pain or frustration in their hearts. Think about how you would want to be handled when you are in pain or frustrated.

Sometimes we speak from our negative experiences, our wounds and faulty perspective and overdramatize our feelings or opinions. When we inject emotive dramatization into the conversation, we increase the risk in the hearts of others. We should seek to avoid these words even if we feel them. Think about what you really want in the conversation so that the moment of conversation is not filled with risk.

Avoid inflammatory speech:
Oftentimes when we become defensive, we will move to hiding and intimidating and the intimidating side takes on the form of inflammatory speech. Words like, "You always get mad when I talk to you." Or "You think of yourself first and no one else." These kinds of statements are used to defeat any response before it is even made. Most often it is not malicious but a subconscious way of defending ourselves. We don't even realize we are doing it.

The problem is that we inflame the defensiveness in others and lead the conversation into a debate about something totally unrelated to the core of the conversation. We need to step back and ask ourselves what it is we really want, so we can communicate.

My daughter, Karrie, and I are opinionated communicators; that is nice speak for aggressive talkers. When we don't agree, which is rare, we tend to over communicate about nonessentials; defensiveness reigns for a moment. The love we have is deep and so our relationship always wins at the end of the day. What is great about our life together is we are learning to communicate without intimidation and the journey is very rewarding.

Use healing speech:
There is nothing like healing speech. It feels like a warm bath after coming in from the cold. When someone reaches your deepest darkest place and makes you feel safe and loved, you are experiencing healing speech. If we are going to be successful in living this life well, we must learn the language of love and healing.

If we are going to learn healing speech, we must first avoid what we will call resistance speech. For example, when you use statements like, "That's ridiculous," or "You've got to be kidding," or "You're simply wrong," these are terms of resistance that cause a reaction in the heart of the person we are talking to and stops meaningful communication.

If we are going to learn healing speech, we must secondly learn the language of healing. For example, when we say, "I can see how you would feel that way," or "I understand, I see what you're saying," or "I like the way you just said that," this kind of language reaches the heart and begins the process of healing. But it must be taken a step further, and we must learn that healing is speaking to people's real fears and creating safety. We must learn to say from our heart things like, "It is okay not to be okay," or "I'm also struggling with the same kind of issues." We must create safety for those who are flawed, broken and afraid.

Getting the most out of love:

The Apostle John teaches a simple contrast: Hate will result in blindness, misdirection and death, whereas love will produce life and emotional stability.

> "9 *Whoever says he is in the light and hates his brother is still in darkness. 10 Whoever loves his brother abides in the light, and in him there is no cause for stumbling. 11 But whoever hates his brother is in the darkness and walks in the darkness, and does not know where he is going, because the darkness has blinded his eyes.*" (1 John 2:9)

> "*We know that we have passed out of death into life, because we love the brothers. Whoever does not love abides in death.*" (1 John 3:14)

It is unwise to underestimate this principle. This is a spiritual law that is as real as the law of gravity. We need to understand our negative emotions can be handled greatly by walking in the "The Principle of Love" and avoiding the "The Principle of Hatred."

> **The Principle of Hatred: If you hate your brother, you will experience the qualities of death.**

> **The Principle of Love: If you love your brother, you will experience the qualities of life.**

The Principle of Hatred: hatred produces two clear experiences: 1) Darkness, blindness and misdirection and 2) Death. As we look at the real meaning, the impact on our lives emotionally becomes clear.

Darkness, blindness and misdirection: Blindness is a condition that John speaks about in his writings that describes a perspective of life. John, in quoting Isaiah, expresses the impact of darkness. John 12:40, "*He has blinded their eyes and hardened their heart, lest they see with their eyes, and understand with their heart, and turn, and I would heal them.*" When understood in the overall context of John's writings, it becomes clear that this blindness is the inability to find the healing of God due to hatred of one's brother. That healing certainly extends to the healing of our emotions.

According to the above passage, 1 John 2:9-11, when hatred toward one's brother is in one's heart, it produces darkness and that causes blindness, which results in the inability to walk without stumbling. **The principle of hatred is clear that our experiences are impacted by our opinion of our brother. Much misery could be avoided if we would esteem our brother as valuable and love him/her.**

Death: The second impact of the principle of hatred is the experience of death. Of course, this death is not physical; it is spiritual/emotional. The scripture, 1 John 3:14, makes it clear that hatred produces death. However, we should look at this more closely and notice that what he actually says is, "*whoever does not love abides in death,*" Abiding in death takes some explanation. The word abide in the original language is the word "*meno,*" meaning, "to settle down and be at home." What John is clearly saying is that when we hate, we will be at home with death and all of its thought and emotions. We become so used to our negative emotions of fear and self-centeredness, we come to believe they are normal.

This concept of living in emotional death is essential to our understanding of negative thinking and emotions. We will never be able to extricate ourselves from negative emotions until we truly love others. In fact, Jesus said that loving your neighbor as yourself was essential to life. We should apply great effort to investing in the lives of others to have meaningful emotional healing come to our lives.

The Principle of Love: love produces two clear experiences: 1) Light, sight and direction and 2) life. When we properly understand the principle of love, we will understand love's impact on our emotions.

Light, sight and direction: There is nothing quite like being able to see when trying to negotiate difficult terrain. The terrain of relationships can be treacherous, and we must have clear sight. When we love, it gives us the clarity to avoid defensiveness and self-protection. John says, "*Whoever loves his brother abides in the light, and in him there is no cause for stumbling*." The light produces the sight so that each step in the relationship can be well-placed and the one who loves won't stumble himself or be a cause for others to stumble.

The second thing about this verse that really brings hope to those struggling with negative emotions is that when you love, you will "*abide in the light.*" Again, that word, "*meno,*" to settle down and be at home in the light. Think of the liberation of being able to really see the importance of loving well, not seeing everything through a need to self-protect or self-promote. What freedom.

Life: In 1 John 3:14, the proof of having passed from death (a self-centered perspective) to life (the ability to see others as God does) is found in love. When we love we abide in life. The meaning of life is found in loving your neighbor as yourself. You become what God has called you to be.

One last word about loving your brother: I'm convinced the only way to love your brother is to first love God. In the epistle of 1 John, it is clear that we must avoid loving the world. 1 John 2:15, "*Do not love the world or the things in the world. If anyone loves the world, the love of the Father is not in him.*" In the next verse he explains the things in the world are the lust principle, 1 John 2:16, "*For all that is in the world the desires of the flesh and the desires of the eyes and pride of life is not from the Father but is from the world.*"

The world operates on the "***lust principle***" not the "***love principle.***" To experience both, love for God and love for others, we have to intentionally take our focus off those things that are about self-gratification. They won't work and won't satisfy.

We need to understand the power of these two contrasting principles: The "*Principle of Hatred*" and the "*Principle of Love.*" Once we discern this, we can realize that life is best when we love well, when we love God with all our hearts, and we love others as ourselves.

Chapter 12 Life Skills:

Take a sheet of paper and divide it into three columns: 1) Things I do for self-gratification, 2) What I do for others, and 3) Things I do solely for God. Quantify by putting a time on each item. You will be able to evaluate your level of love and stress.

Evaluate your conversations this last week. How many of those conversations became high-stakes conversations and how did you handle them? Take a sheet of paper and write down your conversations, evaluating them based on how high-stakes the conversations were and how you handled each.

Memorize the following verses:

> "9 *Whoever says he is in the light and hates his brother is still in darkness. 10 Whoever loves his brother abides in the light, and in him there is no cause for stumbling. 11 But whoever hates his brother is in the darkness and walks in the darkness, and does not know where he is going, because the darkness has blinded his eyes.*" (1 John 2:9-11)

> "*We know that we have passed out of death into life, because we love the brothers. Whoever does not love abides in death.*" (1 John 3:14)

Chapter 13: Living in the Moment

Living Sequentially and Enjoying Life to its Fullest

"Do not worry about tomorrow, for tomorrow will care for itself. Each day has enough trouble of its own."
(Matthew 6:34)

We have been through a process of seeking to think right, of allowing truth to dominate our minds, and now we come to this final chapter of our journey. We now look at the matter of living life in the moment, free from the regrets of the past and fears of the future. This is a struggle but one worth the effort.

In this chapter we will explore how to live sequentially, one moment or experience at a time. We will look at how to extricate ourselves from the past and how to be free from the anxiety over the future. We then look at the power of living life with purpose and how that can cause us to savor the moment.

My Story:

As you might imagine, over the years after Linda's suicide, I struggled with my personal culpability in her death. I struggled with thinking that I should have loved her better. I went between thinking I should have been more forceful or less forceful. I spent hours in silence trying to navigate my thoughts of responsibilities, the "What if," or the "Should haves." I was in an emotional time warp. I couldn't live in the moment because I couldn't extricate myself from the past and Linda's death. I spent an extreme amount of emotional energy on this, but somehow, I had to reconcile my involvement. The longer I thought about it, the less I could resolve.

One day I had a breakthrough; I realized the obsession with trying to resolve my responsibility toward Linda's suicide had nothing to do with Linda or my love for her. I realized I was being selfish and self-protective. I was not taking responsibility for my life at the moment because emotionally I was living in the past, trying to resolve it, trying to rationalize it, trying to fix my responsibility. I wanted to be right not only now, but also in the past. I wanted to be exonerated in my own mind. I was struggling with guilt and shame. I wanted my imaginary world to find me not guilty. I wanted to be found innocent of Linda's death. I was in an idealistic fantasy that would never really work out. Things like love and marriage, life and death are not as clean as that. Life is messy, and strength and weaknesses were factors in all of it.

I know this doesn't seem like such a breakthrough; however, it was for me. Once I realized living in the past would not prove my value as a husband to Linda or even prove I loved her, I was free to stop the selfishness. I couldn't call Linda back to life, she was in the arms of Jesus and I was living this life. The awareness of my own selfish desire to fix the past by obsessing over it was the key to me releasing it. I was trying to validate myself at the expense of the people in my "now world," and they were missing my love in each moment because I couldn't get out of the past. The selfishness of this caused deep repentance and a strategy to move on with life in the "now."

I needed to leave that behind, and I decided one day that I was done. I came to God in humble admission of my complicity with Linda's decline into darkness. I admitted only what I truly believed was my involvement. Even though I had never had malicious intent toward Linda, my insecurity and need be loved along with hers drove our hearts apart. I confessed to God I had been a weak husband and I had not trusted Him with my marriage like I should have. I admitted that emotionally I let our marriage dissolve in the early years, even though outwardly we stayed responsible to each other in a mechanical commitment. I told God I was sorry for my failure to love well like Jesus loves the Church. I asked God to forgive me. I know He did and does.

That day the healing began and the obsession with her suicide and my culpability began to subside in the power of His redemptive work. God began to heal my heart so I could love my family and people in my world in the present. Because of redemption, I was free to live in the moment.

Life in the moment is messy but full of joy, heartaches, and most of all the presence of a God who loves me and calls me to His face for intimate times of refreshing. Life is at the same time good and treacherous, kind and malicious, filled with success and failure, and knowing that life is like this, causes me to always be present in the joy of life. The circumstances will vary but God is the constant in my life, the rock, the hope and the salvation of my life. He is my life in the now, the moment, and the present.

The problem with baggage:
Baggage is an idiom meaning that someone has past issues that impact his/her present relationships. We see people with baggage all the time, in fact, most of us have a cartful being dragged behind us like a homeless man and his grocery cart full of bags of "stuff," worthless but valued. I explain baggage with the following formula:

NE + O x C = Baggage

Here is how baggage develops in the life. It starts with a **negative experience** (NE). This is a real or perceived event in one's life that has impact on the heart. What happens next separates those who develop baggage and those who don't. For many, the negative experience is dealt with maturely. The mature do many different things to deal with negative experiences: they forgive, they resolve, they release and various other things that cause the experience to be left in the past. But for the person on the road to baggage, this event is possessed, that is, they take **ownership**, (NE + O).

Once this event is owned, they begin to "**complain**" (NE + O x C) about it. The complaining takes them back to the event, so they never get over it. When he/she complains about the negative experience, the experience is *multiplied* many times over and creates a barrier in his/her life. He/she now is living with "**baggage,**" (NE + O x C = Baggage). Would you want to date this person? You probably already have. You may have even married someone like this. More importantly, you may be a person with baggage.

Here it is:

> **(Negative Experiences + Ownership x Complaining = Baggage)**

Our complaining drives us back to the negative experience. We can't move on because we are stuck in the past. It impacts our relationships, our job performance and most of all it impacts our ability to savor life and enjoy it to the fullest. Baggage is simply living in the past, which pulls our negative experiences into our present, a sad way to live.

I have always been amazed at man's ability to turn a PE (Positive Experience) into a NE (Negative Experience.) We don't do this because we don't want to have fun or enjoy life, but because of the inability to keep our heads out of the past or the future. Life is now!

Life is now!

Life is not going to happen later when you get what you want. Life is now, this moment, in this place, with these people and with these resources. Your ability to live in the moment will determine your ability to love life and live well. Here are several points to remember about living in the moment:

If you are waiting for life to happen, you are missing it. Savor the moment and live life to its fullest.

The past will steal your present and the fear of tomorrow will transport you to a dangerous, uncontrollable place: the future.

You don't need to be rich, healthy, pain-free or influential to live in the moment. You can do this with intentional savoring and focus, irrespective of your resources.

The motivation for achievement should not be based on hating the moment but rather on a clear purpose for life.

Our problem with trying to live in the moment is that we are constantly feeling the pull of the past and the future. The past calls us with regrets, and the future calls us with its fears and uncontrollable variables. Our desire to control our past and future drives us out of the moment and steals our joy.

The good news, there is a place to visit the past with healthy nostalgia, celebrating past accomplishments and there is a place to visit the future with vision and goal setting. I will address in this chapter how to set goals and remain in the present. I will also address the importance of remembrances. But for now, we need to understand this biblical principle of living in the moment so we can deal with the negative emotions of regret, fear and anxiety.

In the following pages, I will unpack these concepts. But before we go too deeply into the details, it should be understood there is only one way to safely deal with life outside of the moment. This way is to connect with an eternal God who lives on an eternal plane, who is the "*Alpha and the Omega*" the "*beginning and the end*." Even though this is difficult to understand with our finite minds, the scripture is clear that God is in the past, the present and the future. It is God then who can help us resolve regrets from the past through "restoration" and assuage our fears of the future through "hope" in Him.

This chart will help to visualize the process. To go to the past or the future without God is a dangerous journey, but with Him you will find what you need.

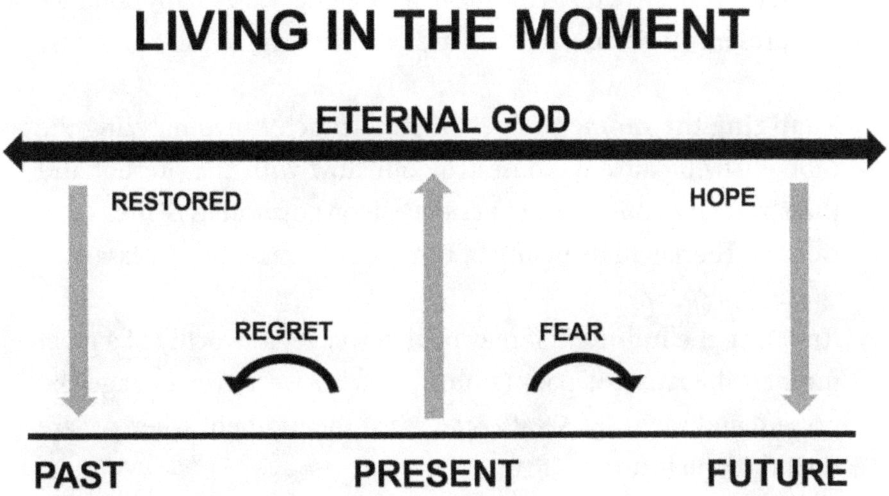

<u>**The way we lose the present:**</u>

The following are a list of ways in which we lose the moment:

Chasing/Contriving the moment: When we try too hard to make the moment happen, we fail to relax and live in the present. Enjoy the process of life; don't chase life. For example, don't force others to perform for your moment. Family reunions may be contrived experiences to recapture the past. Let your family be what they are now.

Comparing the moment: We may tend to compare one moment with a past moment and value it only when it meets that benchmark. The problem is that past moments are sometimes exaggerated in our minds as being better than they actually were. Even if they were monumental, we should not compare the moment.

Idealizing/romanticizing the moment: We have developed ideals about what a great moment is and then project it on our present, and if it doesn't live up to the ideal, we are unable to totally embrace our present (for example, holidays or birthdays).

Analyzing the moment: Spending too much time analyzing the moment will cause us to destroy our flow with the present and thereby take us out of the experience. Don't overanalyze life's experiences. There will be plenty of time later to reflect if necessary.

Resisting the moment: It may be that we feel unworthy of a great moment because of past failures, and so we never engage the present and savor it. We also can resist the moment when we are fearful of the future.

The way we capture the present:

Savor the process of each day: Slow everything down and smell, taste, see, feel and hear each experience. Let your senses embrace all that is happening in the moment (for example, eat more slowly or listen more carefully or watch your children play).

Give up control of the moment and "Flow": Flow happens when you have let go of the control and you are in focused immersion. The best athletes have learned how to do this. This is essential to life in the moment. The best way to do this is to allow imperfection to exist around you and focus on your contribution to the moment.

Don't compare your life to others: Accept God's unique journey for you. Don't feel sorry for yourself as though God is not there, know His presence and embrace Him in the moment. When you compare your situation to another's, you have lost sight of God's unique plan for you. It is helpful to write down your distractions, things outside the moment that call for your attention. Carefully analyze how you have been distracted and recommit to focus on the moment.

Focus and Breathe: When distractions are screaming in your mind (that is, fear of the future or regrets from the past), you can silence them by taking a moment to breathe. Feel each breath, focusing on both inhale and exhale. The power of this is that you are forcing a physical reality to impact your psychological focus.

Believe that God has created this day for you: Psalm 118:24, "*This is the day which the LORD has made; Let us rejoice and be glad in it.*" One of the things I have learned is to quote this verse and claim the truth of it. I will say, "God, You made this day, and I accept what You want in it; this day is enough for me."

Wait on God and strength will come supernaturally: Remember God is the Alpha and the Omega, the beginning and the end, He is eternal and holds the future. Isaiah 40:31, "*Yet those who wait for the Lord will gain new strength; they will mount up with wings like eagles, they will run and not get tired, they will walk and not become weary.*" God promises to show up for the patient soul. God will arrive with supernatural strength for the moment. Notice also Psalm 68:19, "*Blessed be the Lord, who daily bears our burden, The God who is our salvation.*" God bears the burden today; not yesterday and not tomorrow. He bears the moment for you.

Use gratitude to overpower the temptation to leave the moment: Worry is always removed by a combination of prayer and thanksgiving. Philippians 4:6-7, "*Do not be anxious about anything, but in everything by prayer and supplication with thanksgiving let your requests be made known to God. 7 And the peace of God, which surpasses all understanding, will guard your hearts and your minds in Christ Jesus.*" Be thankful intentionally for the moment, and God promises to show up with supernatural peace. Read the verses again and see the connection between thanksgiving and the guarding of your heart by God. This is supernatural.

Kristie's Story:

Kristie wanted the perfect Christmas for her family. Her mother had just been diagnosed with terminal cancer and was told she only had a few months to live. Kristie was confident this was their last Christmas with her mother. The sense of mission was driven with fear of the future. The problem came in trying to get her children to cooperate. They were fighting as usual and characteristically immature and a little ungrateful for their gifts. When Christmas dinnertime came, they were in a hurry to get away from the table to be able to play with their new games.

Kristie's perfect Christmas was falling apart. Instead of flowing with the moment, she was forcing the moment. Instead of loving her family, she was uptight at every immature moment with her kids. Her mother could sense the strain in Kristie and asked her what was wrong. She told her mom about her fears and wanting this to be the best Christmas ever. Her mother gave her sound advice. She told her that she was old enough not to expect that young children are going to cooperate with our desires and that the perfect Christmas is just being with her imperfect family. Kristie cried with her mother and changed her disposition and expectations. Kristie was able to relax and quit trying to make the moment and just love in the moment.

Jesus' logic for freedom from worry:
A commonly taught passage on living in the moment is Matthew 6:34. It is a directive to not worry or be anxious. Without the context this is as helpful as telling a raging man to stop being angry. It won't produce a change of disposition in the heart of the worrier; it will just increase guilt over another failure of life. The good news is that the context gives the reason behind the directive not to worry. Here is the whole passage:

> "25 *Therefore I tell you, do not be anxious about your life, what you will eat or what you will drink, nor about your body, what you will put on. Is not life more than food, and the body more than clothing? 26 Look at the birds of the air: they neither sow nor reap nor gather into barns, and yet your heavenly Father feeds them. Are you not of more value than they? 27 And which of you by being anxious can add a single hour to his span of life? 28 And why are you anxious about clothing? Consider the lilies of the field, how they grow: they neither toil nor spin, 29 yet I tell you,*

> *even Solomon in all his glory was not arrayed like one of these. 30 But if God so clothes the grass of the field, which today is alive and tomorrow is thrown into the oven, will he not much more clothe you, O you of little faith?*" (Matthew 6:25-30)

The power of this passage is that it gives us not only the directive not to worry about tomorrow, but it gives us the incentive, that is the logic of not worrying. Here are Jesus' three points of logic:

Logic #1: If life were more than resources, why would you worry about the lesser?

Jesus explains this in verse 25 when He expresses that life is not about resources, invoking His previous point in verse 24, "...*You cannot serve God and money*." Jesus makes it clear that to focus on resources and not on the real meaning of life, that is, serving God, will lead to worry and all kinds of negative emotions.

Logic #2: If God will care for the lesser, He will most certainly care for the greater.

Jesus explains this in verses 26-30 when He expresses that your life (the greater) is more valuable than the life of animals and plants (the lesser). He compares His care of the birds and the grass of the field with His love for us. This is the impetus for us to be free from worry. Based on this comparison of value, He says, "*Therefore don't worry about tomorrow...*"

Logic #3: Today is not tomorrow; therefore, the worries of tomorrow cannot be managed today.

Jesus in verse 34 says not to be anxious because, "*...tomorrow will be anxious for itself. Sufficient for the day is its own trouble.*" God gives us the power of His grace for today's needs, but never promises to give strength today for the problems of tomorrow.

Clearly, Jesus wants His followers to be free from worry no matter what condition they find themselves in. God certainly will meet His followers' needs when they, "*seek first the Kingdom of God and His righteousness.*" Matthew 6:33.

Change your brain and live in the moment:
Understanding how the brain is wired for thinking is important to living in the moment. When you understand that the brain develops neuro pathways every day, you will understand how to change the pattern of thinking. The brain is rewired in a sense. The patterns of thought have changed. For example, my boys Jesse and Malachi love to surf, and I had not seen them do so for a while. When I saw them surfing after about six months, their improvement was dramatic. This was due to a change in neuro pathways in their minds. They literally have increased their surfing ability through thinking. They focus, no I should say even obsess, about surfing, and that focus turns into increased ability. They will sit for hours together and watch surfer videos on our computer.

Kimberly was with the boys at the beach one day after some recent shark sighting near our San Diego beaches were reported. She watched as Jesse, who was very young at the time, struggled with fear, even though it had been weeks since the last shark sighting. His older brother, Malachi, was out in the surf having a great time, but Jesse couldn't get out past the break for fear of sharks. It actually was an irrational fear because there were no shark threats at the beach where they were surfing.

Jesse walked up on the beach with shoulders down and frustrated by his fear. As he approached Kimberly, who was sitting on the beach praying for him to overcome his fear, he heard her say, "Jesse, you turn around and get out there In Jesus' Name." When Kimberly invokes her old Pentecostal roots, "In Jesus' Name," we all know she means business. She is saying, you're in a spiritual battle for fear or victory and in Jesus' name you will win. Jesse knew he had to overcome the fear to do exactly what he loved. That was a turnaround day for Jesse. He learned that Jesus is there, and an irrational fear should be dismissed. This began a freedom to surf without fear and he has progressively gotten more skillful and enjoys it tremendously.

Putting this in a biblical perspective, Paul says, "*Think on these things*" (Phil. 4:8). He also says, "*Set your mind on things above*" (Col. 3:2). Psalm 1 describes the transformation of the life due to "*meditation*." The word in the original language means to ponder and even mutter to yourself. This is what I call self-talk. But in Psalm 1 it is referring to biblical truth, not various unfocused thoughts.

The key to living well is living in the moment, and we will only live in the moment when we intentionally focus on it. **Thinking is not supposed to be passive; it is supposed to be intentional. You have the power to think on what you want.** Here are some good exercises to mentally focus on the moment. State truths repeatedly and focus on them. You will begin to rewire your mind. Your neuro pathways will change. By just examining one passage, you can gain insight into the power of God's Word and His promises. Consider a few verses from the book of Psalm:

> *"1 God is our refuge and strength, a very present help in trouble. 2 Therefore we will not fear though the*

earth gives way, though the mountains be moved into the heart of the sea. (Psalm 46:1-2)

"10 'Be still, and know that I am God. I will be exalted among the nations; I will be exalted in the earth!' 11 The LORD of hosts is with us; the God of Jacob is our fortress." (Psalm 46:10-11)

Meditate and focus by repeating truths from this passage:

"God is my help in this present moment."

"The troubles around me have no power because God is my strength."

"I'm constantly in God's presence."

"God is over all things and He is with me."

"God is my refuge; He is my strength."

These promises must be repeated over and over in your mind and even spoken out loud. RSTs (Reinforced Strategic Thoughts, Chapter 3) are nothing more than repeating truths and promises, which will displace lies that were your patterns of thought. When this is reinforced, that is, repeated over and over in your mind, you will develop new neuro pathways and, therefore, a new belief system. This is what the Bible refers to as the transforming of the mind.

I want to be clear; I don't mean to imply this is merely a psychological effort. This is actually a biblically prescribed spiritual discipline (for example, "focus," "think," and "meditate"). Just imagine; you can be set free, not through the change of circumstances, but by simply and intentionally focusing on truth. You will then be free to live in the moment.

Two appropriate times to leave the moment:
In most cases, it is dangerous to move outside the moment because life is not there; it is in the now. There are at least two ways in which we should leave the moment to actually optimize and enhance our present experience:

1. **Enhancing the moment through celebrating the past**
2. **Enhancing the moment through setting goals**

Enhancing the moment through celebrating the past:
Scripture gives several examples of celebrating the past to enhance the present. In Joshua 3 the children of Israel miraculously crossed over the Jordan River, and in chapter 4 Joshua was given a directive to make a memorial for the people to remember what God had done for His people. Joshua was so excited about the prospect of a memorial he actually made two: One on the banks as directed by God and one in the Jordan River where the soles of the priest stood when God dried up the river for crossing.

> *"5 Joshua said to them, 'Pass on before the ark of the LORD your God into the midst of the Jordan, and take up each of you a stone upon his shoulder, according to the number of the tribes of the people of Israel, 6 that this may be a sign among you. When your children ask in time to come, "What do those stones mean to you?" 7 then you shall tell them that the waters of the Jordan were cut off before the ark*

> *of the covenant of the LORD. When it passed over the Jordan, the waters of the Jordan were cut off. So, these stones shall be to the people of Israel a memorial forever.'"* (Joshua 4:5-7)

> *"And Joshua set up twelve stones in the midst of the Jordan, in the place where the feet of the priests bearing the ark of the covenant had stood; and they are there to this day."* (Joshua 4:9)

God understands the weakness of man to remember His power and strength in protecting and providing for His people. Memorials were used as reminders of what God has done so that you can understand what God can do today in your present. This really becomes a powerful reminder of God's present power.

It would be powerful to memorialize moments of great blessing from God for your children and yourself. You might create a plaque to be a reminder of the hand of God in your life. Even certain items in your home could be a reminder of God's hand. I would encourage you mothers and fathers to look for creative ways to remember the past dealing of God in your life.

Memorials, when done properly, empower us to live safely in the moment. God wants you to remember those things that got you to this point safely.

Enhancing the moment through setting goals:
Goals often are a reflection of our ambition, and unfortunately an extension of our egos. When our goals are ego-oriented, it is impossible to make them about a divine given purpose. Before I go on any further, let me qualify by saying that at best we will have

mixed motives in our goal setting. We are imperfect and therefore our egos will creep into the motivation.

Time should be spent on analyzing our motives for goal setting, and once we hear the voice of God in the direction we should go, we begin the process of setting goals. These goals need to be oriented around our purpose, not just our desires for more.

"Ambition" is both good and bad, depending on your worldview. The fact of the matter is, "ambition" is a morally neutral word. It is what drives the ambition that makes it good or bad. Ambition may pull you out of the moment. Another problem with ambition is that you are not in control of the variables in the future. Because you don't know what the future holds, you cannot force an outcome toward your ambition. This creates an emotional crisis of need and fear, especially for those who struggle with negative emotions.

Learning to have both goals that look to the future and the ability to live in the moment is one of the secrets to joy. This is so crucial that we must learn these skills or we will live with disappointment, anxiety and even a sense of failure.

Much of the stress and anxiety we feel is due to a flawed life purpose. We are driven by what we believe and what we value. We must discern this and make fundamental adjustments in our belief systems to relieve stress and anxiety as they relate to our futures.

Goal setting will create a thirst for more and that thirst will pull you out of the moment. So then, how do we set goals or have ambition without leaving the moment? The following are keys to setting goals and living in the moment:

1) Set goals that align with purpose. If something is good for Jesus, it's probably good for me. In speaking of His driving purpose, Jesus shared that His life and goals were relegated to His following statement: *"For I have come down from heaven, not to do my own will but the will of him who sent me"* (Jn. 6:38). When we see ourselves as serving God, not ourselves, our motivation in goal setting is free to be oriented to divine purpose.

2) Set goals in submission to God's authority. What would happen if you could control all the variables of the future? If you could control the market, your health, the opinions of others and the weather, you could determine a course of action and then make sure it happens. James addresses this point to his readers when he says, *"Come now, you who say, 'Today or tomorrow we will go into such and such a town and spend a year there and trade and make a profit' yet you do not know what tomorrow will bring. What is your life? For you are a mist that appears for a little time and then vanishes. Instead you ought to say, 'If the Lord wills, we will live and do this or that'"* (Jms. 4:13-15). James is not forbidding goal setting; he is recommending the truth of goal setting. Because you don't control the variables of the future, you should submit all your goals under God's authority, "*If the Lord wills.*" This is a powerful way to live because you see God as in control of the variables, and you are free to trust Him.

3) Set goals with next steps in mind. One of the greatest struggles emotionally with goal setting and ambition is the pull to think in the future only. With a proper focus, with each step we can both move toward the goal and remain in the

moment. Each step toward that goal should be placed on a timeline and enjoyed as a journey toward the goal. In the Apostle Paul's experience, he learned now to live in the moment. He said, "*11 Not that I am speaking of being in need, for I have learned in whatever situation I am to be content. 12 I know how to be brought low, and I know how to abound. In any and every circumstance, I have learned the secret of facing plenty and hunger, abundance and need. 13 I can do (be content) all things through him who strengthens me*" (Phil. 4:11-13). In verse 13, he is not speaking about accomplishment but rather contentment. He is saying the secret of contentment is found in strength from God. When we are able to look at each circumstance (step), we can rejoice in the fact that God has you there and will empower you there. This was Paul's secret.

4) <u>Set goals that can be celebrated as steps to be accomplished.</u> When someone speaks of goals, they are thinking the celebration for the accomplishment will take place when the goals are reached. However, like in the previous point, there is a secret to rejoicing even before the final goals are met. If we truly have set goals with steps along the way, then, when we reach the completion of each step, we can celebrate accomplishment. This will keep us in the moment and at the same time move us toward the goal. The key will be to learn ways to celebrate each step. Get creative and learn to savor the journey toward the goal.

Setting goals for the future and celebrating the past is an important part of all human experience. However, what causes us to be able to do this well is a careful commitment to "living in the moment" while "living for God" and His eternal purpose. God has done wonderful things in your past and will do wonderful things in your future, yet be careful to focus on those in the healthy ways I have described.

Chapter 13 Life skills:

Write down four significant events this week in your life. Write down the distraction from those experiences. How could you have stayed in the moment?

On a blank sheet of paper, write down your goals for life in the following areas:

1) Personal growth
2) Family
3) Financial
4) Professional development

Create a timeline for your goals with specific steps along the way so you can focus on the steps and celebrate them when accomplished.

Go over your Thanksgiving Journal and see how you are doing in emotional growth.

> **Memorize:** *"13 Come now, you who say, 'Today or tomorrow we will go to such and such a city, and spend a year there and engage in business and make a profit.' 14 Yet you do not know what your life will be like tomorrow. You are just a vapor that appears for a little while and then vanishes away. 15 Instead, you ought to say, 'If the Lord wills, we will live and also do this or that.'"* (James 4:13-15)

Take time to go over all thirteen lessons and focus on your weak areas.

Appendix 1:

Truths about Who You are in Christ

How we become united with Christ:

In Romans 3:23 the Bible says, "*...All have sinned and come short of the glory of God,*" and in Romans 6:23 it says, "*For the wages of sin is death, but the free gift of God is eternal life in Christ Jesus our Lord.*" It is clear that the New Testament teaches that all have sinned and the penalty is death. But the great news is that Christ died for our sins and He gives to all who believe in Him the gift of eternal life. When a person acknowledges to God that he is a sinner and expresses to God his need for forgiveness and understands that the gift of life is in Christ Jesus, that person is given the gift of life.

If you have accepted this life in Christ Jesus, you are united with Christ and many things become true about you, your life and your destiny.

Here are a few of the many truths you should learn and speak into your life through RSTs:

Repeat these truths over and over while meditating on them:

"I am alive in Christ"

> "*9 We know that Christ, being raised from the dead, will never die again; death no longer has dominion over him. 10 For the death he died he died to sin, once for all, but the life he lives he lives to God. 11*

So you also must consider yourselves dead to sin and alive to God in Christ Jesus." (Romans 6:9-11)

"I will never be condemned because I'm in Christ"

"There is therefore now no condemnation for those who are in Christ Jesus." (Romans 8:1)

"Nothing can separate me from Christ"

"37 In all these things we are more than conquerors through him who loved us. 38 For I am sure that neither death nor life, nor angels nor rulers, nor things present nor things to come, nor powers, 39 nor height nor depth, nor anything else in all creation, will be able to separate us from the love of God in Christ Jesus our Lord." (Romans 8:37-39)

"I am a new Creature in Christ Jesus"

"Therefore, if anyone is in Christ, he is a new creation. The old has passed away; behold, the new has come." (2 Corinthians 5:17)

"I am God's child"

"for in Christ Jesus you are all sons of God, through faith" (Galatians 3:26)

"But as many as received him, to them gave he power to become the sons of God, even to them that believe on his name: Which were born, not of blood, nor of

the will of the flesh, nor of the will of man, but of God." (John 1:12)

"I have all spiritual blessings"

"Blessed be the God and Father of our Lord Jesus Christ, who has blessed us in Christ with every spiritual blessing in the heavenly places." (Ephesians 1:3)

"My sins are forgiven in Christ"

"In him we have redemption through his blood, the forgiveness of our trespasses, according to the riches of his grace." (Ephesians 1:7)

"But God commended his love toward us, in that, while we were yet sinners, Christ died for us." (Romans 5:8)

"I am chosen by God"

"In him we have obtained an inheritance, having been chosen according to the purpose of him who works all things according to the counsel of his will." (Ephesians 1:11)

"God supplies everything I need"

"19 And my God will supply every need of yours according to his riches in glory in Christ Jesus. 20 To our God and Father be glory forever and ever. Amen." (Philippians 4:19-20)

"My life is safely hidden in Christ"

> *"For you have died, and your life is hidden with Christ in God."* (Colossians 3:3)

"My destiny is to be with Christ in heaven"

> *"When Christ who is your life appears, then you also will appear with him in glory."* (Colossians 3:4)

> *"16 For the Lord himself will descend from heaven with a cry of command, with the voice of an archangel, and with the sound of the trumpet of God. And the dead in Christ will rise first. 17 Then we who are alive, who are left, will be caught up together with them in the clouds to meet the Lord in the air, and so we will always be with the Lord. 18 therefore encourage one another with these words."* (1 Thessalonians 4:16-18)

"I am loved by God the Father"

> *"I in them, and thou in me, that they may be made perfect in one; and that the world may know that thou hast sent me, and hast loved them, as thou hast loved me."* (John 17:23)

"I have peace with God"

> *"Therefore being justified by faith, we have peace with God through our Lord Jesus Christ."* (Romans *5:1*)

"I have eternal Life in Christ"

> *"5 Jesus answered, 'Truly, truly, I say to you, unless one is born of water and the Spirit, he cannot enter the kingdom of God. 6 That which is born of the flesh is flesh, and that which is born of the Spirit is spirit. 7 Do not marvel that I said to you, "You must be born again."'"* (John 3:5-7)

"I have the righteousness of God in Christ"

> *"For our sake he made him to be sin who knew no sin, so that in him we might become the righteousness of God."* (2 Corinthians 5:21)

"I'm seated with Christ in the heavens and I'm safe"

> *"5... When we were dead in our trespasses, He made us alive together with Christ; by grace you have been saved 6 and raised us up with him and seated us with him in the heavenly places in Christ Jesus"* (Ephesians 2:5-6)

Appendix 2

Scriptures on Negative Emotions

Here is a list of negative emotions with appropriate scriptures to memorize:

Anger:

"Be angry and do not sin; do not let the sun go down on your anger," (Ephesians 4:26)

"31 Let all bitterness and wrath and anger and clamor and slander be put away from you, along with all malice. 32 Be kind to one another, tenderhearted, forgiving one another, as God in Christ forgave you." (Ephesians 4:31-32)

"Refrain from anger, and forsake wrath! Fret not yourself; it tends only to evil." (Psalm 37:8)

"For the anger of man does not produce the righteousness of God." (James 1:20)

"A soft answer turns away wrath, but a harsh word stirs up anger." (Proverbs 15:1)

"Be not quick in your spirit to become angry, for anger lodges in the bosom of fools." (Ecclesiastes 7:9)

"Whoever is slow to anger is better than the mighty, and he who rules his spirit than he who takes a city." (Proverbs 16:32)

"*A fool gives full vent to his spirit, but a wise man quietly holds it back.*" (Proverbs 29:11)

"*A hot-tempered man stirs up strife, but he who is slow to anger quiets contention.*" (Proverbs 15:18)

"*Wrath is cruel, anger is overwhelming, but who can stand before jealousy?*" (Proverbs 27:4)

"*8 Refrain from anger, and forsake wrath! Fret not yourself; it tends only to evil. 9 For the evildoers shall be cut off, but those who wait for the Lord shall inherit the land.*" *(Psalm 37:8-9)*

"*4 Love is patient and kind; love does not envy or boast; it is not arrogant 5 or rude. It does not insist on its own way; it is not irritable or resentful.*" (1 Corinthians 13:4-5)

Anxiety:

"*fear not, for I am with you; be not dismayed, for I am your God; I will strengthen you, I will help you, I will uphold you with my righteous right hand.*" (Isaiah 41:10)

"*but whoever listens to me will dwell secure and will be at ease, without dread of disaster.*" (Proverbs 1:33)

"*28 Come to me, all who labor and are heavy laden, and I will give you rest. 29 Take my yoke upon you, and learn from me, for I am gentle and lowly in heart, and you will find rest for your souls. 30 For my yoke is easy, and my burden is light.*" *(Matthew 11:28-29)*

"31 Therefore do not be anxious, saying, 'What shall we eat?' or 'What shall we drink?' or 'What shall we wear?' 32 For the Gentiles seek after all these things, and your heavenly Father knows that you need them all. 33 But seek first the kingdom of God and his righteousness, and all these things will be added to you. 34 "Therefore do not be anxious about tomorrow, for tomorrow will be anxious for itself. Sufficient for the day is its own trouble." (Matthew 6:31-34)

"4 Rejoice in the Lord always; again, I will say, rejoice. 5 Let your reasonableness be known to everyone. The Lord is at hand; 6 do not be anxious about anything, but in everything by prayer and supplication with thanksgiving let your requests be made known to God. 7 And the peace of God, which surpasses all understanding, will guard your hearts and your minds in Christ Jesus. 8 Finally, brothers, whatever is true, whatever is honorable, whatever is just, whatever is pure, whatever is lovely, whatever is commendable, if there is any excellence, if there is anything worthy of praise, think about these things." (Philippians 4:4-8)

"6 Humble yourselves, therefore, under the mighty hand of God so that at the proper time he may exalt you, 7 casting all your anxieties on him, because he cares for you." (1 Peter 5:6-7)

"1 Let not your hearts be troubled. Believe in God; believe also in me. 2 In my Father's house are many rooms. If it were not so, would I have told you that I go to prepare a place for you? 3 And if I go and prepare a place for you, I will come again and will take you to myself, that where I am you may be also. 4 And you know the way to where I am going." (John 14:1-4)

"Peace I leave with you; my peace I give to you. Not as the world gives do I give to you. Let not your hearts be troubled, neither let them be afraid." (John 14:27)

"41 But the Lord answered her, 'Martha, Martha, you are anxious and troubled about many things, 42 but one thing is necessary. Mary has chosen the good portion, which will not be taken away from her.'" (Luke 10:41-42)

"7 Be still before the Lord and wait patiently for him; fret not yourself over the one who prospers in his way, over the man who carries out evil devices! 8 Refrain from anger, and forsake wrath! Fret not yourself; it tends only to evil. 9 For the evildoers shall be cut off, but those who wait for the Lord shall inherit the land." (Psalm 37:7-9)

"Cast your burden on the Lord, and he will sustain you; he will never permit the righteous to be moved." (Psalm 55:22)

"You are a hiding place for me; you preserve me from trouble; you surround me with shouts of deliverance. Selah" (Psalm 32:7)

Bitterness:

"31 Let all bitterness and wrath and anger and clamor and slander be put away from you, along with all malice. 32 Be kind to one another, tenderhearted, forgiving one another, as God in Christ forgave you." (Ephesians 4:31-32)

"A soft answer turns away wrath, but a harsh word stirs up anger." (Proverbs 15:1)

"Do not say, 'I will repay evil'; wait for the Lord, and he will deliver you." (Proverbs 20:22)

"14 For if you forgive others their trespasses, your heavenly Father will also forgive you, 15 but if you do not forgive others their trespasses, neither will your Father forgive your trespasses." (Matthew 6:14-15)

"See to it that no one fails to obtain the grace of God; that no 'root of bitterness' springs up and causes trouble, and by it many become defiled." (Hebrews 12:15)

"Hatred stirs up strife, but love covers all offenses." (Proverbs 10:12)

"Be angry and do not sin; do not let the sun go down on your anger." (Ephesians 4:26)

"17 Repay no one evil for evil, but give thought to do what is honorable in the sight of all. 18 If possible, so far as it depends on you, live peaceably with all. 19 Beloved, never avenge yourselves, but leave it to the wrath of God, for it is written, 'Vengeance is mine, I will repay, says the Lord.'20 To the contrary, 'if your enemy is hungry, feed him; if he is thirsty, give him something to drink; for by so doing you will heap burning coals on his head.' 21 Do not be overcome by evil, but overcome evil with good." (Romans 12:17-21)

"What causes quarrels and what causes fights among you? Is it not this, that your passions are at war within you?" (James 4:1)

"12 So speak and so act as those who are to be judged under the law of liberty. 13 For judgment is without mercy to one who has shown no mercy. Mercy triumphs over judgment." (James 2:12-13)

"5 Blessed are the meek, for they shall inherit the earth. 6 Blessed are those who hunger and thirst for righteousness, for they shall be satisfied. 7 Blessed are the merciful, for they shall receive mercy. 8 Blessed are the pure in heart, for they shall see God. 9 Blessed are the peacemakers, for they shall be called sons of God." (Matthew 5:5-9)

"If you really fulfill the royal law according to the Scripture, 'You shall love your neighbor as yourself,' you are doing well." (James 2:8)

Depression:

"17 When the righteous cry for help, the Lord hears and delivers them out of all their troubles. 18 The Lord is near to the brokenhearted and saves the crushed in spirit." (Psalm 34:17-18)

"Come to me, all who labor and are heavy laden, and I will give you rest." (Matthew 11:28)

"Fear not, for I am with you; be not dismayed, for I am your God; I will strengthen you, I will help you, I will uphold you with my righteous right hand." (Isaiah 41:10)

"Even though I walk through the valley of the shadow of death, I will fear no evil, for you are with me; your rod and your staff, they comfort me." (Psalm 23:4)

"1 The LORD is my shepherd; I shall not want. 2 He makes me lie down in green pastures. He leads me beside still waters. 3 He restores my soul. He leads me in paths of righteousness for his name's sake." (Psalm 23:1-3)

"6 Do not be anxious about anything, but in everything by prayer and supplication with thanksgiving let your requests be made known to God. 7 And the peace of God, which surpasses all understanding, will guard your hearts and your minds in Christ Jesus." (Philippians 4:6-7)

"You have turned for me my mourning into dancing; you have loosed my sackcloth and clothed me with gladness." (Psalm 30:11)

"But they who wait for the Lord shall renew their strength; they shall mount up with wings like eagles; they shall run and not be weary; they shall walk and not faint." (Isaiah 40:31)

"But you, O Lord, are a shield about me, my glory, and the lifter of my head." (Psalm 3:3)

"May the God of hope fill you with all joy and peace in believing, so that by the power of the Holy Spirit you may abound in hope." (Romans 15:13)

"You keep him in perfect peace whose mind is stayed on you, because he trusts in you." (Isaiah 26:3)

"The Lord is near to the brokenhearted and saves the crushed in spirit." (Psalm 34:18)

Encouragement:

"Death and life are in the power of the tongue, and those who love it will eat its fruits." (Proverbs 18:21)

"Like a gold ring or an ornament of gold is a wise reprover to a listening ear." (Proverbs 25:12)

"Iron sharpens iron, and one man sharpens another." (Proverbs 27:17)

"I sought the Lord, and he answered me and delivered me from all my fears." (Psalm 34:4)

"May the God of hope fill you with all joy and peace in believing, so that by the power of the Holy Spirit you may abound in hope." (Romans 15:13)

"Those who sow in tears shall reap with shouts of joy!" (Psalm 126:5)

"Blessed are those who mourn, for they shall be comforted." (Matthew 5:4)

"For whatever was written in former days was written for our instruction, that through endurance and through the encouragement of the Scriptures we might have hope." (Romans 15:4)

"Cast your burden on the Lord, and he will sustain you; he will never permit the righteous to be moved." (Psalm 55:22)

"Now may our Lord Jesus Christ himself, and God our Father, who loved us and gave us eternal comfort and good hope through grace, comfort your hearts and establish them in every good work and word." (2 Thessalonians 2:16)

"So that by two unchangeable things, in which it is impossible for God to lie, we who have fled for refuge might have strong encouragement to hold fast to the hope set before us." (Hebrews 6:18)

Fear:

"Be strong and courageous. Do not fear or be in dread of them, for it is the LORD your God who goes with you. He will not leave you or forsake you." (Deuteronomy 31:6)

"It is the LORD who goes before you. He will be with you; he will not leave you or forsake you. Do not fear or be dismayed." (Deuteronomy 31:8)

"Even though I walk through the valley of the shadow of death, I will fear no evil, for you are with me; your rod and your staff, they comfort me." (Psalm 23:4)

"1 The LORD is my light and my salvation; whom shall I fear? The LORD is the stronghold of my life; of whom shall I be afraid? 2 When evildoers assail me to eat up my flesh, my adversaries and foes, it is they who stumble and fall. 3 Though an army encamp against me, my heart shall not

fear; though war arise against me, yet I will be confident." (Psalm 27:1-3)

"5 For God alone, O my soul, wait in silence, for my hope is from him. 6 He only is my rock and my salvation, my fortress; I shall not be shaken." (Psalm 62:5-6)

"1 God is our refuge and strength, a very present help in trouble. 2 Therefore we will not fear though the earth gives way, though the mountains be moved into the heart of the sea," (Psalm 46:1-2)

"3 When I am afraid, I put my trust in you. 4 In God, whose word I praise, in God I trust; I shall not be afraid. What can flesh do to me?" (Psalm 56:3-4)

"Cast your burden on the LORD, and he will sustain you; he will never permit the righteous to be moved." (Psalm 55:22)

"The LORD is on my side; I will not fear. What can man do to me?" (Psalm 118:6)

" fear not, for I am with you; be not dismayed, for I am your God; I will strengthen you, I will help you, I will uphold you with my righteous right hand." (Isaiah 41:10)

"Peace I leave with you; my peace I give to you. Not as the world gives do I give to you. Let not your hearts be troubled, neither let them be afraid." (John 14:27)

"I have said these things to you, that in me you may have peace. In the world you will have tribulation. But take heart; I have overcome the world." (John 16:33)

"for God gave us a spirit not of fear but of power and love and self-control." (2 Timothy 1:7)

"5 Keep your life free from love of money, and be content with what you have, for he has said, 'I will never leave you nor forsake you.' 6 So we can confidently say, "The Lord is my helper; I will not fear; what can man do to me?" (Hebrews 13:5-6)

"Casting all your anxiety on Him, because He cares for you." (1 Peter 5:7)

"There is no fear in love, but perfect love casts out fear. For fear has to do with punishment, and whoever fears has not been perfected in love." (1 John 4:18)

Guilt

"If we confess our sins, he is faithful and just to forgive us our sins and to cleanse us from all unrighteousness." (1 John 1:9)

"There is therefore now no condemnation for those who are in Christ Jesus." (Romans 8:1)

"My little children, I am writing these things to you so that you may not sin. But if anyone does sin, we have an advocate with the Father, Jesus Christ the righteous." (1 John 2:1)

"*11 For as high as the heavens are above the earth, so great is his steadfast love toward those who fear him; 12 as far as the east is from the west, so far does he remove our transgressions from us.*" (Psalm 103:11-12)

"*He is the propitiation for our sins, and not for ours only but also for the sins of the whole world.*" (1 John 2:2)

"*For our sake he made him to be sin who knew no sin, so that in him we might become the righteousness of God.*" (2 Corinthians 5:21)

"*16 For God so loved the world, that he gave his only Son, that whoever believes in him should not perish but have eternal life. 17 For God did not send his Son into the world to condemn the world, but in order that the world might be saved through him.*" (John 3:16-17)

Insecurity:

"*25 Therefore I tell you, do not be anxious about your life, what you will eat or what you will drink, nor about your body, what you will put on. Is not life more than food, and the body more than clothing? 26 Look at the birds of the air: they neither sow nor reap nor gather into barns, and yet your heavenly Father feeds them. Are you not of more value than they? 27 And which of you by being anxious can add a single hour to his span of life? 28 And why are you anxious about clothing? Consider the lilies of the field, how they grow: they neither toil nor spin, 29 yet I tell you, even Solomon in all his glory was not arrayed like one of these.30 But if God so clothes the grass of the field, which today is alive and tomorrow is thrown into the oven, will he not much more clothe you, O you of little faith? 31 therefore do not be anxious, saying, 'What shall we eat?' or 'What shall we drink?' or 'What shall we wear?'"* (Matthew 6:25-31)

"22 The glory that you have given me I have given to them, that they may be one even as we are one, 23 I in them and you in me, that they may become perfectly one, so that the world may know that you sent me and loved them even as you loved me. 24 Father, I desire that they also, whom you have given me, may be with me where I am, to see my glory that you have given me because you loved me before the foundation of the world." (John 17:22-24)

"1 The LORD is my shepherd; I shall not want. 2 He makes me lie down in green pastures. He leads me beside still waters. 3 He restores my soul. He leads me in paths of righteousness for his name's sake. 4 Even though I walk through the valley of the shadow of death, I will fear no evil, for you are with me; your rod and your staff, they comfort me. 5 You prepare a table before me in the presence of my enemies; you anoint my head with oil; my cup overflows. 6 Surely goodness and mercy shall follow me all the days of my life, and I shall dwell in the house of the LORD forever." (Psalm 23:1-6)

"And you will know the truth, and the truth will set you free." (John 8:32)

"For we are his workmanship, created in Christ Jesus for good works, which God prepared beforehand, that we should walk in them" (Ephesians 2:10)

"I have been crucified with Christ. It is no longer I who live, but Christ who lives in me. And the life I now live in the flesh I live by faith in the Son of God, who loved me and gave himself for me." (Galatians 5:22)

"And let steadfastness have its full effect, that you may be perfect and complete, lacking in nothing." (James 1:4)

Panic attacks:

"1 But now thus says the Lord, he who created you, O Jacob, he who formed you, O Israel: 'Fear not, for I have redeemed you; I have called you by name, you are mine. 2 When you pass through the waters, I will be with you; and through the rivers, they shall not overwhelm you; when you walk through fire you shall not be burned, and the flame shall not consume you.'" (Isaiah 43:1-2)

"Fear not, for I am with you; be not dismayed, for I am your God; I will strengthen you, I will help you, I will uphold you with my righteous right hand." (Isaiah 41:10)

"Do not be anxious about anything, but in everything by prayer and supplication with thanksgiving let your requests be made known to God." (Philippians 4:6)

"Be still, and know that I am God; I will be exalted among the nations, I will be exalted in the earth." (Psalm 46:10)

"16 *Let the word of Christ dwell in you richly, teaching and admonishing one another in all wisdom, singing psalms and hymns and spiritual songs, with thankfulness in your hearts to God. 17 And whatever you do, in word or deed, do everything in the name of the Lord Jesus, giving thanks to God the Father through him.*" (Colossians 3:16-17)

Shame:

"*But the Lord God helps me; therefore, I have not been disgraced; therefore, I have set my face like a flint, and I know that I shall not be put to shame.*" (Isaiah 50:7)

"*if we confess our sins, he is faithful and just to forgive us our sins and to cleanse us from all unrighteousness.*" (1 John 1:9)

"*And he said, 'I heard the sound of you in the garden, and I was afraid, because I was naked, and I hid myself.'*" (Genesis 3:10)

Stress:

"*10 Be still, and know that I am God. I will be exalted among the nations, I will be exalted in the earth!" 11 The LORD of hosts is with us; the God of Jacob is our fortress. Selah*" (Psalm 46:10-11)

"*They who wait for the LORD shall renew their strength; they shall mount up with wings like eagles; they shall run and not be weary; they shall walk and not faint.*" (Isaiah 40:31)

"*41 But the Lord answered her, 'Martha, Martha, you are anxious and troubled about many things, 42 but one thing is necessary. Mary has chosen the good portion, which will not be taken away from her.'*" (Luke 10:41-42)

"Peace I leave with you; my peace I give to you. Not as the world gives do I give to you. Let not your hearts be troubled, neither let them be afraid." (John 14:27)

"28 Come to me, all who labor and are heavy laden, and I will give you rest. 29 Take my yoke upon you, and learn from me, for I am gentle and lowly in heart, and you will find rest for your souls. 30 For my yoke is easy, and my burden is light." (Matthew 11:28-30)

"He is like a man building a house, who dug deep and laid the foundation on the rock. And when a flood arose, the stream broke against that house and could not shake it, because it had been well built." (Luke 6:48)

"But seek first the kingdom of God and his righteousness, and all these things will be added to you." (Matthew 6:33)

"2 Count it all joy, my brothers, when you meet trials of various kinds, 3 for you know that the testing of your faith produces steadfastness. 4 And let steadfastness have its full effect, that you may be perfect and complete, lacking in nothing. 5 If any of you lacks wisdom, let him ask God, who gives generously to all without reproach, and it will be given him." (James 1:2-5)

Thinking on lies, TNTs:

"4 For the weapons of our warfare are not of the flesh but have divine power to destroy strongholds. 5 We destroy arguments and every lofty opinion raised against the knowledge

of God, and take every thought captive to obey Christ." (2 Corinthians 10:4-5)

"Finally, brothers, whatever is true, whatever is honorable, whatever is just, whatever is pure, whatever is lovely, whatever is commendable, if there is any excellence, if there is anything worthy of praise, think about these things." (Philippians 4:8)

"Set your minds on things that are above, not on things that are on earth. 3 For you have died, and your life is hidden with Christ in God." (Colossians 3:2-3)

"For God gave us a spirit not of fear but of power and love and self-control." (2 Timothy 1:7)

"1 Blessed is the man who walks not in the counsel of the wicked, nor stands in the way of sinners, nor sits in the seat of scoffers; 2 but his delight is in the law of the LORD, and on his law he meditates day and night. 3 He is like a tree planted by streams of water that yields its fruit in its season, and its leaf does not wither. In all that he does, he prospers." (Psalm 1:1-3)

"4 Be angry, and do not sin; ponder in your own hearts on your beds, and be silent. Selah 5 Offer right sacrifices, and put your trust in the LORD. 6 There are many who say, 'who will show us some good? Lift up the light of your face upon us, O LORD!' 7 You have put more joy in my heart than they have when their grain and wine abound. 8 In peace I will both lie down and sleep; for you alone, O LORD, makes me dwell in safety." (Psalm 4:4-8)

"6 When I remember you upon my bed, and meditate on you in the watches of the night; 7 for you have been my help, and in the shadow of your wings I will sing for joy. 8 My soul clings to you; your right hand upholds me." (Psalm 63:6-8)

"8 This Book of the Law shall not depart from your mouth, but you shall meditate on it day and night, so that you may be careful to do according to all that is written in it. For then you will make your way prosperous, and then you will have good success." (Joshua 1:8)

"Let the words of my mouth and the meditation of my heart be acceptable in your sight, O Lord, my rock and my redeemer." (Psalm 19:14)

"I will meditate on your precepts and fix my eyes on your ways." (Psalm 119:15)

"20 My son, be attentive to my words; incline your ear to my sayings. 21 Let them not escape from your sight; keep them within your heart, 22 for they are life to those who find them, and healing to all their flesh." (Proverbs 4:20-22)

"You keep him in perfect peace whose mind is stayed on you, because he trusts in you." (Isaiah 26:3)

"I have stored up your word in my heart, that I might not sin against you." (Psalm 119:11)

"13 Until I come, devote yourself to the public reading of Scripture, to exhortation, to teaching. 14 Do not neglect the gift you have, which was given you by prophecy when the

council of elders laid their hands on you. 15 Practice these things, immerse yourself in them, so that all may see your progress." (1 Timothy 4:13-15)

Worry:

"Anxiety in a man's heart weighs him down, but a good word makes him glad." (Proverbs 12:25)

"And he said to his disciples, 'Therefore I tell you, do not be anxious about your life, what you will eat, nor about your body, what you will put on.'" (Luke 12:22)

"Peace I leave with you; my peace I give to you. Not as the world gives do I give to you. Let not your hearts be troubled, neither let them be afraid." (John 14:27)

"Now may the Lord of peace himself give you peace at all times in every way. The Lord be with you all." (2 Thessalonians 3:16)

"1 The LORD is my shepherd; I shall not want. 2 He makes me lie down in green pastures. He leads me beside still waters. 3 He restores my soul. He leads me in paths of righteousness for his name's sake. 4 Even though I walk through the valley of the shadow of death, I will fear no evil, for you are with me; your rod and your staff, they comfort me. 5 You prepare a table before me in the presence of my enemies; you anoint my head with oil; my cup overflows. 6 Surely goodness and mercy shall follow me all the days of my life, and I shall dwell in the house of the LORD forever." (Psalm 23:1-6)

"10 Be still, and know that I am God. I will be exalted among the nations, I will be exalted in the earth!" 11 The LORD of hosts is with us; the God of Jacob is our fortress. Selah" (Psalm 46:10-11)

"1 I lift up my eyes to the hills. From where does my help come? 2 My help comes from the LORD, who made heaven and earth. 3 He will not let your foot be moved; he who keeps you will not slumber." (Psalm 121:1-3)

"5 Trust in the LORD with all your heart, and do not lean on your own understanding. 6 In all your ways acknowledge him, and he will make straight your paths." (Proverbs 3:5-6)

"6 Humble yourselves, therefore, under the mighty hand of God so that at the proper time he may exalt you, 7 casting all your anxieties on him, because he cares for you." (1 Peter 5:6-7)

"28 Come to me, all who labor and are heavy laden, and I will give you rest. 29 Take my yoke upon you, and learn from me, for I am gentle and lowly in heart, and you will find rest for your souls. 30 For my yoke is easy, and my burden is light." (Matthew 11:28-30)

Appendix 3

Truths to Use for RSTs

The following are types of RSTs that you should focus on by speaking truth. There may be difficulties of life, but think on those things that bring the positive into your life. Make sure what you say is true, because your heart will eventually reject self lies.

Philippians 4:8, *"Finally, brothers, whatever is true, whatever is honorable, whatever is just, whatever is pure, whatever is lovely, whatever is commendable, if there is any excellence, if there is anything worthy of praise, think about these things."*

Here are several areas to RST with a few possible examples. Know "your truth" and your situation so you think on the positive truths of life:

1. Reinforced self-praise: Focus on your best qualities
   "I'm kind to others"
   "I care for my family"

2. Reinforced celebration: Focus on the best of situations
   "I have a place to live"
   "I have enough food for today"

3. Reinforced freedom from residual guilt: Focus on God's forgiveness
   "I'm forgiven in Christ"
   "My past is in the past and I stand free in Christ"

4. Reinforced self-nurture and encouragement: Focus on your potential
   "I'm good and worth love"
   "I thank God for my life"

5. Reinforced hope for change: Focus on God's provision for your change
   "With Christ's strength I'm going to overcome"
   "I'm free from the bondage of failure in Christ"

6. Reinforced awareness of the presence of God: Focus on God's love and power
   "God is with me right now, right here"
   "You will never leave me, God, thank You for Your presence here"

7. Reinforced reversal of worry: Focus on solutions
   "I know that all will be well because God is leading me even in the dark times"
   "I thank God for the path, His word is a lamp to my feet and a light for my path."

8. Reinforced release of control: Focus on adjusted expectations
   "I am satisfied with just what God has provided today"
   "I don't need anyone to change for me to be happy, I'm full in Christ"

9. Reinforced identity: Focus on your position in Christ
   "I'm accepted in Christ Jesus"
   "I'm God's child and loved in Christ Jesus"

Appendix 4:

The Filling of the Holy Spirit and RSTs

It is important to see the transformation of your emotions as assisted by supernatural power. Ephesians 5:18 gives the best and only real teaching on the filling of the Holy Spirit. This has become a difficult doctrine to explain in light of many various doctrinal views among Christians. What I want you to see is the clear and undeniable teaching about the filling of the Spirit. I want you to set aside your doctrinal bias for a moment and let scripture teach you. This doctrine is so important to RSTs that you must understand this as a starting place. So here we go:

Ephesians 5:18 is the only place where the filling of the Holy Spirit is specifically taught. Other scriptures give historical narrative of believers being filled with the Holy Spirit. These are primarily in the book of Acts. In these historical narratives we can see the results of the filling of the Spirit, but are not given enough context to know how filling takes place, nor do we see the dynamics of the filling. With this in mind, let's look at several things about this passage:

> *"15 Therefore be careful how you walk, not as unwise men but as wise, 16 making the most of your time, because the days are evil. 17 So then do not be foolish, but understand what the will of the Lord is. 18 And do not get drunk with wine, for that is dissipation, but be filled by the Spirit, 19 speaking to one another in psalms and hymns and spiritual songs, singing and making melody with your heart to the Lord; 20 always giving thanks for all things in the name of our*

> *Lord Jesus Christ to God, even the Father; 21 and be subject to one another in the fear of Christ. 22 wives be subject to your husbands."* (Ephesians 5:15-21)

First, the filling is used in the context of changed behavior. We are told to be careful how we walk, that is, behave, in verse 15. This is the key to understanding transformed living. Ephesians 5 is going to connect our behavior with the filling of the Spirit. Note the grammatical structure here:

Be careful how you walk:
Not as unwise... but wise 5:15
Not as foolish... but understanding 5:17
Not drunk... but filled 5:18

We can see a connection between walking/behavior and filling. Whatever filling means, it impacts our behavior in such a way as to make it careful, which is from the Greek word "*akribos,*" meaning accurate. When we are filled with the Spirit, our behavior is corrected. This is a supernatural transformation.

Second, the filling is used in the context of changed thinking. Notice the progression above. Wise... Understanding... filled. There is a clear connection with wisdom and understanding with this filling. In fact, to make it clearer, the grammatical structure of this passage is in the "instrumental case" in the Greek, which gives a clearer translation of filling. The filling is done by the "instrument" of the Holy Spirit. In other words, you are not being filled with more of the Holy Spirit, but the Holy Spirit is filling you with something. This something is clear when we look at the grammar here. The Holy Spirit is filling you with that which is "wise" and "understanding." We would be best served by a better translation: **"Filled by means of the Holy Spirit."**

By way of analogy, if you had an empty cup and it was going to be filled with water, you would have three aspects of this filling: 1) The cup, 2) The water and 3) The person doing the filling. In the filling of the Spirit, you are the cup; the wisdom and understanding of God's Word is the water, and the Holy Spirit is the one filling you.

Notice the mission of the Holy Spirit in John 16:12-13, when Jesus said, "I will send the Holy Spirit to you and He will 'guide' you into all truth, He will 'speak' to you, He will 'teach' you." The mission of the Holy Spirit is a teacher who is imparting truth to the believer. The filling of the Holy Spirit is to teach and guide in wisdom and understanding with the impact of transformed thinking and living. When we have changed thinking and beliefs, we will inevitably have changed behavior and even changed emotions.

To shore up this concept that the filling is tantamount to teaching, I have included this comparison of a parallel to this passage, Colossians 3:16 ff.

Filling by the Spirit	The Indwelling of the Word of Christ
"18 *And do not get drunk with wine, for that is dissipation, but be filled by the Spirit, 19 speaking to one another in psalms and hymns and spiritual songs, singing and making melody with your heart to the Lord; 20 always giving thanks for all things in the name of our Lord Jesus Christ to God, even the Father; 21 and be subject to one another in the fear of Christ. 22 wives be subject to your husbands."* (Ephesians 5:18-22)	"*16 Let the word of Christ richly dwell within you, with all wisdom, teaching and admonishing one another with psalms and hymns and spiritual songs, singing with thankfulness in your hearts to God. 17 Whatever you do in word or deed, do all in the name of the Lord Jesus, giving thanks through Him to God the Father. 18 Wives, be subject to your husbands, as is fitting in the Lord."* (Colossians 3:16-18)

Notice that in Ephesians 5 where the filling of the Holy Spirit has the same results as in Colossians 3, where the directive is to let the word of Christ dwell in you richly. The results are dynamic transformed thinking, attitude, and emotions.

Notice the five changes:

1. Communication – "Speaking to one another"
2. Joy – "Singing and making melody in your heart"
3. God consciousness – "to the Lord"
4. Thankfulness – "Giving thanks for all things"
5. Mutual submission – "Be subject to one another

Think of the significance of this. A heart filled with these characteristics would result in incredible emotional stability. The filling of/by the Holy Spirit is the supernatural way in which we have transformed emotions.

<u>**Third, the filling is used in the context of changed relationships**</u>. Interestingly, these passages are further paralleled in that both Colossians 3 and Ephesians 5 give the context of specific relationships. These are relationships that are committed relationships. They are not like friendships; they are relationships in which you are "stuck," if you will.

1. **Husband/Wife** Ephesians 5:22-33 and Colossians 3:18-19
2. **Child/Parent** Ephesians 6:1-4 and Colossians 3:20-21
3. **Slave/Master** Ephesians 6:5-9 and Colossians 3:22-4:1

The importance of this is that the passages speak of changed living, changed relationships, and they have the same results of: communication, joy, God-awareness, thankfulness and mutual submission. What if you were married to a man or woman who had these character traits? Your marriage would be greatly improved, especially if you had these Spirit-filled character traits. This filling by means of the Holy Spirit will measurably improve your **behavior**, **thinking**, and **relationships**. So how do we become filled?

<u>**Fourth, the filling of the Spirit is in the context of The Word dwelling within you.**</u> The reason I have taken this time to show the parallel nature of Ephesians 5 and Colossians 3 is so you will be able to understand the way in which someone is filled. Colossians 3 says let the Word of Christ dwell in you and this is the same as Ephesians 5 being filled. We must expose our minds to the scriptures. As we do, the Holy Spirit will implant the truth in our minds, transforming our beliefs, behaviors and relationships. This is the infilling of the Holy Spirit. Set aside your views of this doctrine and read again what you just read and see if you are gaining some new insight into how the Holy Spirit fills us and with what He fills us.

You may say, "But Tim, I have seen many people who have been well taught in the Word of God and yet they don't have changed behavior and they are mean-spirited in relationships. If what you are presenting is true, why do these people not change?" There is a simple reality that truth will only change a life when the word dwells in that life richly. 1 Corinthians 8:1 states, in the context of loving a weaker brother, "Knowledge makes arrogant but love edifies." It is important to remember that the knowledge of the Word of God is not the goal; but rather the goal is to have the Word of God dwelling in us. Some of the most well taught people I have seen are the most judgmental and mean spirited. On the other hand, some new believers who are allowing the truth to change them are experiencing tremendous growth and maturity.

Two important aspects of how to experience the filling by the Holy Spirit:

1. **Study of the Word of God daily**. When we expose our minds to biblical truth, the Holy Spirit can use this truth to implant it into our lives. What happens in many cases is we study the Bible because our goal is to know truth, but this is only the beginning of transformation. This truth must become a part of our lives. The Holy Spirit supernaturally implants this truth in our lives when we take the next step.

2. **Submit to God in prayer**. When we submit to God in prayer, we come to Him, admitting our need for truth to be implanted in our lives. We express our dependency upon the Holy Spirit to not only teach us but to transform us with truth. When this prayer of submission takes place, the Holy Spirit takes the studied Word and begins animating it in the life of the believer.

Appendix 5:

Thought Journal

Negative Thought	Scale 1-10 1 most negative 10 most positive	Reinforced Strategic Thoughts
"I'm going to fail in my presentation tomorrow because they will see my flaws"		"I'm prepared for this presentation and it doesn't have to be perfect, it simply needs to be excellent, which I can and will do"
"My spouse will never love me like I want and need, my life is miserable"		"I'm going to create an environment of safety for my spouse so he/she finds it safe to be intimate and God is meeting all my needs. My life is blessed."
"I will never be good enough to be used by God for His work"		"God has given me His righteousness in Christ Jesus and I'm a saint worthy to serve Him"
"I'm always going to be stuck in fear"		"God has not given me the spirit of fear but of a sound mind"
"I will never be free from my addiction to alcohol, I'm an alcoholic"		"I'm a child of God and even though I struggle with alcohol, God is strengthening me today to live in freedom"
"I'm in bondage to alcohol and will never be free"		"I'm free to serve Christ"
"This is going to be a lousy day today"		"This is the day the Lord has made. I will rejoice and be glad in it"

Appendix 6:

Tools for Overcoming Negative Emotions

<u>Overcoming Negative Thinking:</u>

Use Reinforced Strategic Thinking (RST)

Reinforced: Truth must be reinforced through the discipline of repeated focus. You can't just say once, "*God gave me a sound mind.*" It must be repeated and reinforced over and over throughout the day, and every day for weeks, until the truth takes dominion of your mind and soul.

Strategic: When we focus our thinking, it must have direction. The direction is toward the point of weakness in your soul. For example, if you tend to be fearful, you should focus on this truth: "*For God gave us a spirit not of fear but of power and love and sound mind*" (1 Tim. 1:7) Memorizing this verse, targeting the fear in your soul, so it will give great relief to the anxiety controlling your thoughts, mood, and even your actions. Over time, this focused, "strategic" truth will transform your mind.

Thinking: Thinking is foundational for emotional healing. Scripture says repeatedly, "*Think on these things.*" It is clear from this directive that we have the compacity to change/redirect our thinking. We are not subject to passive thoughts ruling our minds unless we allow them. People who are happier and more filled with joy tend to think about the positive outcomes, whereas the people who struggle with misery tend to think on negative outcomes.

Overcoming Fear

Three steps to overcoming fear:

Step 1 — Identify your fears: You must identify your fear by listing your greatest fears and your view of yourself in this world. Write them down so you can identify them and expose them.

Step 2 — Take each fear to its logical conclusion: You must take fear to its logical conclusion and ask yourself: Is this manageable? Could I handle this if it happened? Would God provide grace for me in this situation? How much of this is a real threat to me?

Step 3 — Replace lies with truth: You must replace the lies you are believing with truth about who you really are. What you know God says about you: for example, "I'm loved," "I'm chosen," or "I'm God's child." State these truths to yourself over and over throughout the day until your mind is convinced of these truths.

Overcoming Bitterness:

> "*31 Let all bitterness and wrath and anger and clamor and slander be put away from you, along with all malice. 32 Be kind to one another, tender-hearted, forgiving one another, as God in Christ forgave you.*" (Ephesians 4:31-32)

Bitterness is something you don't just decide to let go. You must take the steps recommended in Ephesians 4:31-32. Bitterness, and all the related negative emotions, are eradicated from the soul through the following three steps:

1. **Be kind**: When letting go of an offense, even an egregious one, you should show kindness toward the one who offended you. As recommended in chapter 5, if this person is a predator you should stay away, but other than that you should look for ways to show kindness to your offender. This takes their power away from them and gives it to you by viewing them as human, not a force.

   When we act in kindness, we affirm the humanity of our offender.
   When we act in kindness, we take back our power.
   When we act in kindness, we become free to live.

2. **Commiserate**: When we show compassion and understanding for why the offender does what he/she does. This gives you your power back, as you are free not to judge the person but only the behavior.

   When we commiserate, we acknowledge that our offender is flawed.
   When we commiserate, we allow mitigating circumstances to soften our hearts.
   When we commiserate, we acknowledge our own flaws.

3. **Forgive**: We need to forgive and release our offender for our own healing, while maintaining a high standard of behavior for others and ourselves. You can, at the same time, forgive and see the abuse given to you as egregious. We should be able to see the bad behavior for what it is and still be able to forgive.

When we forgive, we are free to live in the present.
When we forgive, we free the heart to heal.
When we forgive, we function as sons and daughters of God.

Overcoming Guilt and Shame

The Five Rs of overcoming guilt and shame:

1. **Repent**: Change your mind about your sin and God's character. Agree with God that this behavior is not good for your life.

2. **Return**: Journey back to our offense and discover how best to resolve the offense.

3. **Restore**: Make amends or repayment when possible. If a simple apology is appropriate, give it! If financial restoration is appropriate, give it! If other forms of restoration are in order, freely give it! You want freedom.

4. **Release:** Receiving forgiveness from God and others. People will most often forgive you; however, there are times where you will not be forgiven. Don't let this impede your freedom. God has forgiven you and you must acknowledge this.

5. **Resolve**: Leave the offense in the past through RSTs. Acknowledge your freedom through God's forgiveness. In fact, repeat this to yourself over and over, "I am forgiven by God." (Note: You don't need to forgive yourself, but rather receive God's forgiveness; this will free you.)

Overcoming Nonorganic Depression:

Three steps to overcome depression: T.C.A. Nonorganic depression is a matter of thinking, but if you have depression, please see a physician and get a complete physical. T.C.A. is not meant to be a substitute for therapy, but is meant to be a tool to help to alleviate depression and its pain.

1. **Think**: Depressed people need better disciplined thinking. Thinking is the core problem of all of us who have suffered from depression. Depressed people must train themselves in truth. Every time there is a decline in thinking toward negativity, they should apply RSTs with tenacity. Memorizing truth from Scripture and meditating on these is crucial for recovery. (See appendix 2 for specific scriptures)

2. **Connect**: One of the major problems depressed people have in common is disconnection from others. They tend to have either no relationships or only shallow, non-meaningful relationships. They do life alone. The depressed should intentionally pursue meaningful relationships with trusted and healthy people. Depressed people feel they must self-isolate because others will not be able to tolerate their negativity.

   It is crucial to push past these fears and find connection. Develop at least one meaningful authentic relationship with a trusted friend. Don't wait until you feel better; do it now.

3. **Act**: Every human being is here for a purpose. We all need to serve something bigger than ourselves. Depressed

people usually are so self-focused they have little to no purpose in life, other than survival.

Do something today for someone else. Small or large acts of kindness will take your mind off of self and put meaning back in your life.

Overcoming Anxiety:

To overcome anxiety, it will take an intentional approach over an extended period of time (my estimate is ninety days), but at the end you will have substantial change. Here are six biblical ways to overcome anxiety from Philippians 4:

> "6 *Be anxious for nothing, but in everything by prayer and supplication with thanksgiving let your requests be made known to God. 7 And the peace of God, which surpasses all comprehension, will guard your hearts and your minds in Christ Jesus. 8 Finally, brothers, whatever is true, whatever is honorable, whatever is just, whatever is pure, whatever is lovely, whatever is commendable, if there is any excellence, if there is anything worthy of praise, think about these things.*" (Philippians 4:6-8)

1. **Prayer**: Come before God in humble adoration and find intimacy with Him to be satisfying. Seek Him with all your heart. Pray not for nothing else but to connect to Him.

2. **Thanksgiving**: Give thanks for what is. Do this until the vision of what you want is very dim. Whenever you begin to experience dissatisfaction with what you have, focus on what is already yours (Phil. 4:6).

3. **Request**: Make the request in full surrender to the will of God. Tell Him, "Whatever You want for my life is sufficient," (Phil. 4:6).

4. **Focus**: Dwell on all that is good. Make a list of all the good you see around you and in your life. Read that list over and over until the list is "top of the mind" for you (Phil. 4:8).

5. **Worship**: Speak to God's provision and His character. Who is God? What has He done? State it over and over in your mind. Speak to God about His greatness and power over your life (Phil. 4:8).

6. **Submit**: Speak specifically to God's care for you and tell God whatever He provides is enough. Tell Him repeatedly that you are satisfied with His provision today. Submit to His care of you and seek nothing other than His kingdom and His righteousness.

Overcoming Panic Attacks:

Panic attacks are scary but not too dangerous. Our reaction to them is what causes most of the problems; they seem to come out of nowhere. Here are six ways to overcome panic attacks:

1. **Accept the attack**: Roll with the attack. Know that it is harmless and will be over in a few moments. In doing this, you will remove its power.

2. **Practice RST**: Apply Reinforced Strategic Thoughts from Appendix 2. Choose those RSTs that apply to your specific fears, and repeat them over and over until they are first on your mind. If you make a list you can read at any given

moment, keep it in your purse or wallet so they are readily accessible.

3. **Practice Diaphragmatic Breathing**: Breathe from your diaphragm, inhale through your nose and count to four, then exhale through your mouth slowly and count to six. Do this repeatedly and the symptoms of the panic attack will go away. This slowing of your breathing will bring relief to the physical symptoms of a panic attack, always.

4. **Focused relaxation**: Relax your muscles, limb by limb. You can do this in almost any environment. When the body is relaxed, your vulnerability to panic attacks recurring is greatly diminished.

5. **Take action**: Get up and move if possible. Change your environment.

6. **Thankfulness to God**: Express gratitude to God for who He is and what He has done. Make a list of God's faithfulness to you, so it is available to you.

Overcoming Irrational Thoughts:
Irrational thoughts range from thoughts of doing harm to yourself and others to thoughts of acting unkind toward others. They don't make sense to us, because in most cases we know we would never do such a thing. You may need to revisit chapter 8 to understand how irrational thoughts develop and manifest.

In short, irrational thoughts develop from threats in our lives. Here is how; the problem is what I refer to as "uncontrollable threats" in our lives that create psychological distress. (For example: the threat of being exposed for a sexual affair, or being exposed for the money you stole from your company, or cheating on your taxes.) This distress causes an often unconscious reaction. We unknowingly develop "controllable threats" or "controllable scenarios." These can be irrational thoughts of harming your husband; it is irrational because violence is foreign to your character. The threat or scenario is controllable because at your core, you know you would never be violent toward him. However, because this was developed unconsciously it seems so irrational, you think you are going crazy.

Follow the five ways to quiet the mind:

1. **Acknowledge the thoughts for what they are**: controllable scenarios.

2. **Find the root of the problem**: What are you feeling guilt or shame about?

3. **Evaluate irrational thoughts**: Is this something I would ever really do?

4. **Talk to a counselor**: Tell your counselor your irrational thoughts and get feedback on how unlikely the thoughts are as actual threats. This should not be casually shared with a friend; you should seek counsel.

5. **Meditate on truth to displace fear**. (See chapter 8 for how to meditate)

Overcoming Stress:
Practice C.O.P.E.:

Contentment: Reinterpret life with a heart of gratitude. Focus on what you are thankful for by keeping your thanksgiving journal.

Organize: Often stress is avoidable by organizing our commitments. Create your ABC list and be diligent to follow it every day: A list: urgent and required, top priority list. B list: important but not required, secondary list. C list: Are not directly related to our goals or our responsibilities, wait list.

Prevent: Stop stressors before they take over. Once you know what your stressors are, make a list of causes that bring about those stressors. Once you have this list, begin to prevent these causes by taking evasive action and making wise decisions before they turn into stressors.

Express: Assert yourself when you are being pushed for work beyond your ability to accomplish it. We often fall into the stressor by not speaking to our real need. We need to speak up and have the uncomfortable conversation to avoid a world of ongoing stress.

Overcoming perfectionism
Overcome the pain of perfection is through the "LET GO" principle in the Lord's Prayer:

> "*9 Pray then like this: 'Our Father in heaven, hallowed be your name. 10 Your kingdom come, your will be done, on earth as it is in heaven. 11 Give*

us this day our daily bread, 12 and forgive us our debts, as we also have forgiven our debtors. 13 And lead us not into temptation, but deliver us from evil.'" (Matthew 6:9–13)

L–Let God be God
E–Expect God's will to be done
T–Thank God for today's provisions

G–Give room for reconciliation
O–Overcome temptation by God's power

Let God be God: "Our Father who is in heaven, Hallowed be Your name." Worshiping God is putting God in His proper place. We, in truth, say, "God is God and I am not." If God is God, then He can handle the control, and if I'm not, I don't need to control. As well, God is perfect, but I don't need to be because I'm not God. What a relief!

Expect God's will to be done: "Your Kingdom come. Your will be done, on earth as it is in heaven." The problem with the need to control is that we want our will to be done. When we pray properly, we are transferring our agendas from our outcomes to His. We become free from this transfer to enjoy whatever God chooses to do.

Thank God for today's provisions: "Give us this day our daily bread." Jesus teaches us to ask for the simple provision of the day's needs. We are constantly striving for more, but to be thankful dislodges the stronghold of selfish ambition. The freedom to be overwhelmingly satisfied with what you have comes from an intentional and reinforced thankfulness.

Give room for reconciliation: "And forgive us our debts, as we also have forgiven our debtors." So much guilt can be avoided by having our debts taken care of, creating room for reconciliation. To release others of their obligations is to have freedom from "justice control." Justice control is what perfectionists strive for in life. Perfectionists are always trying to set things straight, make things right. This is a lot of pressure and creates stress for the perfectionist. When we seek forgiveness of our debts to God, we are reminded of our need; and then when we release others, we release the justice control of life. You don't have to control all the injustices in the world.

Overcome temptation by God's power: "And do not lead us into temptation, but deliver us from evil." The sense of obligation to perform for God is intense in most of us. What a relief that when we submit to God, He will lead us away from evil. Our primary goal should be to submit to God, and He will produce strength in the temptation as He leads us away from evil.

CPSIA information can be obtained
at www.ICGtesting.com
Printed in the USA
FSHW011932030521
81005FS

9 781662 815102